Over the Highest Mountains:

A Memoir of Unexpected Heroism in France during World War II

Intentional
Productions

Pasadena, California
2005

Over the Highest Mountains:

A Memoir of Unexpected Heroism in France during World War II

Alice Resch Synnestvedt

Edited by Aase Ingerslev (1998)
and Claire Gorfinkel (2004)

Translated from the Norwegian, French and Danish
by Ann Kunish (2000)

With a preface by Howard Wriggins

Cover photographs:
Hardanger Fjord, Norway, ca. 1930
and Jewish children at Aspet, 1942
Book and cover design by Anne Richardson-Daniel, 2004

Library of Congress Cataloging-in-Publication Data

Synnestvedt, Alice Resch, 1908-

Over the highest mountains : a memoir of unexpected heroism in France
during World War II / Alice Resch Synnestvedt ; edited by Aase Ingerslev
and Claire Gorfinkel ; translated from the Norwegian, French and Danish
by Ann Kunish ; with a preface by Howard Wriggins.

p. cm.

Includes bibliographical references and index.

Summary: "Alice Resch Synnestvedt became an unlikely hero upon
discovering Quaker relief workers in France in 1939. She spent six years
assisting Jewish and other refugees escaping from the Nazis. She wrote
this detailed memoir for her deaf mother in 1945. Over fifty years later
she was honored by those whose lives she saved"--Provided by publisher.

ISBN 0-9648042-6-3 (alk. paper)

1. Synnestvedt, Alice Resch, 1908- 2. World War, 1939-1945--Refugees--
France. 3. World War, 1939-1945--Children--France. 4. Child concentration
camp inmates--Care--France. 5. World War, 1939-1945--Jews--Rescue. 6.
World War, 1939-1945--Underground movements--France. 7. World War,
1939-1945--Personal narratives, Norwegian. 8. France--History--German
occupation, 1940-1945. 9. Nurses--Norway--Biography. I. Ingerslev, Aase.
II. Gorfinkel, Claire. III. Title.

D809.F7S96 2005
940.53'1835'092--dc22

2004021969

Intentional Productions
PO Box 94814, Pasadena, CA 91109
... publishing stories of courage ...
human responses to adversity and evil.

Dedicated to the memory of Helga Holbek,
whose generous spirit and outstanding leadership
made the work possible.

The view over Hardanger Fjord from Alice Resch's childhood home

Over the highest mountains ...

I cried on my twelfth birthday. I couldn't bear the thought that childhood was ending and I was on the way to adulthood! Mother came in, comforted me, and then she gave me a necklace with Roman pearls. I was so happy and proud! When summer came, my mood shifted. On a delightful, warm day I climbed up to my favorite place, a large rock in the far corner of the garden, where the landscape fell steeply downward. As I sat and gazed over to Folkefonnen on the other side of Hardanger Fjord, my thoughts turned to Bjøernstjerne Bjørnson's poem:

> Out, I *do wish* − *Oh so far far away over the highest mountains.*
> *What will I see over the highest mountains ...*

And I wondered what I would experience. I wanted to experience everything, everything in life. And life became filled with much joy, but also with darker times.

Many years later I learned the expression: "Beware what you ask for, that is what you will get."

- Alice Resch

Table of Contents

Jacques Lligonya and young Spanish workers
bringing food for French children (see chapter IV)

Preface

This gripping account of international rescue and relief work in southern France under Nazi occupation shows how an individual with warmth and charm, quiet courage and willingness to run risks, could perform extraordinary service to harassed refugees and quite unexpected acts of heroism. From 1940 through 1945, Alice Resch Synnestvedt worked tirelessly along with Helga Holbek in the Quaker center in Toulouse, in the notorious Gurs internment camp and in other camps holding Jews, foreigners and political prisoners, in children's colonies and wherever else she could be of use.

Alice was fond of saying that she was born in the United States, spent her "growing up" years in Norway, her adulthood in France and her retirement in Denmark. She had an idyllic childhood and adolescence in a small town at the edge of a Norwegian fjord where she first looked out "over the highest mountains," and embraced the physical and emotional challenges that her life would bring. Following graduation from high school, her parents gave her a year in Europe to "think things over". She studied at German and French universities, while enjoying picnics, parties, theater and museum visits.

Then, almost by chance, she applied to nursing school at the American Hospital in Paris. After some fairly glamorous years of international travel as a private-duty nurse, she returned to Paris. In 1939 Alice encountered the Quakers and joined their efforts to feed hungry French children. She would spend the next six years feeding, clothing and assisting refugees, and rescuing men, women and children from the Nazis, during which time she also married and formed a network of lifelong friendships.

Alice is a sharp observer of people under great pressure, a good raconteur, a person open to adventure. She rose to meet the wholly unanticipated challenges that came her way with great courage and creativity and – when her dangerous and complicated life permitted – she enjoyed travel, nice clothes, good food and wine.

She describes the intensifying hunger as rations decline, the misery of the trapped and interned refugees who had already lost everything. But her story also shows the light that can come from a dedicated, gifted individual who was able to improvise, and talk her way around the regulations in chaotic, defeated France. With her we visit refugee camps, see her and her colleagues distributing clothing to the most needy, assisting harassed doctors in camp clinics, and watching helplessly as refugee friends and even staff members are deported in cattle cars to almost certain death. Alice and her colleagues brought food and water to the departing trains and accepted prisoners' messages and tokens for safekeeping. She negotiated with the Father Secretary of a Trappist monastery to hide a young Jewish man. She helped some very colorful artists, musicians, members of the Resistance and children escape into Spain and Switzerland.

We are with her as she escorts a group of German Jewish children out of Camp de Gurs to an orphanage in Aspet. She stays on to comfort those who wonder why their parents were willing to send them away. She tells of her dangerous attempts to whisk several of them to safety in Switzerland. Most of her children eventually found new lives in Israel or America; all of the parents perished at Auschwitz. More than fifty years later, some of those who would always think of her as their "Angel of Aspet," re-located Alice. They hosted reunions, and she was honored in Israel as one of the Righteous Gentiles.

The telling of this remarkable memoir of unexpected heroism has a unique twist. In 1918, Alice's mother had lost her hearing in the flu epidemic, and even though she learned to read lips, every conversation took time. Thus, in 1945, when Alice was finally reunited with her beloved parents in Norway, it was easier to communicate with her mother in writing than orally. So Alice sat down to write about all her adventures during the war and she said: I *wrote one long paragraph non-stop, almost a thousand pages! The events were fresh in my memory, and everything, from the best to the most painful of events, ended up on the page.*

After reading her account, her parents felt the material ought to be used in some way. But for Alice "the very thought of writing any more was too much to bear. Why bother? Thoughts of that time were repressed. No one wanted, or could stand, to talk about the war. It was time to think about the future. We thought we were going start a new life, build a new and better world."

And with the modesty that characterizes so many rescuers, Alice sought no recognition for her work. She said: "I only did what anyone would have done" and insisted that Helga Holbek deserved any praise that was due.

Alice began the work of editing her memoir many years ago, with the inspiration, advice and support of her brother, Wilhelm H. Resch. In 1998 her Danish friend Aase Ingerslev helped her edit the hand-written manuscript. Then Hal Myers, one of the children whom Alice cared for in Aspet, wanted to thank and honor her.

In 2000 he arranged for Ann Kunish to translate her story from Norwegian into English, and with the help of Jack Sutters, Archivist of the American Friends Service Committee in Philadelphia, he arranged to have the memoir published. His version of the Aspet story appears in the Epilogue.

Now the world can finally learn about the unexpected heroism of Alice Resch Synnestvedt.

- Howard Wriggins

Howard Wriggins is Bryce Professor Emeritus of the History of International Relations at Columbia University, and author of *Picking Up the Pieces from Portugal to Palestine: Quaker Refugee Relief in World War II* (University Press of America, Lanham, MD, 2004).

Over the Highest Mountains:

A Memoir of Unexpected Heroism in France during World War II

Alice and her brother Wilhelm in 1916

I. Childhood and Youth

When asked about my life, I sometimes say: "I began as an American, spent my childhood and youth in Norway, my active adult life and marriage in France, and my old age in Denmark." But in my heart, I am and will always be Norwegian.

My parents, Knut and Frida Resch, met in Germany, where my father attended a Technical College, and my mother the *Fröbelschule*. When my father finished his schooling, like so many other young people, he went to America to make his fortune. He was lucky, finding employment at the Westinghouse electrical company, where he quickly climbed the corporate ladder. In 1903, my mother's parents reluctantly gave their blessing, and she traveled over the ocean to her Knut. But they insisted: "A young lady from a good family cannot just take off alone to America!" Her father's younger brother agreed to accompany her.

Father and Mother married, and thanks to my father's work they saw much of the United States. He was responsible for the Westinghouse pavilion at the World's Fair in St. Louis in 1904. They settled down in Chicago, where I was born on December 14, 1908 and my brother Wilhelm Herman was born in November, 1910. They had planned to stay in the U.S., but my father received a tempting offer to help

Alice and her mother in traditional Norwegian dress

build the electrical power station "Aura" in Sunndalsøren, Norway and in the fall of 1913 we moved to Norway. Work on Aura stopped when the First World War broke out in September of 1914, and my father was unemployed. He returned to the U.S., where Westinghouse had said there would always be a job for him.

Fate drew my father back to Norway to become the administrative head of Tyssefaldene Inc., which was building a power station at the famous waterfall. In April of 1915, we relocated to the tiny fjord village of Tyssedal, spread among the pine trees at the lower end of the falls. There was no access by road so all travel was by boat.

Childhood

During my childhood the village grew from a simple farming community to an international town. Both Norwegians and foreigners came to build the new factories and houses. There was a lively social life, but the words "environment" and "pollution" were not yet known, and smoke from the industrial areas was too much for the pine forests.

Tyssedal was isolated. The southern boundary was called "The World's End" and the northern boundary was at Bos renden, just beyond the power station. If we wanted to go to Odda, the small urban area six kilometers up the fjord, we traveled by boat. When important delegations visited, the garbage collector's horse was groomed till he shone, and then harnessed to a small basket-like contraption on wheels in which he pulled the guests up the hill from the dock to the hotel. The garbage collector, in his Sunday best, walked alongside holding the reins, and crowds of curious youngsters brought up the procession at the rear.

Knut and Frida Resch in 1920

Ours was a happy home, and my childhood was safe and pleasant. The village children found that "up at the Resch's" was a fun place to be with a vegetable garden, a meadow and a forest with blueberry and cranberry bushes during the summer. Rock-strewn slopes from an avalanche at Tveitenuten supplied us with interesting nooks and crannies in which to hide.

My mother had a special way with children. She invented games, made up exciting stories, and sang and played for us. My brother Wilhelm and I took our wonderful parents for granted, but she was like flypaper to the children of the neighborhood, even after she lost her hearing in the horrible influenza epidemic of 1918-1919. My father was incredibly generous. Thanks to his foresight we didn't even notice the First World War. Despite strict rationing we were well stocked with sugar, rice and the like. He had built a barn for fifty cows, so the village had milk and meat when a cow was butchered. We grew potatoes and other vegetables.

Our home was also a sort of cultural center. Both my parents were fluent in many languages and they had books in the Scandinavian languages, in English, French, and German. We also borrowed regularly from the university library in Oslo. In the beginning of the 1920's, roads were built both to the south and the north. We were the first to

The Resch home in Tyssedal

have a car, which made possible many interesting trips both in Norway and throughout Europe.

School

I began my schooling in the little white schoolhouse with two classrooms, attending classes every other day. The schoolyard was hidden in the pine forest. Soon the flock of children grew too large, and a new schoolhouse was built where the forest had been. I was one of the first to graduate. To get to the middle school, we first had to travel up the fjord to the tiny community of Odda. The school purchased a 1908 Opel for a school bus in the winter. In the summer, we traveled by bicycle.

The middle school had two rooms in the Hardanger Hotel, Norway's largest wooden building. Our three excellent teachers were genuinely interested in us. The principal gave many entertaining lectures to expand our horizons and to teach us to think independently. One of his lectures on morals made a huge impression on me: "There is only one sin in this life, to act against one's conscience." But how was I to live up to that?

Upon graduating from middle school, the principal addressed us with the formal pronoun "De." We were adults, at the age of 15! As a reward for doing well on my final examinations, I accompanied my parents on a trip to

Oslo. It was thrilling to attend a concert with excited patrons dressed in their finery. My father was elegant in his tails. My mother wore an expensive ball gown, and I had a princess dress, with a lace collar draped over my shoulders, and my hair pinned up in braids for the first time! We sat in the front and had a perfect view of King Haakon and Queen Maud in the royal box, with the handsome Crown Prince Olav between them in his cadet uniform. The second evening, we saw *Vendetta*, with Gerd Egede Nissen, and I was transported yet again. I couldn't sleep that night: I was going to be Norway's greatest actress! Then I saw my chubby body and my moon face in the mirror, and ruled out life as an actress, once and for all.

Along with three of my friends, I ended up at Hegdehaugens High School in Oslo (then known as *Kristiania*), and our illusions of having reached adulthood were quickly stripped away! The high school was as boring and uninspiring as the middle school had been stimulating. But the quiet and interesting Principal Alfsen managed to teach me mathematics, and the friendly, entertaining Pande, who claimed not to understand Norwegian, forced us to make ourselves understood in French. We didn't have a single lesson in grammar, so I speak and write French fluently, but I never learned grammar.

We were forbidden to leave the school grounds. But we ran across the road to Wendelboe to eat the incredible Napoleons anyway. And outside of school, life was bubbling with interesting new friends, new discoveries, and wonderful evenings at the theater. Life was good. At 18, I graduated and had to figure out what I wanted to do with my life. Mother and Father gave me a year abroad, "To think things through."

My childhood was now in the past. I had grown up surrounded by love, security, and understanding. Of course it had not been without its sorrows, illnesses and disappointments. We children made mistakes and got into trouble, but in my memories, the days are filled with sunshine. Now I would have a year abroad, to think things over!

My Adventure Begins

I boarded the Astréa in Bergen, headed for a life of luxury in Hamburg where my Norwegian uncle ran a lucrative lumberyard. We had wonderful expeditions including the opera, theater, and nightclubs. I got to see Berthold Brecht's Threepenny Opera, which had just had its world premier.

In Cologne, I stayed with another uncle who was the distinguished Herr Professor Dr. of Geology. Mother and Father came to celebrate their silver wedding anniversary. In an elegant restaurant we ate Rheinsalm salmon, before the poor fish died from the pollution in the Rhine River. Then they left me with a marvelous family in Heidelberg where I enrolled in a University course in German literature and culture. But I was having much too much fun to concentrate on my studies. With fellow students from Germany and abroad, I went dancing and spent magical summer days canoeing on the Neckar. It was simply a wonderful time!

The high point was a huge demonstration for returning the Saar region to Germany. After the First World War, the Saar was occupied by French troops, but the wish to be reunited with Germany grew stronger and stronger. The Neckar was full of small boats with colored lights. The famous castle ruins and the beautiful old bridge were lit with floodlights, and along side it, spelled out in fireworks, one could read, "Deutchland, die Saar Ruft Dich!" It seemed that half of Germany had gathered for this celebration, and I felt a lump in my throat when I heard the crowds on all the boats burst into patriotic songs.

I followed a series of lectures on the history of philosophy, by Professor Karl Jaspers, with great interest. I had no idea how famous he was, but his idea that man only finds himself through interaction with others, not through books, made a deep impression on me. He occasionally led our excursions, and the students often invited him for private discussions. He was a great admirer of Ibsen.

When the course at the university drew to a close, to my father's great consternation I wrote home and announced, "Tomorrow I leave for Paris!" My mother sensibly commented that the child had to learn to stand on her own two feet! For the first time in my life, I was truly alone. By some miracle I found the K.F.U.K. house (the Danish equivalent of the YWCA) in Paris. I had a vague plan to take an intensive French course in Grenoble, but I thought I should take a look at Paris first. The girls at the K.F.U.K were friendly, but they thought I was a strange country bumpkin because I went around from museum to museum, and did things like climb the Eiffel Tower. One of the girls laughed herself silly when I wanted a ticket to Gounod's *Faust* at the Paris Opera, but Kaia Eide Norena was singing Margareta and I was spellbound!

The American Hospital in Paris

I shared a room with a very withdrawn and silent beautiful Danish girl. One day, she started talking, and after that it was practically impossible to stop her! She spoke incessantly of the American Hospital in Paris. All her life, she had dreamed of being a nurse, and she had been accepted at the most wonderful nursing school in the world. She had been so happy there! But she had many friends and an active social life, and one free evening per week was not enough for her. So she sneaked out and her friends helped her over the high wall when she came home late at night, until she was discovered. She was called into the school office and told: "We have few rules, but those we have must be obeyed. How can we trust you in important matters, when you are not capable of following a simple rule?" She had to leave the same day. She felt she had ruined her life.

9

She talked and talked about this fantastic hospital, and wanted me to look at it. Being a nurse was one of the few things I *hadn't* thought of. "You're crazy," I said, "Why should I go there? I don't want to be a nurse!" "But you could just pop in and take a peek at the wonderful lobby, and have a stroll in the beautiful garden." To keep the peace, I put on my best rags and went out to this paradise on earth.

"I wish to speak to the principal of the nursing school," I informed the receptionist. And I was led into a well-furnished room with deep leather chairs, beautiful carpets and costly paintings on the walls. I suddenly wondered why I was there. What would I say? Should I just cheerfully suggest that the principal show me around?

And then Miss Winnifred Kaltenbach came in. She was tall, slender, gorgeous, with dark, curly hair, wearing perfect white starched clothing from head to shoelaces, and she had intense, dark eyes that could see right into my soul. "What can I do for you, Miss Resch? Would you like to be a nurse?" she asked. I didn't have the nerve to say that I just wanted to see the place. "Well, the next class is full; would you like to begin in February of next year?" At last I was able to find my tongue. "Yes please, and then I can go to Grenoble this winter to perfect my French."

"An excellent idea," said Miss Kaltenbach. And I was led to her secretary's office, where I received an enormous pile of application materials. So I left without seeing anything but the waiting room and the lobby. Was this fate, or just a coincidence? Nursing had never crossed my mind, and I was uncomfortable with the idea of illness and patients. Strangely enough, it did not occur to me to simply rip up the applications and drop them in the wastepaper basket. I felt trapped. When I got back to the K.F.U.K. house, my Danish friend laughed and said: "I knew it."

Two days later, I left Paris for three months in Grenoble, followed by a wonderful Christmas vacation at home. In a little industrial town, the only fun you have is the fun you make yourself, and that's just what we did, dancing in someone's home almost every evening and saying goodbye to our teenage years. Then I went off to my new education with all the necessary equipment. My mother, knowing how much I hated darning, sent me off with twelve pairs of white cotton socks.

Alice in Paris, 1929

II. Nursing Days

On February 1, 1929 I found myself filled with anticipation, waiting along with nineteen other young women of many different nationalities. The future could begin.

We worked hard at the hospital, but what I remember best is the kindness and understanding and help with which we were met, the enduring friendships we made, the interesting patients, and last but not least the wonderful babies! I remember happiness, fun and laughter, the elegant balls and the more intimate gatherings, but when I dig deeper in my chest of memories, I also find three and a half years of long days, endless night shifts, mistakes, despair and sometimes inhuman exertion. Many of us became ill from overexertion, but we took it in stride. We loved our hospital.

I can't remember how many times one of us said, "I can't take anymore. I'm leaving!" And many did leave. I remember overhearing my dear parents as they discussed my decision to become a nurse. They were convinced that I would soon tire of that idea. "I'll show them," I thought to myself, and I grit my teeth and made it through. Soon I felt the same love for the American Hospital that my roommate had shown, but unfortunately, she disappeared from my life.

The school was strict. Absolute honesty was expected, and we knew that the fear of making a mistake might very well be the difference between life and death. Many dramatic and occasionally sad things happened, but also strange and idiotic things. For example: a Russian student in her last year was unfortunate enough to forget a kettle on the stove in the utility room. She had been in a great hurry, and the kettle burned. She couldn't make herself report the incident, so she hid the kettle! Naturally, it was discovered. The reaction was clear and brutal: "if you can't admit such an inconsequential mistake, we can't trust you in a serious situation." She had to pack and leave the hospital that very day. We were all horrified and dismayed. It was a tragedy for a poor Russian refugee. A delegation of her classmates appealed to the administration, but it didn't help.

A couple of weeks later, I arrived on my wing at the hospital after a much-too-short break. The duties were endless: serve the tea, give the afternoon medicine, answer the patients' rings, and give a high colonic irrigation before dinner. Everything was prepared in the utility room. The container with sterile hot water, the rubber hoses, and the extra waterproof sheet were arranged on a cart to be wheeled in to the patient. Catastrophe struck. Just as I was about to insert the hose, it loosened from the container hanging high up on a pole, and four liters of hot water sprayed over the patient, the bed, and me! A colleague helped me to change the patient's robe, and I ran back down to warm up more water and sterilize the hoses. That would take ten minutes, so I thought I could manage to get something else done in the meantime, even though it was strictly forbidden to leave something on the burner unattended. After a half hour's hectic work, I suddenly remembered the hose on the burner! I practically flew down the long corridor back to the utility room, where all my worst fears were confirmed: through the thick soot, I could make out the outline of a colleague. The water had boiled away, and the hose was gone! It had turned to ash and ruined the paint on the walls, which were now black!

I felt like jumping out the window. Now it was *my* turn to be expelled, and I desperately wanted to finish my education. My next thought was: *honesty*. Admit my mistake. So I marched off to Miss Harrell, the principal, with my wet hat dripping over my ears, and purple in the face from anxiety. "What is the meaning of this, bursting in here in such disarray?" she demanded. "Miss Harrell, I've burned up the utility room!" She strode calmly and majestically out

The life of a nursing student was full of scrubbing and dusting - by Alice Resch

of her office, with me trailing after. In the utility room we found a horrified head nurse and a group of students. Miss Harrell looked around in dismay, and said, "Well, Miss Resch, I must say, when you do something, you do it *thoroughly*. What do you suggest we do about this?" I thought she wanted me to choose my own punishment, but I squeaked, "Perhaps we ought to paint the room again?" Silence. Then came a surprise. With a twinkle in her eye she put her arm around my shoulder and said, "Miss Resch, accidents happen in the best families." And that was that! One of my classmates commented on how I always seemed to land on my feet, no matter what.

Nurse and Physical Therapist

My student days had drawn to a close. One beautiful spring day in 1932 I was summoned, at morning prayers. I was both nervous and excited. Why did Miss Harrel want to see me? "It has been interesting to follow Miss Resch's progress on the road to her nursing degree." This was followed by more complimentary words about my temperament and my endurance. Then she pinned the small gold insignia on my brand-new white uniform, to identify me as a nurse from the American Hospital in Paris. It consisted of a white ring with a cross, an anchor and a heart inside: faith, hope and love. How I wanted to be able to live up to that insignia! It was a very emotional moment, and my thoughts went back to the three and a half years of hard work and all the experience I had accumulated to earn my pin!

But the biggest surprise had been saved for last: I was offered the position of head nurse of the Electro- and Hydrotherapy department. I worked there for a year, and then returned home to complete a two-year physical therapy degree at The Oslo Institute of Orthopedics. I had planned to work in Norway, but there was a great shortage of nurses in France and the hospital in Paris wrote asking me to help them.

I returned to Paris, to a position in the maternity ward, where I practically worked myself to death. One summer night the night nurse found me flat on the floor. I was so tired; I *had* to rest my back! I jumped up, but she said nothing. A few days later, I was called into the office. I felt a little nervous. They had received a letter from a doctor in Brides les Bains in Savoy who needed a multilingual physical therapist for his private patients. "You have been working quite hard the last few months, and are obviously exhausted. We will give you a leave of absence if you wish to take the appointment." If I wanted the appointment? I felt like hugging Miss Harrell then and there!

The Spa at Brides les Bain

I traveled down to the fashionable spa in the Alps, where people came to get rid of a few extra pounds through various treatments and by drinking the disgusting, smelly water from a well. For me, it was a welcome change. The work and fresh air helped me lose some weight and made me healthy as a horse. I wrote to my parents:

Here I can go on the most wonderful walks. One day I had a long break before my first patient, so I wandered up the hills on the sunny side of the valley past tiny, picturesque, filthy villages and up, thorough vineyards and fields, chatting with the farmers who paused in their work out of curiosity. It was quite steep. I came to a tiny chapel 1250 meters above sea level, with a magnificent view over the valley and out toward the snow-capped peaks. I could even see my favorite peak – Mont Blanc. The terrain got wilder, the forest more sparse. Soon it disappeared in back of me, and I ran up in the mountain grass, among the grazing cows and sheep. It had taken me three and a half hours to get to the top – the trip down took only 50 minutes. I skipped over roots and stones, and took every imaginable short cut. My goodness, I felt that trip down in my thighs for days!

I make my own breakfast in my room from the spa's own special honey and the most wonderful chocolate truffles. The confectioner's that makes and sells them ought to be out of bounds at a spa such as Brides – they should see the clients' embarrassed faces when they sneak into the store because they can't resist the temptation! Personally, I have to walk past the store in a huge arc to avoid being sucked in! I've tasted the horrible water people keep gulping down, but I've decided that I'd rather be fat and happy the rest of my days than drink that disgusting stuff.

I have all sorts of patients. I begin each day at 7 a.m. with a middle-class French family in a small hotel. The fat and jolly father shuffles around in his slippers and a short-sleeved shirt. The mother is unpleasant in the mornings – her nightcap on her head, her hair on the dresser – and she does not like massage! The father follows the whole process with great interest. He has to massage his wife with a mitten made of knitted twine whenever she demands it, so he wants to learn how to do it properly.

At 7:45 a.m. I hurry over to the large Hotel des Thermes, to a sweet young Armenian girl who is always very sleepy, because she has been out dancing in the casino most of the night. Thin *as a stick, so I have to look hard for the so-called extra kilos. After that, it's on to a French woman who talks me to death – a real aristocrat – she knows everyone worth knowing in France, and I feel like I know them, too! I have to work hard to sneak away from her – she follows me down the hallway in her bright red nightgown...*

Hitler's Shadow on the Horizon

The season in Brides came to a close and in the beginning of September I went back to the hospital. It was a busy time. In addition to nursing, I acquired quite a few massage clients from among the Parisians who had been to Brides. I was unexpectedly offered a position as physical therapist at the von Norden's private clinic in Vienna! I left my position at the American Hospital, spent a nice Christmas at home with my parents, and then left for Vienna in the beginning of 1935.

Wonderful Vienna! Thanks to an acquaintance who had secured the job for me, I found good friends who did their best to show me the city as it had been in the good old days. However, they felt that Vienna hadn't been the same since 1918. There was certainly nothing wrong with the musical life! I heard more or less everything worth hearing in those years between the wars, including the American Negro singer Marian Anderson, at her first performance in Vienna. The Viennese wrinkled their noses in outrage: a Negro, singing Schubert in Vienna! I heard her first and third concerts. The first was in a tiny concert hall, half full. The Viennese were amazed. It seemed that the applause would never end! Miss Anderson was asked to give another concert, then yet another. The last was in the large hall and it was a full house. She became the toast of the town.

Hitler's shadow was already on the horizon. In Vienna, opinion was divided. I treated a very regal lady who said, "Oh, I would be willing to get down on my knees and scrub the floor for that man!" My Jewish friends tried not to attract too much attention. They all had friends or relatives in Germany, and had heard how Jews were being treated there. Several had been arrested, and those who had managed to get out had lost everything. "We are lucky not to be in Germany," they said.

In the spring of 1935, after six months in Vienna, I went back to Paris. It was a beautiful Sunday morning, and on the way, the train passed through Stuttgart. I obeyed my instinct, and got off the train to look up a friend from the hospital who had married a German. Unfortunately they weren't at home, and the next train to Paris wouldn't leave until evening, so I sat down on my suitcase. A nice woman in the house next door saw me, and came out to tell me that the Giesslers were out for the day with friends from Paris. She invited me to go with her and her husband and child for a drive through Stuttgart and the surrounding area. Among other things, we saw a huge camp where Hitler Youth were engaged in hard physical training with shovels and picks in lieu of weapons. The family invited me back for tea in their home. Afterwards, the husband left us, dressed in his brown shirt and tall boots, with a medal on his chest. When I asked him how he had gotten it, he literally clicked his heels together, stood at attention, and said formally, "The Fürher gave me this himself!" It turned out that he had been in the Putsch in Munich, and was one of Hitler's closest friends. I wonder what became of him.

Private Nurse in Paris

Back in Paris, I tried to build up a clientele as a physical therapist. Several of my patients from Vienna were interested in continuing treatment, but the physical therapy work wasn't enough to live on, so I added to my income with private nursing jobs in the evenings. Of course this was too much for one person, so I decided to limit myself to private nursing, a decision I didn't regret, even though I came close to giving up at times. I had one difficult patient after another.

From my diary:

> 1935 *ended with depression and three patient deaths in a row.
> … New Year's Eve I was terribly sick all day, when the telephone
> rang at 5 p.m. It was Thévoz, the second in command of the
> nurses, who beseeched me: "Please, please, at least think it over
> before you say no…" and on and on. I said that I would take the
> night shift, even though I was woozy. I arrived in the isolation
> unit and found a truly beautiful child, only six months old,
> critically ill with croup. I stayed with that child for two hours
> before it was seized with cramps and died. It sounds awful – and
> it was – but never before had I cleaned up so quickly after an
> experience with a patient. It was pure superstition. I felt I had to
> get out of there before the New Year was upon me, so it wouldn't
> be sullied by evil. At 11:45 p.m., still in my white uniform, I
> stormed over to Zaren Wang's, and just managed to raise my
> champagne glass to toast the New Year. At 2:30 a.m. I collapsed
> into bed. Something strange had happened. All signs of
> depression were gone. I had the distinct feeling that now I was rid
> of evil for a while. I actually said to myself, "1936 will be a good
> year for me!" and proceeded to sleep my way into the new year.*

There were fun times, too. Being a private nurse in Paris in
the 1930's was an entertaining experience. The telephone
would ring, and someone would ask: "Can you accompany a
patient to a clinic in Munich this evening?" "Can you
accompany a family by motorboat through the canal from
Le Havre to Marseille to take care of a baby?" "Can you
leave for Le Havre to take care of an elderly woman on a
yacht that's going to Biarritz?" Or: "Can you accompany a
seriously ill patient to America on the Queen Mary?"

It was, in a word, fairly hectic. The only way to travel
between America and Europe at that time was by boat, so
if Americans or prominent members of society became ill
in France, they came to "our" hospital in Neuilly, right
outside of Paris. There was always work for us. Most of us
were fluent in several languages, and we were fairly
sophisticated. We became personally acquainted with
many politicians, film actresses and actors, millionaires

and aristocrats. We lived in fashionable hotels or their amazing private residences, traveled with them, and we were exposed to a lifestyle we otherwise would never have experienced. When we weren't in uniform, we had to be well dressed. This was not particularly difficult, because good seamstresses saw the advertising value of our proximity to our rich clients and gave us good prices. What woman can resist an accomplished seamstress at a bargain price? I'll never forget the time one of my patients and I turned up wearing the same hat! I had given her the address of my little milliner. How we laughed! But neither of us wore that hat again, and we never went back to that particular milliner.

I had a circle of friends, and when we weren't working, we went to bars or to *thé dansant*, and ate in the popular restaurants. Along with three other private nurses from the American Hospital, I rented four rooms with a shared bath and a kitchen above the stalls at Marymont, the convent school in Neuilly. We never thought to save money. When our money ran out, we borrowed from each other. New sources of income would soon turn up and then it would be our turn to loan to others. Live while you can — who knows what tomorrow will bring!

Two of us were relaxing over a lazy breakfast after a long and difficult case, looking forward to a few days of enjoying the wonderful May weather in Paris, when the telephone rang. We looked at each other. Who should answer? It *could* be a private call, but I dragged myself over to the infernal telephone to answer. Of course, it was the hospital. "How long is your passport valid, Miss Resch?" My angelic disposition took off, and I snarled, "My God, Miss Andrews, isn't it enough that you are always after us for our French Identity Cards? Do you have to involve yourself with our passports as well?" "Now, now, take it easy. I'm just asking!" I found my passport. "It's valid for six more months." "Good, can you be ready to accompany a seriously ill patient to America at 2:00 this afternoon?" You bet I could!

It was 11 a.m. Three hours to go. I called my good friend
Anne Crawshay, who had a car. That wonderful creature
was outside my door in 10 minutes. She drove me to the
American Consulate and continued on to my tailor where
my new spring outfit was ready, and then on to Madame
Suzanne, to pick up my new Easter hat. She bought three
pairs of stockings, and zoomed back to the consulate,
where I had just convinced them to give me the necessary
visa immediately. "I'm leaving for the States at 2 p.m. –
please give me a tourist visa!" I said, as I put my Norwegian
passport on the counter in front of me. The fellow behind
the counter looked at it, and said, "I'm sorry, but we can't
give you a visa with a foreign passport. You were born in
Chicago, so you are an American citizen. Therefore, your
Norwegian passport is a foreign passport as far as we are
concerned." I did my best to control my temper, which was
at the boiling point. "No! I'm *not* an American citizen, I'm
Norwegian, and that's why I have a Norwegian passport!"
Was my trip to America going to disappear before my very
eyes because of this man's inability to grasp the situation?
I asked to speak with the Consul.

"Sit down and wait, and I'll see what I can do." I don't know
how long I waited, but it seemed like an eternity.
Eventually, a woman appeared, with her arms full of
papers. "We can give you a visa on one condition," she
said. "That you sign these papers renouncing all rights to
apply for American citizenship again!" I had never before in
my life felt as European as I did at that moment, as I gave
up my birthright as fast as I could sign my name, and got
permission to enter the United States as a tourist, at the
last possible minute.

Anne rushed me back to Marymont, helped me pack, and at
exactly 2 p.m. I arrived in the office of the hospital director,
Dr. Lawrence Fuller, somewhat out of breath.
"Congratulations!" he said with a smile, which made my
day. A compliment from him was something we all valued.
Dr. Fuller introduced me to Dr. William Jason Mixter, a
famous brain specialist from Boston, Miss Robbins, a

friend of the patient, and Miss Dorothy Howard, the patient herself. She suffered from a terrible case of leukemia, and was extremely weak. Miss Robbins and Dr. Mixter would also be accompanying the patient on her trip home. My heart was pounding, as was usual before a new case. Would I measure up? Would I make the right decisions in an emergency? But Miss Howard turned out to be a good person, and to my great relief, we got along well. An ambulance took us to the boat train, and for the first time I saw beautiful Normandy roll past through the windows in the train. A special luxury car had been reserved for us. I felt like I was playing a part in a film.

It was dark when we arrived in Cherbourg. From the dock, we could see the unforgettable sight of enormous Queen Mary, lit up with floodlights. A motorboat took us out to the giant ship, where we were met by the ship's doctor. Two men carried Miss Howard on a stretcher to her cabin, which turned out to be a spacious, comfortable salon with an alcove for the bed. My cabin had an adjoining door. And what a bathroom! There were three faucets over the bathtub, for hot, cold, and seawater! I had all this luxury to myself, because Miss Howard was so weak, she had to have sponge baths in bed. She was very easy to deal with. Besides a morning and evening toilet and an injection, all I had to do was make her as comfortable as possible. She was too tired to talk much, and what little energy she had she saved for friends who visited. Her condition seemed to improve during the journey, and towards the end of the trip I even took her up on deck in a wheelchair.

Miss Howard was a seasoned traveler, who had been to most of the jungles in the world. She had just come from Java, Sumatra and Borneo, and her cabin was full of the most grotesque masks, spears, fetishes, bows and arrows, that were headed for the ethnological museum in Boston. I had lots of time for myself, and used the opportunity to explore the huge ship. You could forget you were on the sea. The Queen Mary appeared to have everything: a long shopping avenue, a swimming pool, a gym, a playroom for the children, shuffleboard, and equipment for shooting clay pigeons.

Some passengers tried to be friendly, but I was working, and couldn't allow myself to socialize. I sat on the deck in a deck chair, wrote countless letters on the ship stationery, saw movies, or took in an afternoon concert. Time flew by as we headed toward the New World. The days had 25 hours instead of the customary 24, in order to eliminate the time difference between east and west. I was up very early on Monday May 9, and was richly rewarded. Sailing into New York harbor was like a dream! The morning sun cast a golden sheen on the Statue of Liberty, and the skyscrapers glowed pink. Strange that a world of stone could be so beautiful!

There was plenty of time to prepare Miss Howard for the docking, and we proceeded through customs without the usual formalities. After a drive in an ambulance to the station, we boarded a deluxe Pullman to Boston. I wished I had eyes on the back of my head in order to be able to capture all the wonderful sights. On the train, I experienced my first typical American lunch: chicken salad and ice water! The interesting landscape passed by the train windows. It varied from "the wrong side of the tracks" so often described in American literature, to beautiful forests and fields. I was surprised. I thought that the eastern U.S. was comprised of towns and factories.

Finally we arrived in Boston, "the most European city in the U.S.A." Mrs. Mixter said: "I hope you will stay with us for a few days before your return journey. We would so like you to see a true, old-fashioned New England home, and take back a good impression of our country." She was a large woman with a deep voice and a heart of gold. We drove to the impressive Massachusetts General Hospital, and with the help of a couple of the local nurses, I installed Miss Howard in a private section there. Our good-byes were warm. She was wonderful person, and we had become good friends.

The Mixter's charming old family home was in Brookline, a pleasant suburb. I was given a cozy room with a four-poster bed, a private bath, and a view out over the harbor. Everyone wanted to give me the best possible impression of their America. It was like one long party! But finally, I took the train back to New York, where I found a room at The Pickwick Arms, a hotel for women. My last days in the city were spent with friends who had a beautiful apartment in Greenwich Village. We saw the sights, including the Empire State Building. The view from the top took my breath away. There was a meter showing how the building swayed in the wind. It was very scary! What if the elevator stopped working? We ate lunch in a drugstore: more chicken salad, ice water, and ice cream. Another highlight was Rockefeller Center, where we ate dinner in a restaurant on the top floor, and we had an amazing view of New York by night, with millions of lights as far as the eye could see. The skyscrapers looked as if they were lit from the inside. The starlight above was icing on the cake.

After breakfast on May 18, my friends drove me to my ship, the Normandie. It was huge. Farewell, New York! Farewell, America! Farewell, friends old and new! Your generosity warmed my heart! On the Queen Mary we had traveled First Class, but the trip home was Tourist Class. And even that was very comfortable, and I was *free*! The first day, there were no locked doors between classes and everyone could wander throughout the ship.

The ship was booked to capacity. For some reason, we had had to pick up passengers from another ship, resulting in three to a tourist-class cabin instead of two. I shared my lodgings with two very nice girls. The days floated by. Play a round of shuffleboard, sit in a chair on deck and read, have cocktails in the bar at lunch, a movie or a concert in the afternoon, more cocktails before dinner, and then dancing all night. In the beautiful concert hall I heard the famous pianist Arthur Rubinstein for the first time. He was on his way to a concert tour in Europe.

Months later, back at the hospital on the night shift, I encountered Rubinstein again. A small polyp was removed from his vocal cords, and he had been given strict orders not to use his voice. Other than that, he was in great shape, so I can't imagine why he needed a private nurse. He was very nice and cheerful. He had to write everything down in order to communicate, which caused a lot of laughter. Finally, I said he had to write down the laughter, as well!

We finally docked in Le Havre. My wonderful journey was at an end. But nothing compares to Paris! The next morning I left for the hospital to report to Dr. Fuller, and deliver the gifts and messages I had been given for him. Of course I ran right into Miss Andrews, who said, "Oh, you're back. Can you leave for Vienna this evening to pick up a sick child?"

Anne and Jack Crawshay

On January 20, 1937, I was back at the home of the Crawshay family, with my very best friends, Anne and Jack Crawshay. Our acquaintance began when I was hired to nurse Jack Crawshay during the several months he was ill. But the friendship lasted a lifetime. Anne Crawshay was the daughter of Lord Tyrell, the former ambassador to France and Permanent Under Secretary in the British Office of Foreign Affairs. As a young woman, Anne accompanied her father to Paris during the peace negotiations following World War I and served as his hostess when he became ambassador. She knew all the politicians and journalists. Her husband, Captain Jack Crawshay, became very ill, and I came to their home as a private nurse from January until November 1936. They remained my dear friends their whole lives, and came to mean very much to me. It was Anne who got me involved with the Quakers.

One day, someone will no doubt write a biography of Anne. She was a unique human being. I copied part of an article in the *Paris Daily Mail* about her:

> Miss Anne Tyrrell, … *really belongs to the Diplomatic Service.*
> *While Sir William was Permanent Under Secretary at the Foreign*
> *Office, she acted for some time as his secretary. Now she is*
> *carrying on the good work in Paris, and I cannot help thinking*
> *that she will probably be our first lady diplomat.*

But Anne laughed. "Professional diplomat? No, one has much more influence when one pulls the strings behind the scenes – cherchéz la femme." She had real influence, because people listened to her opinions.

Anne grew up on an estate in the south of England, with two brothers and a sister. There were true children of nature, surrounded by all sorts of animals. One Sunday, she horrified the parish by wandering in to church with her favorite goat! Her mother was the daughter of another well-known British diplomat, David Urquhart. Lady Tyrrell had very modern ideas concerning bringing up children, but didn't have much time for her own. Instead, she wrote history books, and impressed many with her charitable work.

So Anne gravitated toward her father. Sir William Tyrrell took her along on his travels to France, Italy and Germany, and she had a long stay in America. It was not easy for the young single woman. No one took her seriously! She was invited to boring teas with schoolgirls, so she hurriedly married a young English diplomat. But the marriage of convenience was a mistake, and was annulled without difficulty by the Pope. Some years later, Anne met the love of her life, the young Captain Jack Crawshay, who came to work as Assistant Military Attaché at the British Embassy. Jack was one of the 1920's "Lost Generation." In 1914, he enlisted immediately upon finishing at Eton, even though he was under the legal age. He served during all four years of the war. Then he inherited a sizable fortune from an uncle, and spent the next several years just having fun. But then he met Anne, and was content to settle down and build a beautiful home with her.

We young people followed the political and social changes closely, and our discussions were lively when we got together. We talked about Adolf Hitler, who had managed to win the election in 1933 in Germany, and who slowly gained so much power that he thought he could ignore the Versailles Treaty. We didn't spend much time thinking about Mussolini and Fascism. "Musse" had, after all, been in power since we were children, and had "straightened up" things in Italy. But we were aghast that England and France looked the other way when he invaded poor Ethiopia in February 1935. And we were firmly on the side of the government in Spain, when Franco started the Civil War. Several of us volunteered for the International Brigade. We talked and talked but we didn't lift a finger!

Occasionally, we felt a cold wind from the east. Hitler was a threatening cloud on the horizon. But war? Hitler couldn't possibly be strong enough to stand up to the Allies. France was invincible with its Maginot Line*! As we sat at the sidewalk cafés on the Champs Élysées we were worried. We heard only German and Yiddish around us. Thousands of Jewish refugees had come to France, which had generously taken them in.

I wrote to my parents, on the occasion of Pa's sixtieth birthday, in March 1938:

> Dear Pa...
>
> I send you all possible good wishes for your 60th birthday, and for the next 30 years!

---

* A fortified line of defense along the eastern border of France, constructed after World War I, the Maginot Line includes aboveground fortresses and underground hospitals, communications systems, living quarters and storage spaces. Thanks to the Maginot Line, France was considered "impenetrable" until 1940 when the Germans successfully invaded in three weeks by going through Belgium, and north and behind the Maginot Line.

...we are slowly becoming optimistic again. Hitler gets whatever he points at, so at the moment he has no reason to go to war. War will most likely not break out before autumn, at any rate – he needs some time to finish with Austria, before he can wander into Czechoslovakia. Other than that, it's awful that Hitler can just reach out and take whatever he wants.

The Crawshays lunched the other day with a well-known American journalist, Knickerbocker, who has been in Vienna for quite a while, and he told them that the foreign journalists were literally locked into their hotel rooms during the excitement so that the foreign papers would only have access to the official news – ergo, no true information about the situation would get out.

I strolled down the Champs Élysées yesterday afternoon ... It was strange to see how many Austrian refugees have managed to get in. I heard Austrian everywhere – just like in 1933, after the "clean up" in Germany. But the French don't want them here this time – they feel that there are enough Jews here already ... So far, there hasn't been much anti-Semitic feeling here, but you can feel it start to bubble up.

Then Hitler threatened to invade Sudentenland and Chamberlain flew to Berlin to mediate. 1938 was difficult. We nurses were no longer needed. The Americans went home, and everyone who could leave did so. 1,800 Americans tried in vain to get out on the Queen Mary when it left from Le Havre. Paris was under a blackout. Businesses closed. Historical buildings and monuments were covered with sandbags. The streets were empty. Would there be war? We crossed our fingers and promised to be good the rest of our lives if only there wouldn't be war!

More and more refugees from Czechoslovakia streamed into Paris. I was unemployed, so the hospital asked me to go out to Gare de l'Est together with the hospital's chauffeur in a large bus, to pick up American refugees. We just waved an American flag and offered to take them to the American Hospital in Paris. But when the other refugees saw the American flag, we were bombarded. We managed to get our Americans on the bus, and told the confused, desperate others to take a taxi to the hospital, and we would try to find a solution for them. This didn't please the hospital's administration. They telephoned everywhere to try to find places for them. We drove two rounds, and imagined we were making a difference.

From my diary, September 28, 1938:

> What a day! I woke to the headlines in the paper, announcing that Germany had given Prague an ultimatum – and if an answer wasn't received by two o'clock, the order to mobilize and invade Czechoslovakia would be given! It was announced on the radio at ten o'clock.
>
> In the hospital, everyone went around with long faces. Some nurses had already received telegrams telling them to come home. … All the hospital employees had picked up their gas masks!
>
> Then we heard the latest news! It was broadcast that Mussolini (most likely at the request of England) had asked for a conference with Hitler tomorrow. So now they will meet with Chamberlain and Daladier in Munich!
>
> Perhaps the question can be settled peacefully, after all! We can almost dare to breathe again. These last days have been awful. It is depressing to see nothing but overburdened trucks in town – filled with luggage, people and dogs leaving Paris.

A man named Rothschild asked the hospital director for an ambulance to take him and his family to Switzerland. "You can't have an ambulance, even if you pay your weight in gold!" was the answer, but Rothschild turned up in front of the hospital at two o'clock with an ambulance!

September 30, 1938

> What a pleasure to wake up this morning! The sun was shining, the birds singing, and everything seemed peaceful.
>
> The treaty in Munich was signed last night at 1:30 a.m. Hitler gets what he wanted, unfortunately, but at least there is peace! We cried and cheered and went to the Champs Élysées to celebrate

with champagne – you could see signs everywhere that said "Merci Daladier. Thank you Chamberlain!" And innumerable English and French flags – the street was filled with happy, celebrating citizens. "Peace in our time!" Chamberlain had proclaimed!

The day after the Munich Treaty, Anne Crawshay took me and some other friends out to lunch at Fouquets, one of the big restaurants on the Champs Élysées. It was packed, but we had a good table, and could see Daladier wander up toward the Arc du Triomphe to re-light the flame over the grave of the Unknown Soldier. A hysterical crowd followed him, cheering and crying and singing and laughing. They fell into each other's arms in ecstasy and relief and emotion and gratefulness. The people's reactions to the 1918 Armistice couldn't have been much more enthusiastic. It was an incredible experience. The choreography was perfect. Just as Daladier lit the flame, two spotlights were turned on, lighting up a huge tricolor French flag, which hung from the top of the arch almost to the ground beneath. Dusk was descending, and the illuminated flag had an amazing effect. Tens of thousands of people who had just been cheering, were moved to silence.

Anne invited me home for dinner. Dinners in the Crawshay home were always exciting with so many interesting and influential people. The discussions were lively, the stories entertaining. Questions and problems were examined in depth, and Anne's opinion was always heard. This particular evening, after the victory parade, several English diplomats came by. The enthusiasm from the street had disappeared. Chamberlain had said "Peace in our time," but who would pay for it? His intentions were so good, but we had weakened in our promises to Czechoslovakia, and Hitler had got his Sudetenland. It was too bad we weren't already at war now while Hitler was still ill prepared. The war would come, sooner or later. We would have to place our hopes on Churchill.

From my diary, October 10, 1938

Was with Anne (Crawshay) down at the British Embassy, to help write addresses on letters from Chamberlain – A nice letter he wrote, copied thousands of times – to be sent out to all who have written to thank him for having saved the peace. So here in France, the job falls on the Embassy, which has in turn mobilized all the help it can! But when we left, Anne said, "Poor old Chamberlain, he is a peaceful, naive soul who is convinced he did the only right thing. But we'll never hear the end of how we gave up Czechoslovakia just like that – and the war is unavoidable – Chamberlain won't last much longer – Churchill is the up-and-coming man in England."

It's strange to think back and realize that Anne Crawshay had a unique sense of what was to come; time proved her right. And Hitler's insanity went on and on. We shuddered when we heard his horrible voice on the radio. On November 7, 1938, a young Polish Jewish student whose parents had been arrested and sent to a concentration camp murdered von Rath, a secretary at the German Embassy. Was this the murder that unleashed Kristallnacht, the night of fear, November 10 and 11?

On November 13, I wrote in my diary:

It's terrible that we are running around having fun when the Jews in Germany are enduring such horrible persecution – it's almost too awful to even read about. The terror knows no bounds – it's the work of Göring – it's too bad it wasn't he who was shot, instead of the little secretary at the German Embassy here.

Although Hitler yelled at the top of his lungs that he wanted peace, and that he had no more territorial wishes, he still scared us. In March, he entered Prague, and neither France nor England reacted. The winter of 1938-1939 was hard. I had huge amounts of work, with tiring, hopeless patients. In June, I went home for the most wonderful summer vacation with my parents in Lofthus, Norway. I decided that I would come home every year. But when I left on August 1, I had a feeling it would be a long time before I was back, despite my resolution to come home every summer. The world was more unstable than ever. It would be almost six years before I saw Norway and my dear parents again.

III. The War Years Begin

The American Hospital

I did nothing but wait during those ten days between August 20, 1939 when I returned to Paris after my wonderful summer vacation in Norway, and the outbreak of the war on September 1. I couldn't stand the thought of any tiring work. There wasn't much work to be found either. The feeling in the air was much as it had been in September of the previous year.

Hitler was ranting about Danzig and the Polish Corridor. What would happen? People left the city. Windows were protected with sandbags and strips of paper. We picked up our gas masks and bought blackout flashlights with dark blue bulbs. I visited my friends, or hung out at bistros with my colleagues and talked about the war. Should we go home, or should we stay? Then, Germany invaded Poland. France and England declared war on Germany.

As early as 1938 the American Hospital in Paris (AHP) had registered the private nurses who were interested in working if it became necessary. Naturally, most of us were willing. Now the hospital called and we responded. I must admit that I enjoyed the unusual situation. The administration fell all over itself trying to make sure that

The provisional hospital in Etretat

everything went smoothly. The Americans and French-Americans who were still in the city loaned their cars to evacuate civilian patients to the Golf Hotel, located in the tiny resort town of Etretat on the Normandy coast. A year earlier, the AHP had rented it "to be on the safe side."

The hotel had been turned into a modern hospital, with an operating room and an x-ray division. We left for Etretat, a long caravan of more or less luxury cars, with a couple of patients, nurses and as much luggage as there was room for. The sun shone, and Isle de France and Normandy were at their best. It felt more like a carefree tourist outing than the night shift with difficult patients! The stay in Etretat was like a vacation. I was responsible for obstetrics at night, but both the mothers and babies slept peacefully, so my work was easy. I swam at the beach and went on hikes with the other nurses and doctors. All the hotels were full of "luxury refugees." They felt fairly safe in such close proximity to the AHP.

One afternoon a group of English R.A.F. officers came over from Dieppe. They were bored, and they wanted to meet the American nurses. We ended up drinking and dancing. They were so young – between 19 and 23 – good looking and friendly. They were proud of belonging to "The Crack Squadron," and acted like they were the very first to come over to help the French fight against the "Fritzes." But this life of luxury was far removed from the war. Why should I take care of civilian patients for free? I had enlisted of my own free will, but this was war work. After a few weeks I asked to be allowed to return to AHP, which had become a military hospital with just a small section for civilians. The trains and buses were reserved for military purposes, so the only way to get to Paris was to hitchhike in a private car.

Gas Mask Storage and Bomb Shelter

I returned to the AHP in Neuilly, and was assigned to the storage room for gas masks which also served as the hospital's bomb shelter. The hospital had been built on the site of King Louis Philippe's Chateau de Neuilly. It had an underground tunnel from the castle to the Seine. Perhaps it had been an escape route. Now it ended even with the neighbor's garden wall, and had been furnished as an excellent bomb shelter.

The air-raid sirens always screamed out their miserable warning at night. I stumbled out of bed and spread the alarm. The first time, a couple of sleepy people joined me, but after that I was always alone except for a million starving mosquitoes. My colleagues just laughed, turned over in bed, and slept on. Paris was never bombed while I was responsible for the bomb shelter. The gas mask storage room was something else entirely. This was where we received wounded soldiers from the front. We washed and deloused them, and sent them up to the appropriate departments. One of the less popular jobs was sorting the stinking clothing and marking them with the appropriate names before sending them to be disinfected.

We passed the time as best we could by doing the same things over and over again: scrubbing bathtubs, dusting invisible dust on the medicine bottles, piling swabs and compresses into containers, sewing face masks, telling stories, eating candy and knitting. The hospital was teeming with American and French society ladies who had volunteered for war work. I put several of them to work in the storage room, but there was so little to do! They were eager and willing, but most likely disappointed that there was so little need for them.

Refugees from Alsace-Lorraine

I saw a lot of Anne Crawshay during that period. Jack had been mobilized, and was serving as adjunct for Lord Gort, the top commander for the British troops in France.

With the declaration of war, the French government had decided to evacuate half a million people from Alsace-Lorraine into the southern and western parts of France. Anne couldn't get the fate of those poor people out of her mind. We kept hearing about the dire conditions they found themselves in. During the first days of September, they were forced to leave their homes with only a couple of hours' notice, and only what they could carry. Refugees had to be put up in castle ruins and dilapidated farms that had been uninhabited for the last 40 years, in schools where there were no beds, and in churches that were no longer used for worship. The poor evacuees were bitter and disappointed. They protested, but to no avail. Why were they not allowed to return home, just to collect the necessities from their homes so long as nothing was happening at the front?

Several private citizens tried to help, and a few organized charities started their own social work. One of the first was the Protestant organization CIMADE (*Comité InterMouvements Aupres des Evacués*), under the leadership of prominent French Protestants, Pastor Boegner and Mademoiselle Madeleine Barot, who installed themselves in La Rochelle in Charente Maritime. We would eventually work closely with them.

We discussed the evacuee problem from every angle, and decided that we needed to see the conditions ourselves in order to determine what could be done. Anne mobilized some of her friends and I gathered some of the women volunteers from the storage room. We collected all the usable clothing we could find and eight of us drove in five cars down to the Dordogne. Anne had contacted the Prefect in Périgueux ahead of time. I had no problem getting the time off from the hospital, as the work was so obviously necessary.

Our departure fell on a beautiful October day. It was as if we were all going sightseeing in the Dordogne but for the bundles of clothing strapped to the roof of the car. We were met in style by the Mayor of Strasbourg, his deputy Mr. Eccard, and Mrs. Eccard, who was the self-appointed director for *Les Oeuvres de Secours pour Les Alsaciens en Dordogne*. They treated us to a magnificent dinner and then installed us in the Hotel Commerce and the Hotel Domino.

The next morning, we loaded the packages of clothing and shoes into an empty room, and the Mayor of Strasbourg and his secretary took us sightseeing in one of the most beautiful areas in all of France. They said they wanted us to "...get a personal impression of the misery among the evacuees." We were taken through Brantôme, which I remembered well from the previous year when I had spent the night there with my parents. The atmosphere now was less idyllic; it was after all filled to bursting with refugees! We continued through Verteillac, Ribérac and St. Astier.

The idea was to meet the evacuees and see their living conditions for ourselves. When we stopped at a dilapidated farm with rotting buildings, a few blond children were climbing on an old gate. Upon our arrival, they stopped their play in surprise, stared at us, and ran into one of the houses. The children's mother and grandfather came out, regarded us suspiciously, and their faces darkened when our guide asked them if we could see how they lived. They feared we were voyeurs, come to stare at their miserable, humiliating existence. They were clean and well dressed, but we were told that they were wearing their only belongings. Since they had been allowed to take only what they could carry, the choice naturally fell on items with sentimental value. The father had been mobilized.

They became somewhat more receptive when they heard that we hoped to help. We were shown into the house.

The kitchen was fairly large, but completely dark because of the tiny windows. The only furniture was a few chairs and a table, a kitchen counter and a few cupboards, but we saw no appliances or trappings of an everyday kitchen. The young woman began to cry, and the man asked us why in the world he hadn't been allowed to return home to pick up some clothing and a few household essentials. Winter was coming and they needed warmer clothes. He pointed out that the Germans were being held back at the Maginot line, and he couldn't believe that rail transportation no longer existed for civilians. We stood there speechless, and left them the little we had in the car: a pan, some towels, some children's clothing. We made a note of the supplies they needed most, and promised to return. A little of the initial bitterness was clearly gone when we drove on.

The more we saw, the deeper the silence among us became. We were faced with sad reality. Embarrassed, we saw ourselves as "well-meaning ladies," and I considered how easily I could have ended up as a refugee. Why must these people suffer so, while I traveled around like some kind of tourist? This was my first encounter with the refugee problem.

Albert Schweizer wrote:

> Wer viel schönes im Leben erfahren hat, muss entsprechend viel dafür hergeben.
> Wer von eigenem Leid verschontist, 'hat sich berufen zu fühlen, zu helfen
> das Leid der anderen zu lindern.
> Alle müssen wir an der Last von Weh, die auf der Welt liegt, mittragen.

[He who has experienced beauty in life must be grateful. And he who has been spared suffering, must take responsibility for helping those who are suffering.
We must all share the weight of the burdens of this world.]

I would throw myself whole-heartedly into Anne's aid work.

We were shown around Périgueux, where the refugees had a more "official" status. The hospitals were overflowing. We met Doctors Faucher and Pautrier who were in charge of the large hospitals in Strasbourg. They invited us to see *Clairvivre*, where the evacuated Strasbourg hospitals were located. For one day, our group was divided into two, so some could attend a formal tea at the Prefecture and discuss the charitable aid work with the two Prefects.

Dr. Pautrier gave us a sad tour of *Clairvivre*. Patients had spent weeks lying on straw mattresses on the floor. They needed everything. The two doctors saw the situation as hopeless. They had begged for a car so that they could pick up necessary equipment from Strasbourg, but had not yet had any luck. The army had first priority. They had been promised several railroad cars to transport material, but the two institutions were not on the same rail line.

The Doctor lit up when I did as Anne had instructed, and asked if he would like an ambulance. Madame Venizelos, the widow of a Greek Prime Minister, lived in Paris, and had made an ambulance available for Anne. It came a week later. At the time, the gift was anonymous, but I don't think there's any harm in revealing that it was from Madame Venizelos who had lived in exile in France for many years and wanted to return some of the hospitality she had been shown.

It was an anticlimax to return to my storage room. I had some physical therapy patients among the soldiers, which was nice for a change. Then I was asked to treat a civilian in the small section reserved for "normal" people. I was willing, but made it clear I would send a bill. Soldiers were treated with the greatest pleasure, but why should I treat rich patients for free? The result of all this was the discovery that I had been "volunteering" my services since September. Soon my name was included on the list of those to receive a salary, and I would be paid from the first of November. But after one week, I left the hospital for good!

Société des Amis

I had a special experience: Anne Crawshay managed to secure a travel pass to Troyes, a town in the forbidden military zone, made up almost entirely of underwear factories and stores. She gave me a sizable sum of money. One of the volunteers from the storage room and I took the truck as well as the woman's own private car to Troyes, which was humming with soldiers. The factories were ecstatic when they realized we were there to purchase such large amounts. They rolled out the red carpet and we were extravagantly wined and dined. It was a miracle that we made it out in one piece, our vehicles filled with underwear in all shapes and sizes. We didn't even need to unpack; the next day we drove directly to the Dordogne, a marvelous sight with all the autumn colors. The refugees greeted us as if we were old friends, and we became re-acquainted with the misery there. Luckily there was enough food, so no one was starving. Rationing had not yet begun.

In the meantime, Anne Crawshay visited various organizations to offer her help. One of these was the French/Quaker organization *Société des Amis*, or Society of Friends, where she met one of our future co-workers, Toot Bleuland van Oordt. This tiny organization had a tight budget, which they were using to help those fleeing Hitler's Germany, mostly political exiles, but also some Jews. Toot sent Anne on to Mr. Howard Kershner, an American Quaker who was in charge of the *Comité International d'Aide aux Enfants de France* (The International Commission for Assistance of Child Refugees). This organization, made up of Quakers from various countries, had worked in Spain during the Civil War. Michael Hansson, a Norwegian judge, was the Commission's president.

When Franco assumed power and the Civil War ended, between four and five hundred thousand Spanish republicans fled to France. The Commission chose France as its base, and opened sixteen colonies for Spanish children in western and southern France. Anne's offer of help interested Mr. Kershner. He offered her a few rooms in his large complex where she could work independently. The result was the birth of Anne's *Comité*. Anne mobilized her friends quickly. Because she was quite influential in Paris, and personally acquainted with many important people, she quickly secured all the necessary permits and papers without bureaucratic interference. She collected large amounts of money, both in France and England. Queen Elizabeth gave a thousand pounds, which was a sizable sum in 1939.

In Paris, I set up a meeting between Anne and Dr. Fuller of the AHP, who was also very concerned about the refugees from Alsace-Lorraine. Together, they visited several of the Prefects in the inner departments, which resulted in medicine and social service aid from five of the departments. Dr. Fuller was to organize the medical service in the department in Indre.

Refugees at Châteauroux in Indre

Anne asked if I would help Dr. Fuller, which I was of course happy to do. Luckily, I found three good helpers immediately: my colleague Lisa Nilssen from the AHP; Tob Jensen, a Norwegian Red Cross nurse; and Jeanette Siefert, a nurse from Alsace. Lisa had returned home to Norway after she completed her nursing studies at the hospital, but when her beloved France entered the war, she wanted to return. She said she practically begged the French Embassy on her knees to give her a travel permit, and after a while they couldn't stand the sight of her, and gave her the permit just to get rid of her!

Lisa said she went into the office at the AHP with a smile: "Here I am, what can I do?" "Yes, well Miss Nilssen, you see, we are up to our ears in volunteers who have so little to do that they just end up leaving. We just don't need any more help." "All right," she replied, "I'll find something *else* to do!" Lisa even managed to smile when she said goodbye. But I was happy they turned her down, because that meant she could accompany me to Châteauroux in Indre. Tob Jensen was from Bergen and had done her nursing studies in southern Norway. Jeanette Siefert was a social worker as well as a nurse, and had been at the AHP for a while when we met.

The team consisted of two young American doctors and Dr. Fuller who made long lists of medications and instruments. Anne and her helpers took care of clothing, kitchen equipment, some food, and the funds. I was allotted a car, and finally, on December 8, we three Norwegian girls drove over icy winter roads through thick fog to Châteauroux with all the material the car could hold. The Prefect, Monsieur Grimal, came in person to welcome us over a drink. He looked like he was trying to figure out what in the world he would do with this unlikely gang of giggling youngsters!

In Indre alone there were over twenty thousand refugees from the border departments, and just as many from the other Prefectures, and all the doctors had been mobilized to the front. Because we had two cars, we were asked to go to the villages that were farthest away. We arranged to treat refugees twice a week at each of them. The work was hard, but we had the feeling that what we were doing mattered. The first times we made it out to the outlying villages, we got the impression that the refugees had come out of curiosity to see if the American was a *real* doctor. They soon discovered that he was indeed the real thing, and after that they came only when they needed medical help. We saw forty patients a day on average.

The consulting room was a story in itself. 150 people now lived in the ruin of *Chateau de Clion*, where no one had lived for the past forty years. We had the only room with four walls and an intact roof. The inhabitants soon became accustomed to our presence, and did what they could to improve it for us by finding curtains and painting the walls. At another place, we worked in the kitchen. And at a third, our room was a space behind two sheets suspended from the ceiling in the corner of the dormitory room of a nursing home for the aged. Twenty bed-ridden patients listened with great interest to every sound that came from behind the sheets!

In the other Prefectures where Anne's *Comité* worked, some large buses which she had acquired from England were furnished as mobile consulting rooms, but we carried everything we needed in a suitcase. In the beginning, transportation was a sore point. Jeanette Siefert, who took care of the social work, needed a car. A large, fancy Ford that had been purchased for a sightseeing trip in Asia was donated to us. But the chauffeur had forgotten to fill the radiator with anti-freeze. It was far below zero, and at night the block cracked! Everything had been taken for the army, so there were no extra parts. Buying a new car was impossible as well.

Anne managed to secure five ambulances from England. They came with ten female military chauffeurs known as WAAFs or Women's Auxiliary Ambulance Force. When they came breezing in one evening, we received them joyfully, thinking our transportation problems were gone. When they heard that we were only to be allotted two of the cars (the others were bound for Charente and Les Landes) the intelligent leader of these women said, "We are a group, and shall not be separated." In the end, Dr. Fuller rescued us. AHP also had an ambulance park with volunteer female chauffeurs in smart uniforms. They were embarrassed that they had so little to do, so they were happy to help when Dr. Fuller suggested sending an ambulance down to us. It arrived with two friendly female chauffeurs who got as much work as their hearts desired.

The hospital in Châteauroux was bursting at the seams. Dr. Fuller felt we should establish our own hospital, and he managed to convince the Prefect to let us use a large old clinic that had been empty for some time. We were given a field hospital from Etretat. Nothing was happening at the front, so it hadn't even been unpacked. I contacted an operating room nurse at the AHP who became director of our little hospital with pleasure. She worked practically around the clock with Lisa Nilssen and Tob Jensen to set everything up. Jeanette and I helped when our hours at work were over. How well that turned out! We had a hyper-modern, American hospital with the finest operating room and the latest X-ray equipment, along with thirty-six beds with shining American sheets and accessories. The first patients arrived in the middle of February, and on March 1, 1940, we had a formal opening ceremony. In time, it would have ample opportunity to show its worth.

The directors from the hospital in Paris were of course present at the ceremony, as was Anne, along with various helpers and dignitaries from the town and the Prefecture. The Prefect, Monsieur Grimal, said a few complimentary words: "It is a good feeling to experience an organization that does something other that just talk, like so many of the well-meaning ladies who come to have their picture taken with me on the steps of the castle." This wasn't completely fair, because the "well-meaning ladies" had brought sewing machines for the evacuees, even though every one of them had a brass plate inscribed with "Gift from Mrs. X."

After the cold winter with temperatures down to 20 below, it was good to feel that spring was on the way. It comes early in central France, and we had some enjoyable lunches in villages on our travels. Once in a while, we were invited to dinner in the ruins of *Chateau de Clion*, where a married couple from Alsace, Monsieur and Madame Friedmann cooked for the 150 evacuees who now lived there. Once we were invited to lunch in the beautiful, historic castle *Chateau de Valancay*, which had belonged to the famous statesman Talleyrand. We ate in the "small" dining room, where the table was set with marvelous porcelain and silver, but instead of a damask tablecloth, there was an oilcloth. The food was simple, but beautifully prepared and a welcome change from the hotel food, which almost always included white beans. Even a household in a castle began to feel the restrictions, for example on soap.

One dinner guest was the conservator from one of the Paris museums who complained about the treasures from the various museums having been hastily packed and sent to various castles around the country. He now lived in the castle at Valancay to keep an eye on the irreplaceable paintings from the Louvre, which had been placed there for safekeeping.

Another village we visited was full of Gypsies. Perhaps they were the saddest of all the evacuees from Alsace, because they had had to leave behind their beloved caravans, and live in houses. Their horses and men had been sent to the front. Everywhere we went, wonderful, black-eyed, lively, curious children immediately surrounded us. One day, a sixteen-year-old girl approached us. She was heavily pregnant, so after her consultation, we rushed her straight to the nearest hospital. Three days later, the happy, smiling sixteen-year-old came to find us, carrying twins! The day after they were born, she took one child in each arm, got on the bus, and returned to the village. She was homesick and didn't like the hospital. The twins became our special mascots.

Harriet Marple

Harriet Marple

Dr. Fuller let us know that a new American colleague had asked if there was anything she could do for the French war effort. Miss Harriet Marple loved France, and wanted to help. "Buy a car and come to Indre so you can drive for my girls" was his reply. She managed to get a brand new Peugeot, a miracle at that time. Poor Harriet, what she must have thought when she turned up at our dinner table one evening, and she saw our surprised faces! We were speechless. She was so beautiful, with the bluest eyes filled with friendliness, humor and laughter. Her gray hair was perfectly coifed, her clothing discreetly elegant. Compared to her, we were bums. But Harriet fit in immediately and became very popular. She was around fifty, which seemed ancient to us at the time and we were impressed that she came down to breakfast every morning at 7:30, and then went right to work.

Harriet Marple was quite wealthy and with the help of Jeanette Siefert she immediately started up her own social work. She started workshops with the sewing machines from the well-meaning ladies, and piles of good material the famous haute couture Edward Molyneux had given to Anne Crawshay. Harriet returned happy and red-cheeked for dinner after being out all day collecting equipment for daycare centers. Her clear eyes shone, and she had lots of interesting stories to tell.

Harriet told us of her experiences in the First World War, when she and her good friend Ruth Draper entertained the soldiers behind the front lines. Ruth Draper was my favorite actress! I had gone to every single performance when Ruth Draper had her show in Paris. I sat up in the highest balcony, and once I gathered up the courage to go and thank her. Once, a friend and I got to the theater early but the show was sold out. We were so disappointed! We were standing in the lobby, when Ruth Draper came in. She had a friendly conversation with the woman behind the ticket counter, and then turned to us with a charming smile. We managed to stammer something about how disappointed we were that we wouldn't be able to see her that evening. Then she arranged to give us her own private seats. We had the best seats in the house, and imagined that Miss Draper smiled at us. It was the best of all her performances.

It was always fun when Anne Crawshay came by. She and Dr. Fuller exchanged funny stories and witty banter. She was the guest of honor at a large banquet when her little hospital, the Princess Elizabeth Hospital, opened in Angoulëme. Dr. Joseph Weill, later our good friend and helper in the work we did for the Jews in Toulouse, presided. Anne was crowned "*La Fée des Landes.*"

The Germans Invade Denmark and Norway

It seemed like there was still nothing happening at the front. We were concerned about the fighting in Finland, and had done as much as we could by collecting and sending skis and backpacks, and we knit socks and mittens. But the fighting seemed so distant until April 9, when the Germans invaded Denmark and Norway and the war became a bitter reality for Johanne Winkler, Tob, and me. My first thoughts went automatically to my father, mother and Willie. We three Scandinavians all wished we could go home to share these difficult times with our families.

It was unbearable to hear German spoken with the Alsacian dialect around us, but the poor refugees couldn't be held accountable for the Germans' actions. Tob and I wrote to the Norwegian delegations, asking to go home with the French troops being sent to Narvik. But we were told: "Continue your work where you are." Our work was slow and hard, despite the spring weather. We kept our worries to ourselves, and the events in Scandinavia soon became just another news item in the French papers.

Nothing important happened in Indre, until the routine ended for me, in a terrible way. I was nervous and distraught because of the war in Norway, and not knowing how my family was doing. One day, I argued with one of the doctors over nothing. It got so out of hand that we ended up by telling each other that we could no longer work together. I went right home, packed, finished up the accounts, and turned over the books, inventory lists and money to Jeanette Siefert. I told Harriet the whole ridiculous story. I cried a bit and said I wished I was as calm as she was. "Oh, I understand you," she said, "I've had some hard knocks that have made me the way I am." So I left Châteauroux and the work I loved, and moved slowly toward Paris. There was nothing to look forward to.

There was war at home, and I was alone in a foreign land, with no employment in sight. How could I face the hospital, or Anne, after what had happened? Luckily, there was a room at Marymont, where I had lived earlier. All I wanted to do was to go to bed and get some sleep.

Paris - More Refugees

May 10, 1940. I turned on the radio when I awoke and got the scare of my life: the Germans had gone over the border, into Holland and Belgium! Bourge, Poitiers and Châteauroux had been bombed! Now it was happening here, too. I was distressed that I wasn't in Châteauroux, where I could be of use.

Not knowing what else to do, I went to visit a friend in Vichy, then continued south. The roads were packed with cars filled with belongings – mattresses on the roofs, in traffic jams so long that I turned back and headed north. It was strange to be going the "wrong" way, against the flow. It got more and more crowded the closer I got to Paris.

The next day at Gare du Nord it was practically impossible to move around due to the panicked crowds trying desperately to figure out how to get out of Paris. The few trains leaving for the south were crammed with passengers. I joined a group of worried people who were taking care of small children who had been separated from their parents in the confusion, but the parents soon discovered the children's center, so they got sorted out in the end. The Red Cross, Scouts and other humanitarian organizations were trying to help as much as possible. Those who didn't manage to get a seat on a train were gathered in gymnasiums or schools.

Despite everything, the general feeling in Paris on May 10 was fairly optimistic. The Germans were advancing quickly, but France had one of the world's best armies, and the Maginot line. At the end of the day I turned on the radio, spinning the knobs round and round. Things were happening in Holland. All that could be heard on the French stations was music. From London, a concert was being broadcast – Mozart ABC variations – but suddenly: "*Achtung, achtung wichtige Sondermeldung! Rotterdam ist gefallen! Die Holländer kämpfen nicht mehr!*" ("Attention, attention, special announcement! Rotterdam has fallen! The Dutch have ceased fighting!") After some details, and there was endless military music again. Holland had capitulated after only a very few days. I shuddered, and was suddenly less sure about France.

An air raid woke me at dawn the next day. The sirens in Paris howled in a way that went right through my bones. I pulled the duvet up over my head and waited for things to start. I heard the crack of guns and some planes, but nothing seemed to happen. I supposed "they" were too busy elsewhere to worry too much about Paris, at least for now.

At Marymont I met a Canadian girl, Meg Blair, who had come to France in September of 1939 to get away from a hopeless love affair. She volunteered at the AHP, was not needed after a while, and was asked to leave. Her only possession was a return ticket to Canada, but she didn't want to go home. She followed me like a shadow. On May 16, I found Anne Crawshay back in her office. "Oh, Alice, what luck, you can go down to Agen in Lot et Garonne. I promised to send someone down to help with the new invasion of refugees!" Once again, Anne's instructions were like divine intervention. "Find someone who'd like to go with you, so you won't be all alone," she said. So I called Meg. At around 10 p.m. Anne called to tell us that the British Embassy had sent orders that all women and families affiliated with the Embassy were to evacuate France immediately and unfortunately, she had to obey. The British were pessimistic. An unhappy Anne flew to England that same evening. The next morning, Meg and I drove south in the beautiful summer weather and reached Châteauroux around lunchtime.

Refugees in Agen from northern France, Holland, Belgium

When we reached the highland over Agen, we looked out over the small town bathed in the evening sun. Luckily, we found a room at Hotel de Bordeux et Croix de Marbre. (French hotels had such strange names!) The next morning, we paid a visit to Dr. Delteil, the head of social services and managed to secure an old Peugeot for Meg.

Dr. Delteil introduced us to the Prefect, Monsieur Cumminges, and to his wife, who was responsible for the distribution of materials to the refugees. Like the refugees we had met in September of 1939, all they owned were the shirts on their backs. They had either lost their baggage along the way, or been forced to abandon it at some point. Even the lightest burden becomes unbearable when one walks along country roads for hundreds of kilometers in the scorching sun with sore feet and worn-out shoes. What stories of pain and suffering these refugees had to tell! The worst was when the German planes whooshed down the road to shoot at them with machine guns. Many had lost their loved ones.

Several times a day, the train came through Agen. 50 – 60 cars crammed with tired, hungry thirsty people who had driven around all of France for days in order to avoid military lines. Half of Agen was mobilized to cook food at the station, to relieve the worst hunger and thirst. You couldn't hear yourself think. The passengers cried and moaned; they were so frightened that they wouldn't get any food. Unfortunately, the train didn't always stop long enough and sometimes we did run out before everyone had been served. There were long lines in front of the drinking fountains on the platform because everyone wanted to wash off the worst of the filth, or fill a thermos with water. Meg and I used all of our free time down at the station. This work with the refugees was good physical training. We developed muscles in our arms by slicing bread and preparing sandwiches. It felt like all the food in the entire department ended up there at the station.

I wondered why all these trains were headed for Toulouse, and Perpignan. Those towns must have been too crowded already. Eventually, they stopped in Agen, too. Some of the saddest trains that stopped at the station were cattle cars filled with people from prisons and concentration camps in Belgium, with the words "Fifth Column" written on the sides. They were on their way to St. Cyprien and Argelès concentration camps on the Mediterranean coast, and they were much like the deportation trains that were to come later, but of course we didn't know that then. We had orders from the highest authority not to give any precious food to these "deceitful traitors." Luckily, the Prefect was willing to ignore these orders, so we managed to sneak in a little water and food through the tiny opening up in the corner of the cars. Through these openings we saw the thin, exhausted, unshaven faces, eyes bright with fever, begging for a little water. It was unbearable. We cried ourselves to sleep at night in frustration over being so powerless to relieve their misery. Later I was to meet some people at Camp de Gurs who had been transported in this way. They told me that they weren't spies or traitors, but Jews and political refugees who had managed to escape from Hiltler's Germany to Holland or Belgium. Many of them were later sent from France to the extermination camps in Poland and East Germany. These indescribable journeys always took place in cattle cars.

Military trains brought young Belgian boys who were being sent to the south of France to be trained and equipped as soldiers, then north-bound again to fight against the Germans. They ended up in military camps in the south of France, and never got any farther.

Lot et Garonne was well organized for receiving refugees. All empty properties and houses were prepared, equipped with primitive bed frames, straw ticking for mattresses, woolen blankets and even sheets in a few places. Kitchens were improvised, with large cauldrons for cooking, and the department had rustled up all the silverware it could get its hands on. One day we made use of the town's theater. The next day, it was a large garage, and yet another day we would follow a convoy with new refugees out to a new station for refugees in the country. Strange situations occurred now and then. Some refugees who had money took off as soon as the train stopped, thinking they were normal people again, and they would live at a hotel! They always ended up coming back to us because there wasn't a single room free in the whole town.

Since I had a car and I could speak with the Belgians (in German), I was given an awkward assignment. I was to stop trucks and buses crammed with refugees, and convince them to drive into Agen, and leave us their vehicles! They must have thought I was crazy. I saw the grotesque humor in it. Here was this girl from Hardanger on a country road in the south of France, negotiating with fat, angry Belgian chauffeurs, trying to convince them that they didn't need their cars. "We are Belgians, the French cannot requisition our vehicles!" Where were they headed? "South." They didn't know how far it was, but they had heard about Toulouse. "Why not just stay here in Lot et Garonne, it's far enough south, isn't it? You'll be well received here. That way, you can do both your countrymen and us a service by moving the refugees out of Agen to the various centers." I managed to convince a few of them, and was quite proud when I drove back into town with a line of trucks behind me!

I must admit I was enjoying myself, even as I felt compassion for the poor refugees and everything they were going through. I realized how privileged I was. I could drive around this strange district and be welcomed with open arms everywhere. Of course I realized it wasn't me they were happy to see, rather the useful and necessary supplies I brought with me. But why not have a good time? It wouldn't help to go around with a sad expression on my face in those beautiful surroundings.

One day, I was to take a load of clothing to the village of Bruch, then continue on to Montagnac. In Bruch, the people were talking fearfully about the dangerous spies they thought had arrived by parachute. No one could find them. Germans could disguise themselves as anything, even as priests and old women, hiding their weapons under their robes or dresses. I drove along a narrow, difficult gravel road through the meadows and down a steep hill until five middle-aged gendarmes appeared with their guns slung over their shoulders. They were working so hard; they were practically blue in the face. Sweat ran down their faces. They certainly didn't look intimidating! "Stop," they called out, and I braked so suddenly that the car skidded on the gravel. Had I seen any suspicious types lurking about? I told them that I had not, and they told me that some dangerous elements had parachuted into that very meadow. "Oh dear!" I said, feigning fear. What did I have in the car? "Clothes for the refugees in Montagnac." They searched to see if I'd hidden the paratroopers. They thought it was strange that a foreign girl was driving around on those tiny roads, but relaxed when they saw my papers from the Prefect. I had to smile. What would these exhausted men have done if I really *had* been harboring the spies?

On Friday, May 31, I made my last drive to Paris. I was curious to see the never-ending stream of refugees, and how my beloved Paris was doing. The roads were filled with strange vehicles. Many people were on bicycles, and many were on foot, dragging their belongings. But there was still no panic, until June 10 when the Germans began to approach Paris. I paid a duty visit to the office in rue de Gramont, and there, to my amazement, I found Anne Crawshay! She had sneaked back from England the previous evening, via St. Malo. She couldn't stand just sitting in London with her hands in her lap when there was so much to be done. We ate dinner at La Crémaillére and walked along the Seine in the dusk. The streets were almost empty, and a cloud of sadness hung over the city. Sunday morning I drove south again after saying farewell to Paris. God only knew when I would see this dear city again.

Helga Holbek in her office at 16 Boulevard Bonrepos

IV. Helga Holbek and the Quakers

One day, while I was sitting in the car looking through the paper, a woman suddenly appeared in front of me. "Are you Miss Resch?" she asked with a smile. "My name is Helga Holbek from the Toulouse office of the International Commission*" she said in Danish. Thus began a friendship that continued until her death in November, 1983.

Helga Holbek grew up in a wealthy home in Copenhagen. After graduation she lived for several years in Italy and France. Between 1929 and 1939 she had a travel agency called "International Holiday and Study Tours" in London. She convinced the British and foreign Departments of Education to invite groups of teachers and students to meet with colleagues from the Baltic States, Denmark,

---

* The International Commission (*Comité International d'Aide aux Enfants de France*) was initially set up in 1937 to assist children in Spain who were displaced by the Spanish Civil war. With the end of that war and the flight of half a million Spanish refugees into France in 1939 it became the International Commission for the Assistance of Spanish Child Reguees. Then with the challenges of WWII, it extended its efforts to include French children and those of other nationalities who found themselves in France, and became the International Commission for the Assistance of Child Refugees.

Czechoslovakia, England, France, Italy and Germany to promote international understanding and tolerance.

Helga had a marvelous sense of humor and many amusing stories from her travels. She took an interpreter along when she visited the Minister of Education on her first trip to Italy. It had been a long time since she had lived there, and she didn't consider her Italian to be up to the occasion. She had to wait a week before everything was arranged. When she returned – without the interpreter – and spoke fluent Italian, the Minister's jaw dropped. "But, you didn't speak Italian when you last were here...?" Helga replied: "Yes, well, I've been here a whole week now after all, I ought to be able to speak the language by this time!"

The outbreak of the war meant the end of Helga's travel agency, so she looked around for meaningful work. One of those she approached was Edith Pye, from the English Quakers who asked her to go to Paris to talk with Howard Kershner at the International Commission for the Assistance of Child Refugees. In November 1939, she began work with Mrs. Gertrude Kershner, who was responsible for sixteen Spanish children's colonies throughout France.

One of Helga's wonderful ideas illustrates the kind of person she was. In Denmark right after the war, she met the young, promising architect Jørn Utzon, who was later to become famous for the Opera House in Sydney. She told him of an idea she had for an international house, where people from all over the world could meet, and understanding between peoples would grow. It should include everything: a lecture hall, conference center, theater, cinema, restaurant, and a hotel. Utzon was immediately swept up by the idea and drew the plans. Helga paid him from her savings. But the idea was too early. The world was worn out, and had to build up again first. It was impossible to find adequate interest and capital for the project. The drawings were hidden away and forgotten. Now, there are international houses everywhere. But the idea was Helga's.

Helga Holbek

We ate lunch together to celebrate our acquaintance, and Helga told me of her work in Toulouse. Mr. Schwartz, from the American Joint Jewish Distribution Committee, had recently turned up in her office. Unfortunately he was on his way back to America, but he had managed to withdraw the organization's funds just before all foreign accounts were frozen, and he had the money in his briefcase. He couldn't possibly take the money out of France; it would be confiscated at the border. Could Miss Holbek make use of the funds? "Oh yes," Helga said, and three million francs moved from the briefcase to her desk drawer! That was about $60,000.00 in 1940 terms. Mr. Schwartz only requested that she use them as quickly as possible for the benefit of refugees! The next day, she rented a cab and drove around to the Prefects in the southern departments to discuss the refugee issue and to distribute funds to cover "unforeseen expenses."

Agen and Bordeaux

After lunch we went to see Monsieur Cumminges, the Prefect in Agen. Helga gave Madame Cumminges 100,000 francs toward the purchase of children's clothing. I was to oversee the project. We practically emptied Agen of children's clothing, and I had the pleasure of driving around to distribute it.

At dinnertime on June 15, a message arrived from Helga on her way from Toulouse to Bordeaux with her helper, Miss Betty Cox. Could we meet them when they passed Agen? We knew what *that* meant. The Italians were on the French border, and the Germans had marched into a deserted Paris. The government offices, embassies and other official institutions had been evacuated to Bordeaux and with them the offices in rue de Bramont together with the tiny French Quaker office. Now all the British had to get out of France as quickly as possible, because the Germans were storming southward, right on the heels of the retreating French army.

We reached Bordeaux that evening, and eventually found the address we had been given. The city was in a blackout and filled to bursting. The confusion was just as great as in Toulouse. Co-workers from all over were arriving at the meeting place. The only ones I knew were Anne Crawshay and a few of her helpers. The others were from the International Commission or from the French Quakers. I met Edith Pye, who was famous for her wonderful work with the British Friends Service Council at Chalons sur Marne during the First World War. Now, she was tired and depressed. Toot Bleuland van Oordt from the French Quakers was there. She was Dutch, and ended up working in Toulouse for the entire war. Margaret Frawley was from the Quakers in Philadelphia.

Helga and Betty Cox stayed overnight in the building. Meg and I were given an address where a small room might be available. We drove around a bit in the dark streets, asked for directions, but no one could help us. So we parked on a tiny country road for the night. Meg took the back seat, and I curled up around the steering wheel in front. It was foggy and quiet, except for the frogs croaking in a nearby creek. We woke at dawn, stiff from a night on our unconventional bed. A red sun was rising.

My only acquaintance in Bordeaux was Elizabeth Montague Scott, whom I had met through Anne Crawshay. She was green with envy when she heard that Meg hadn't had to leave the country. She didn't want to go back to England! So Elizabeth and Meg found common ground in their wish to remain in France. Elizabeth wondered why we three couldn't just pop over to Switzerland and work for the International Red Cross. But both she and Meg ended up having to leave.

I followed Anne Crawshay to various temporary embassies, where she tried to secure a permit to stay. She had spent so many happy years in France, and the thought of leaving the worthwhile work she had been doing was unbearable, especially with the stream of refugees from the north, and her mobile clinics ready to accommodate them. She asked me to come to England with her, but England was a foreign country to me, I knew no one there, and I

Margaret Frawley

couldn't just hang on Anne's apron strings. I belonged in France. "I won't go!" she said. "If worst comes to worst, I can always drive to Spain," but she only said this to make the parting more bearable.

In the afternoon we went down to the main railway station in Bordeaux, where the scene was much the same as in the rest of France. Tired people spread their parcels out over all the available benches and floor space in the station. We distributed food to them and milk to their children. Evening came, and again our only alternative for sleep was the car. Anne said, "There is nothing you can do here, go back to your work in Agen, I'll be sure to let you know if you should leave for Spain." So we said *au revoir*, and tried to be brave; we had no way of knowing when we would see each other again. Anne gave me her little blue Simca 5. We called it the jalopy, in contrast to the large Packard. I drove in my newly-acquired car back to Agen, full of sad thoughts.

The next day, Anne really did have to leave. Back in England, she founded the group, "Friends of the French Volunteers" (*Amis des Volontaires Francais*, popularly called A.V.F.). This organization was of great help to the French troops in England. After the war ended, Anne Crawshay came back to France to set up mobile clinics in the war-ravaged area around Normandy, and to provide large transport trucks for materials to build up the ruined farms and homes, continuing the work the Quakers had begun in January of 1945. Helga Holbek eventually led this work during the winter of 1945-46.

Helga arrived late at night. In Bordeaux, she had been able to take over the supply of food and clothing that the International Commission had had enough foresight to bring from Paris, and she had managed to buy several tons of soap. She inherited three three-ton trucks plus some Spanish helpers. Helga insisted again that I come to Toulouse, and the next evening I discovered my suitcases in the lobby! The French army had taken over the entire hotel, as well as all the available rooms in Agen. What was I to do? I drove to the garage and asked the friendly owner if I could sleep in the car that night (I had experience sleeping in cars, after all). "Absolutely not," was his answer, and my heart sank. "You must come home with me. We are expecting family from the north, but you are welcome to come for a few days." What a relief! He drove on ahead and I followed, and we pulled up in front of the finest villa in all of Agen. I had often admired the house from the town below. I was given the guestroom with its own bath, as well as the most beautiful view of the surrounding area. My hosts were incredibly kind, although everyone was affected by the news we heard on the radio: that Pétain* was to form a government. "He gave himself to France." Laval was to be Prime Minister. They had requested a ceasefire. Poor old Pétain !

---

* Henri Phillippe Pétain (1856-1951) was a national hero, thanks to his WWI command. He served as Ambassador to Spain (1939-40) and was accused of being sympathetic to Franco. Following the German invasion of France, Pétain became vice premier and then, in June 1940, Premier. When the French government moved to Vichy, Pétain became "chief of state" willingly collaborating with the Germans by persecuting Jews and forcing many Frenchmen to work in Germany. He tried to maintain the illusion of French sovereignty. In 1945 he was convicted of treason. He died in prison.

On June 18, I was not in a mood to work, but I tried unsuccessfully to find a room. So I returned, depressed, to my temporary home. We sat there in the big kitchen and chatted, while the radio told us what was going on around us. We tuned in to London, "*General de Gaulle vous parle,*" and heard the General's wonderful appeal to France and to Frenchmen: "The battle is not lost, we will fight on!" My hosts cheered. It didn't strike me at the time just how important this appeal was. I was more interested in the other news: all main roads were now reserved for military use, no private transportation allowed. I was frightened. Was my connection to Toulouse now broken? Was I to be stranded here alone, a foreigner in France, in wartime?

The next morning I told Dr. Delteil that I would be leaving for Toulouse. He seemed truly sorry, and offered me full salary and a place with his family. Until then, Meg and I hadn't cost him a cent. He wrote the nicest letter "to Miss Resch's superior," but I took my leave of him and of my new friends. I drove by way of the strangest routes, along back roads, to Toulouse on June 19, 1940. A new chapter had begun. I didn't know that I would spend the next eight years in this city.

La Coume

I went up to the office, and ran into Madame Sérrié, Miss Holbek's secretary. When she realized I had a car, she told me that her husband, a Russian communist, was a prisoner in the strict Camp de Vernet in Ariége, and their two children were at *La Coume*, a Quaker farm in the Pyrenees. Now the Germans were expected at any moment and she was worried: would she ever see her children again? How would she manage to get them to Toulouse, so that they could at least be together? I got the hint, and said, "All right, we'll drive down and pick them up tomorrow." One day more or less before I started my new work couldn't make a difference.

The next morning, we drove south. The sun was shining, and I enjoyed the countryside and mountains. Near Aix les Thermes, we saw a narrow yellow road on the map. It wound around, but was a much shorter route to the little Quaker farm in the tiny, picturesque, walled-in Middle Age village of Mosset. But that "yellow" road turned out to be a steep, curvy path through the woods. We went as quickly as we could in first gear. I was worried the car wouldn't be able to navigate the steep hills on the awful wartime gasoline. Finally, we were rewarded with an amazing view of the snow-clad Pyrenees, dominated by Mont Canigou.

We managed fine on the way down to *La Coume*. In 1933, Edith Pye had bought the farm on behalf of the Quakers, and in 1934 she loaned it to Pitt and Yvès Krueger, a pair of intellectual refugees from Berlin. The Kruegers had fled to Paris with their two small children, Janine and Kiki, when Hitler came to power in 1933, not because they were Jews, but on principle. He was as Aryan as anyone could be, and she had been born in Switzerland. They were both teachers who had worked at a large school for children with learning disabilities. She played the piano beautifully, and Pitt played the flute.

La Coume was no guarantee for an easy life; they worked extremely hard to make ends meet. Something was always happening to thwart their attempts to eke a living out of the land. There wasn't much arable earth in the small valley, but floods washed the soil away and droughts ruined the crops. The ground was strewn with debris from the erosion of the surrounding mountains. During the floods, stone fences would suddenly fall apart and end up far out in the fields. Eventually, they came upon the idea of outfitting a haymow into two small rooms, and advertised them for rent for students. It was a huge success.

For many years they had up to twelve English and American students, both young men and women. *La Coume* became quite famous as a friendly international meeting place. The facilities were primitive, but the climate was ideal and the food was good. The beautiful area was perfect for walks; there was a small center for children and plenty of spiritual nourishment. With the onset of war, all activity at the center came to a halt. Then Miss Mary Elmes, an Irish Quaker, sent several Spanish children to *La Coume*, and it became a colony for children, including Madame Sérrié's Pitchou and Nadine. Mary Elmes had worked for the International Commission in Spain. She had accompanied the Spanish refugees over to France after the Spanish Civil War, and settled down in Perpignan.

We loaded the children and started home, driving as fast as we could. Dark clouds appeared on the horizon, and the wind started to blow. When we reached the "red" main road, the heavens opened and rain poured down! The river Aude flooded, and the road became a waterfall between the steep mountain wall on the one side and the river on the other. Finally, we could make out the gray walls surrounding Carcassonne. We reached the main road to Toulouse, and got home without further incident.

Toulouse

In April of 1940, Howard Kershner, the head of the Quakers' office in France, and his wife Gertrude, left for a speaking tour and vacation in the U.S.A. Helga Holbek was given responsibility for supervising the sixteen institutions for Spanish refugee children in southern France. Their locations made Toulouse a natural choice for a base, and she found it a good place to settle. She contacted Monsieur Augustin Callebat, the architect from Toulouse who had begun a Catholic Committee in 1939 to help the Spaniards who were streaming into France as the Spanish Civil War was nearing its end.

The head of the Committee was another architect and refugee from Spain, José Maria Trias. These two gentlemen agreed to coordinate their work to help the Spanish refugees, under the leadership of the International

Commission, led by Helga Holbek. Mr. Callebat introduced Helga to Bishop Monseigneur de Courréges, who made two small rooms in the Episcopal palace available to her while the young priest who usually worked there was at the front. The Bishop also gave her the run of an old, dilapidated building with the pompous name *Chateau de Larade*, a building that had been empty for ages. He said that Helga wouldn't have to pay rent as long as she fixed it up herself, an arrangement that turned out to be quite expensive! Under Mr. Callebat's leadership, the house was restored to a reasonable standard, with a kitchen and bathrooms, and in the middle of May forty Spanish children moved in. Soon there were sixty. When the persecution of the Jews began in southern France, the *Chateau de Larade* made an excellent hiding place for Jewish children.

Then came the shock. Hitler began his offensive toward the west on May 9, and people from Holland, Belgium and northern France fled in panic. Toulouse, which under normal circumstances had a population of 200,000, suddenly became a city of a million. Exhausted, terrified people wandered around in the streets without any idea of what was to become of them, or where they could seek help. They set up camp anywhere they could find room, in the parks, the back courtyards of dwellings, any available seat in a restaurant, even along the outer walls of buildings. The city government lost all control; nothing was being done to receive or help the refugees.

Helga arrived, and she was furious. Something *had* to be done! With the help of Mr. Callebat, she found an empty store, and opened a soup kitchen. Monseigneur de Courréges found two wonderful women from Toulouse, Madame Chaban and Mademoiselle Maurette, to run the kitchen practically around the clock with the help of boy and girl scouts. Later, the women told us how terrified they were when Monseigneur asked them to run the soup kitchen. They had absolutely no experience with this type of work! One of them had had a millinery shop, and the other sold chocolates. "Show me what you're good for!"

66

Monseigneur had said. "I've already promised you to Miss Holbek!"

Augustin Callebat

When that small establishment was overrun by hungry refugees, Mr. Callebat appropriated *Halle aux Grains*, a large warehouse, ideally situated in the heart of the city. He and his assistants transformed it into a refuge in no time at all. Inside, the building resembled a Shakespearean theater from the 1600's, with a round floor, and galleries around the next two floors. "Stalls" were transformed into bedrooms by placing straw mattresses on the floors, and several other rooms became a kitchen, a dining room and a storage area, infirmaries, offices for information and bureaucratic work, and so on. The doors opened for the first time on June 1. 4,000 hot dinners were served on average every day until the kitchen closed in the beginning of August, and countless refugees passed through.

Many a young man bicycled through France with a red army-issue wool blanket rolled up over his shoulder, on his way to military training. Of course they were perfect targets for the German Stukas flying along the roadways, bombarding refugees. Some came to Toulouse, spent the night in *Halle aux Grains*, and continued on to the camps. The idea was to send them north again in order to fight the Germans, but it didn't quite work out that way. Quite a few of them simply stayed with us! We organized the boys for kitchen duty, under the supervision of the talented Chaban and Maurette. Some took care of the washing up, and yet others kept order in the lines.

An amazing Spaniard named Jacques Lligonya was in charge of purchasing food for *Halle aux Grains*, *Chateaux de Larade*, and later for other centers and organizations. Every day when the open-air market opened at 4 a.m, he was ready and waiting. He kept us all supplied with vegetables and even meat, which hadn't yet been rationed. It seemed to us that he and his Spanish helpers worked day and night! Helga would implore: "You must rest, my dear Lligonya! Don't exhaust yourself!" He replied, "Rest? I, who am so privileged to be able to help, instead of just having to receive, like all of these unhappy people!" He just buckled down and continued with his work.

Helga contacted the Greek buyer Mr. Vafiades, who had worked for the International Commission in Paris, and then settled in Marseille. He had excellent contacts in Eastern Europe, especially Hungary, and managed to find rice, sugar,

Alice organizing food from the American Friends Service Committee

oil, condensed sugared milk, dried vegetables and lentils for the Toulouse delegation. He even managed to arrange rail transportation! We bought 600 tons through him, and used it all during those summer months.

But all this was expensive. I've already mentioned the money from the "Joint" representative. In Bordeaux, Helga received several months' worth of "Commission" money, and from Philadelphia came a telegram from the head of the AFSC, Rufus Jones: *"Spare no effort to spend money usefully and more will be sent. We want these people to feel that they are living in a world that is essentially friendly."* Rufus Jones' words became our slogan. We received a monthly allotment of funds and approximately seven tons of food every month from the AFSC in Marseille until the Germans' total occupation of the free zone* in November

---

* From 1940 to 1944 Germany occupied northern and western France; southern France – also known as "Vichy France" or the free zone – remained under French control, with its capital at Vichy, until 1942, when it too was occupied by Germany.

of 1942, when all rations were drastically reduced.

My involvement began on June 21, the day after my memorable drive to pick up Madame Sérrié's children. "Oh, how wonderful to see you," Helga said. "Can you take over at *Halle aux Grains*, find out what *Larade* needs and buy it, and could you take care of the accounts, as well?" There was no alternative; I just had to roll up my sleeves and start. But the accounts! No one had done anything with them since Betty Cox had left. There was no

Mr. Daniel and Mr. Lligonya

system, everyone just went around with cash in his or her pockets, and Helga's drawer was filled to the brim with receipts. Dead tired after a day filled with new impressions, new tasks and new people, I took the accounts home with me to look them over, but my attempt was futile. I opened the books and saw that the last entry was dated June 13. I shut my weary eyes as I shut the book, and decided that it would have to wait until the morning.

The next day there was so much new work to take care of that there wasn't time to start the accounts. I had to keep changing roles: supervisor, policeman, information service; I needed eyes in the back of my head, and was expected to be everywhere at once. The poor souls resting in deck chairs were so stunned by all of their terrifying experiences during their flight along the French roads. They needed someone to listen to them, but hearing them tell what they had been through was almost too much to bear. Like Jacques Lligonya, I felt privileged to have been spared their experiences.

Toot Bleuland and Margaret Frawley took over Howard Kershner's work when he left Paris for the States. They had used their time well, and had managed to send almost all the inventory from The Commission's storage facility to Toulouse. Toot was also an extremely competent chauffeur. She went right up to the newly established *Orts Kommando* (local police under German control) introduced herself as a Quaker, and asked to speak with the person in charge. She was admitted immediately. As a child after the First World War, the Colonel had been fed *die Kvekersuppe** and it made a lasting impression on him. Toot was issued passes for the remaining members of the Commission, as well as for their luggage and vehicles. Then Toot came to Toulouse, where, to my great relief, she was appointed head cashier.

Toot was a Dutch noblewoman, with the pompous name Catharina Guillemina Bleuland van Oordt. "Toot" was undeniably easier for everyone. She had been educated as a portrait photographer in Berlin before taking a position at Woodbrooke, a Quaker study center in England. She then returned to Berlin, where she worked at the German Quaker office until Hitler came to power. In 1933 she was transferred to the tiny French Quaker office in Paris to assist the steady stream of refugees coming from Germany. In June of 1939 she was evacuated to Bordeaux together with the French Quakers and the International Commission. Finally, in the end of June, she and Margaret Frawley came to Toulouse, where they stayed until one year after the end of the war.

I was so glad to see her! But I was nervous as I attempted to explain to her the state of the accounts. "Who cares," she said, "we'll start from scratch tomorrow," at which point I gave her a huge hug! Soon, she was swamped with Jewish and political refugees who knew her from her compassionate work in the small French Quaker office.

---

* Between August 1921 and October 1924, British and American Quakers provided a nourishing "chocolate soup" known as die *Kvekersuppe* and other basic foodstuffs (*Quakerspeisung*) to between 500,000 and one million German children per day.

Toni Gärtner was our amazing chauffeur from Alsace. He had lost one arm in the Spanish Civil War against Franco in 1939, and later been invaluable in the evacuation of Spaniards, driving between Barcelona and the end of the roadway in the Pyrenees, near the French border. For some reason, the Spaniards stopped the roads before the border, so the refugees had a horrible time plowing through deep snow in their attempt to reach safety in France. Since Toni was French, he had not been imprisoned as the Spanish were. He ended up as a chauffeur for the Commission in Paris, and was involved in the evacuation of Bordeaux. He would wave his hook and scream, "QUAAAAAKER!" and the guards would let him pass.

Margaret Frawley was an American journalist, and a member of the Quaker community in Philadelphia, even though she was a Catholic and not a Quaker. She didn't discuss her beliefs, so we weren't aware of her faith until after her death several years later. She was wise, practical, diplomatic and extremely elegant. She always wore a smart pillbox hat with a small white bird's wing on either side. One client asked respectfully if it was the Quaker uniform. Margaret remained only a few days to confer and observe Helga's work, which impressed her greatly. Then she traveled on to Marseille to start up a main office for the International Commission, which was no longer international, apart from the participation of the American Quakers. She changed the name to The American Friends Service Committee, or the *"Quakers Americains"* and later *Secours Quaker**.

The situation for the refugees improved after a while. New, capable people opened *Cours Dillon*, a large center for men, and a center for mothers and small children in the empty veterinary school. I had my hands full with work, and felt

---

* For a more detailed description of Secours Quaker and many of the individuals involved see *Picking Up the Pieces from Portugal to Palestine; Quaker Refugee Relief in World War II*, a memoir by Howard Wriggins (Lanham, Maryland, University Press of America, 2004)

that things were running smoothly, especially after Toot assumed responsibility for the accounting nightmare! But everything is relative. I had never experienced so many lice and fleas! All of Toulouse was overrun with them that summer. When I put my feet on the floor in the morning, I watched as they hopped up the way raindrops ricocheted off the sidewalk. We all had bloody scratches on our legs.

I was constantly looking for more facilities for bedrooms. When Mr. Callebat mentioned that a gym might be available, I went immediately to speak with the owner. It turned out to be a huge cellar with a low ceiling, a stone floor, walls covered with soot and a few small openings for windows. It was full of spider webs, and had just one toilet in a corner, hidden behind a curtain. The water faucet was out back. But we needed all the space we could get, and were given permission to use it. We supplied it with wool blankets and straw mattresses and in no time at all several hundred women and children moved in. Luckily, I found a Belgian kindergarten teacher, Miss Sterno who came in, kept order, and played with the children. Their meals were served in *Halle aux Grains*.

The building over the basement was falling down. It was in such bad shape that it was dangerous, and we were forbidden to enter it, but the refugees discovered it, and soon it too was full! Families, and the mattresses they had taken from our various centers, occupied every single inch of space on every floor. When the Prefecture finally began to dole out a little economic support (10 francs per day per person), the poor inhabitants felt that their existence had finally gotten a little brighter. Unfortunately, the police got wind of the situation and came after me saying it was extremely dangerous and absolutely forbidden to allow people in that condemned house. I had the occupants go out for a walk, and as soon as the police turned their collective back, all the residents moved "home" again. After a few visits of this type, the police finally let them stay.

Eventually, the Prefecture sent many refugees to the surrounding villages, where it was easier to find a place to stay, and easier to keep the situation under control. They all received their ten francs per day per person, so conditions actually became livable. When the battles in the north were long past, the occupation authorities announced that those who wished to go home could do so. Many did, even though they felt unsure about what they would find when they returned. Many long trains were set up, and one of our last jobs in *Halle aux Grains* was to prepare thousands of sack lunches to distribute to those who were leaving.

Quaker offices at 16 Boulevard Bonrepos

16 *Boulevard Bonrepos*

We were hearing stories about the complete destruction of the town of Dunkirk. We heard scornful accounts in the newspapers that were sympathetic to the Germans, and proud accounts of heroic deeds from the BBC in London. Although every seaworthy vessel was sent over to fetch the British and French soldiers, countless men were left behind. Some were captured and others managed to flee on their own. By the first days of July, many British soldiers had made their way to Toulouse in the hope of getting over the border to Spain, and from there, home to England.

Ernest Bennet, a charming American Mennonite, joined our ranks. He had a truly pleasant disposition, and would say, "keep smiling" instead of goodbye. Soon, we were all saying it. He was very good at his work, and soon found a large building in which to hold classes for our Spanish coworkers. He said, "In this space, there is always room for one more!" Well, "one more" turned out to be many more as English boys were staying for a night or two after their exhausting march through France. After resting, they were then equipped to continue over the border to Spain. Naturally, they had to be careful on the streets. Many of the French police were very helpful, but they still ran the risk of being caught and sent to Germany as prisoners of war.

By now, I had acquired three cars for Toulouse: my own "Fanny", a two-seater Simca, and the impressive Wolseley, which I had inherited from Anne's chauffeur, who had in turn received it from an English woman when she had been forced to leave for England. In those days, it was completely natural to accept a car in much the same way one would accept a box of candy! But soon both the Wolseley and Fanny had to be put up on blocks – they were too expensive to run.

Monseigneur de Courréges became more and more nervous about having us in his center. He was therefore relieved

when Ernest Bennet reported with a huge smile that he had found a closed-down shoelace factory along the Canal du Midi, right across from the train station, at 16 Boulevard Bonrepos. It was ideal for our purpose, with its large storage rooms, many offices, dining room and a large courtyard for our vehicles.

The AFSC Star

Moving day was a momentous occasion! Finally we had our own location, and could hang up an impressive sign over the gate with the words "The American Friends Service Committee" around the AFSC star. Underneath, in parenthesis, were written the words *Quakers Americains*, although there was only *one* Quaker, Toot Bleuland, and *one* American, Harriet Marple. We were also able to offer a room to Monsieur Callebat. It was on the top-most landing, just by the stairway, and I could see that he came and went at somewhat irregular intervals. But when he was there, men frequently came to see him. Who they were and what they wanted was of course none of our concern. He was our good friend and a great support, but he had his own business to attend to.

Later we learned that Callebat started one of the first resistance groups in southern France as early as June 1940. Many groups formed after that, and all of them eventually joined forces. But we knew nothing of this in 1940. He was a deeply religious man, and humanitarian work was very important to him. He had helped refugees from France during the Spanish Civil War.

When Helga Holbek came to Toulouse, he was thrilled to be able to cooperate with her. He had given up his office when the Germans invaded southern France, so as not to expose us to any danger. His office was made into a workshop for seamstresses, led by Madame Garriga, from the well-known Balenciaga fashion house. What amazing clothes we would have been able to get if only we had had access to material! Now the sewing work was restricted to repair and alteration. Philadelphia sent tons of used clothing to the Quakers in the south of France, along with food, medicines and – last but not least – money.

Autumn came, and the character of our worked changed. The problem of the refugees was no longer acute; some were placed in outlying villages, and quite a few remained in Toulouse. Various nations had established aid programs for their own countrymen, but they all came to us when they needed clothing or additional food rations, so we ended up augmenting these programs, especially for the Spaniards.

When the war broke out in September of 1939, all the able-bodied Spaniards were released from the camps into which they had been placed following the Spanish Civil War. They were put to work in various war production factories, to take the place of the French who were at the front. In

Toulouse they were placed in an ammunition factory, and were lodged in the Récébédou camp. This marked the beginning of a relatively good period for the Spaniards. They received a salary, and were able to support their families. The small Catholic committee lead by José Maria Trias helped them find accommodations for their families.

This good period was unfortunately short-lived. France gave up; the soldiers were demobilized and returned to their jobs in the factories, which had been taken over by the Germans. The Spaniards were now unemployed and unable to support their families. Récébédou was limited to refugees who were old or ill. Prices rose, food and household supplies were strictly rationed. The Spanish mothers were finding it increasingly difficult to feed themselves and their children. The Quakers organized food distribution for those who had ration cards. Monsieur Trias and his associates made lists of the needy, and Lligonya acquired what was needed. We augmented the rationed goods with the same food rations we made available to schools and orphanages: rice, oil, sugar, macaroni, and fresh vegetables. Approximately 800 Spanish families collected their food from us three times a week for the duration of the war.

Countless French families were also in need. The breadwinner had either been killed at the front, or was a prisoner of war. Helping these families was a major part of our work, either individually or through the schools. Helga offered our help to the educational authorities and the official *Secours Nationale* and in return they supplied vegetables and whatever other unrationed foodstuffs they could find (a little fish, but meat was out of the question). Thanks to the Greek Vafiades, we provided our standard packages of rice, macaroni, oil, sugar, dried vegetables, sardines, and condensed sugared milk.

We worked closely with the Swiss aid organization *Caritas*. Their leaders in the free zone of France were Maurice and Elanore Dubois, who shared offices with us in Bonrepos until they found space of their own. They had several colonies for children, and arranged a foster parent system between Swiss families and poor French children. Eventually, *Caritas* had approximately 9,000 French foster children in the free zone. The Quakers had something similar, providing proper meals six days a week to children in schools and orphanages. The first winter, we had approximately 8,000 children. Within a year, this increased to approximately 30,000 in Toulouse and the districts of Gers and Herault. In the summer, we fed the same number in the summer camps. I remember one camp director who turned up at the office and asked "Is it possible to get aid this summer as well? Otherwise, I don't dare to open the camp…"

Refugees and Aid Workers in the Free Zone

The concentration camps in southern France were full of Germans and Austrians who had been arrested by the French in September 1939. They were released after the armistice, but many Jews and political opponents of Hitler's regime preferred to remain in the camps. Quite a few of those who chose to leave came to us in Toulouse for help and advice. They thought the war was over!

The war may have been over for the French, but sadness prevailed. They were pained by the total collapse of France's proud army, and by the fact that there was no use for the Maginot line. One million two hundred thousand Frenchmen were prisoners of war, and poor old Pétain was in charge of the country. General de Gaulle's brave speech gave the people comfort. H*e* was a true Frenchman!

Most of the French, Dutch and Belgian refugees had gone home, but many still felt threatened by Hitler's regime, and preferred to stay in the free zone, be it in concentration camps or by placement in villages from which they were not allowed to leave without special permission. All "foreigners" (including us) were required to have special circulation permits. Of course quite a few refugees had managed to find places to live right in Toulouse. Craftsmen were especially able to secure false French papers, and were therefore able to support themselves. Most of them had connections because of their earlier acquaintance with Toot.

The AFSC in Philadelphia had collected quite a bit of money from families who wanted to help *les pauvres honteux* (the honorable poor) French children from good, middle class families, who didn't dare – or who were too proud – to ask for help. The result was a sponsorship system. Rose Thorndike, one of the American delegates in Marseille, asked me if I would take on the job of finding appropriate "candidates" in Toulouse and the outlying area. Of course I was interested in helping, and there were more than enough candidates including many widows with tiny pensions and women whose husbands were in German prisoner of war camps, who were trying to provide their children with enough to eat and some education.

Augustin Callebat was once again an invaluable help. After a month I had ten foster children, and by 1944 I had nearly 200. I met some unusually interesting people. In the beginning, they were embarrassed to come to the office to receive a small sum of money and a sack lunch (the same ration all the children received). It didn't take long to establish friendships, some of which endured long after the war. A mother and a child would come by the office to chat, or to bring a bouquet of flowers from the garden. Many of them turned out to be true friends when we suddenly needed to hide the Jews who were wanted by the Germans. "Of course," they said without a second thought, when we asked if they knew of a good hiding place. Many of them took both Jewish adults and children into their own homes despite the fact that they would be imprisoned and deported if they were discovered.

Autumn came, and unfortunately for us Margaret Frawley returned to the U.S.A. Howard Kershner came back to take over in Marseille, and direct the Quakers' work in Europe.

He was a wise and friendly man, who unfortunately lacked Helga Holbek's flexibility and ability to do the right thing at the right time. We had worked independently all summer, so it took some adjusting suddenly to have to ask permission for everything. When and if permission was granted, it was often too late. Helga insisted on having a Quaker delegate in permanent residence at Camp de Gurs (see Chapter V). That finally went through a year later. The office in Marseille became the administrative link between the main AFSC office in Philadelphia and the delegations in the south of France. They helped the refugees acquire emigration papers and arranged permits from the United States.

A Short Vacation

Our existence became somewhat calmer in September of 1940, and we began to plan a little vacation time after what had been quite a stressful year. The last few hectic months we had worked every day of the week, and into each night.

I left for my vacation on a pleasant Saturday afternoon, taking the train to Ax les Thermes in Ariége. I had my backpack alongside me and my bicycle in the baggage car. Gasoline was rationed and poor quality even when it was available, so my dear "Fanny" was up on blocks, well hidden. But I had been lucky; I had managed to get a beautiful Peugeot bicycle with three gears. I slept until ten o'clock the next morning in the fresh mountain air, so the sun was creeping toward noon when I finally pulled myself together and continued on my way. I secured my backpack on the back of my bicycle and off I went, up out of the picturesque area famous for its naturally warmed water, where people suffering from rheumatism and other ailments would come to be cured. Its other attraction seemed to be enormous laundries that washed the clothing of the entire Pyrenee district.

The road was quite steep, and despite the three gears on my fine bicycle, it was tiring. I ended up walking more than once! The sun beat down – I soon looked like a boiled lobster – without a hint of a breeze or a drop of water! I continued around all the curves – there was no short cut – until I came to the Andorra bend in the road, where I rested for a looooooooong time. I debated whether or not to continue. It was tempting to go farther on in this strange countryside, but there was a war on after all, and I didn't have my passport with me. Only refugees passed this way these days, and they had to sneak in. So I continued on, up to Col de Puymorens, 1,915 meters above sea level, where there was a huge hotel, which was unfortunately closed. I looked around. There was a small building and a workshop, where an old man was planing boards. I asked him if there was a place nearby where I could get something to eat, and he said I could eat right there, and he made me a wonderful meal with meat! He was the only person I saw in that area, and I was lucky to run into him. I looked around while he made the food. There were all sorts of flowers – wild geraniums, crocuses – and a spring with clear water! I knelt down and drank and drank. It was just like the clearest, coldest Norwegian mountain water, nothing better in the whole world. There was a large jug on the table filled with this wonderful water, which I emptied.

I truly enjoyed the view of the French and Spanish Pyrenees. I would have liked to stay right there, but I went on to Font Romeu, where I found a cozy hotel, and slept like a log. I spent all of Sunday there. But there is no rest for the weary; the road continued upward. My muscles were so sore that I could hardly move; I had to be careful not to move too quickly, especially going up or down stairs. Suddenly, I realized why I felt so uncomfortable. I had had too much ice water at Col de Puymorens! My liver was complaining, and seemed to take all the space inside of me! It was incredibly uncomfortable, and lasted almost until I got home to Toulouse.

On Monday morning I continued past Mont Louis, whizzing down all the hills toward Prades so quickly that I almost didn't have time to take a look at the snow-covered Pic de

Canigou. I would have loved to go *there* but there wasn't
enough time. In Prades a bus was just leaving on its way
to Mosset, and my liver affected my decision to be on it.
Mosset was a picturesque little town, falling down around
itself. It looked like a fortress when approached from
below. I went right through and up to *La Coume*, where the
Kruegers were quite surprised to see me. They
remembered me from my short visit in June when Mme.
Sérrié and I came over to collect her children, but that day
the only youngsters were Kiki and Janine Krueger. They
were sweet children, in touch with their natural
surroundings, who knew the names of all the flowers and
were friends with all of the animals in the area. The gray
hills were an ideal playground for them. I had a wonderful
time with them there, and was reluctant to leave after just
a few days. We kept in touch by writing every single
Christmas since.

More About Aid Work in Toulouse

Dr. Joseph Weill was one of the leaders of the Jewish
organizations, and our faithful friend through the entire
war. He suggested that we ought to open a canteen for the
hungry students, so one was established at Terrain Maury,
and Madame Georgette Cassagnavère assumed leadership.
The canteen was a help to many, including Professor
Frédéric Hammel, who led many young men over the
Pyrenees to Spain, either in order to continue on to
Palestine, or to join the free French troops in England.
They got a meal in the student canteen, and even slept a
night on the floor before continuing on their tiring journey.

Madame Cassagnavère – called "Cassa" – was naturally
involved in the resistance movement, and as a result her
well-filled bag contained many things such as false
identification papers, ration cards etc. From the summer of
1943 on she was often bothered by the Gestapo inquiring
into her activities, but with her angelic face and her big

innocent blue eyes, she always managed to talk her way out of trouble.

Once, the Gestapo came into the canteen looking for a student. He happened to be right there, eating. Cassa looked at the officer with a surprised look on her face, and said, "Who, him? All right, wait a minute; we'll take a look at the list." She ran her index finger down the list of names. "Hmm, yes, see? There he is; he's here almost every day, a big, strong fellow, with blond hair. Yes, take a look, there's his name!" Then she looked out over the students eating in the canteen, and said, "No, he doesn't seem to be here today, I can't see him anywhere." Because she was so clear and unreserved in her attempt to "help" them, the officers didn't pursue the matter then, but instead hung around until the meal was over, and started to check the students' papers. The boy they were looking for was short and dark, not tall and blond, and he strolled right out under their noses, surrounded by his friends, and disappeared quickly.

Madame Cassagnavère was unequalled in her fight for those in need. She visited us almost daily in order to get material help for someone. She always managed to find excellent hiding places for those she came into contact with. Her piece de resistance was when she waltzed right into St. Michel prison and took a prisoner out with her! It was quite an old prison, but the Germans utilized every building.

Two affluent people in the resistance had been picked up by the Gestapo, and thrown into solitary confinement where they were denied visitors and packages. There was a chapel in the prison yard. Cassa went in to say a prayer and check out the building where she found a small door leading into the prison. Of course it was locked. One day she smuggled a little bit of wax in to a guard named Juan and asked him to make an imprint of the key to the chapel and the two keys to the cells. Cassa managed to smuggle civilian clothing into one of the laundry exchanges, and on an agreed-upon day, Juan kept the guards distracted with funny stories while Cassa wandered right through the chapel and unlocked her prisoner! Later, she said that her heart had been hammering like a locomotive. She thought it would burst; she had never been so frightened. But they made it through the chapel and out on to the street to freedom. The Germans never discovered their method. Juan didn't even know, since his participation was limited to diverting the attention of the guards. Shortly thereafter all the guard details were changed.

We acquired most of our food supplies from sources outside the country, so as not to unduly tax the French economy. Every month we received the seven-ton shipment of American food from the main Quaker office in Marseille, and our faithful friend Mr. Vafiades imported the rest for us. The wares generally reached us in good shape, but we gave up on one occasion when a five-ton shipment of sugar from Hungary was six months late.

One day, I got quite a shock when two German soldiers came storming up the stairway to my office. I was sure that this was it, although the tired, older men in ill-fitting, worn-out uniforms really didn't look all that frightening. They certainly didn't belong to the elite troops that had been sent to the south of France. "What do you know about this?" one of them asked, as he handed me a crumpled piece of paper covered with scribbling and stamps. It was no easy task, but I finally established that it was the transportation receipt for the Hungarian sugar! No wonder it hadn't reached us, it was addressed to Mr. Vafiades in Toulouse, but he lived in Marseille. The truck had been parked for several months on a side road. The German guard at the roadblock had contacted practically all the aid organizations as well as City Hall, but no one had known anything about the sugar. Finally, they thought of us. I was very happy, but the soldiers were disappointed. "Now we've gotten your five tons of sugar, but what about us?" We happen to like sugar, too." "*Jawohl*," I said, and went down to the storerooms and asked for half-kilo bags of

back row: Alice Resch, Harriet Marple
front row: Ima Lieven, Helga Holbek, Toot Bleuland van Oordt,
Toulouse, 1940

sugar cubes for two German soldiers. The look on the storeroom leader's face was unforgettable; he managed to show surprise, shock and disgust all at once. But I got the sugar. The last I knew of the two Germans was the backs of their ridiculous uniforms and the stomping of their boots on the stairway as they went back down, chomping their sugar cubes loudly. Those two half-kilo bags were well worth it. We got five tons, after all!

Towards the end of September 1940, Harriet Marple asked me if I would accompany her to Montauban. She was going to collect three small boys from a children's colony and deliver them to their mother. Of course I wanted to go with her. I had heard so much about Celine Rott de Neufville and her work, so I was looking forward to meeting her. Celine was of Swiss and French descent but later she became an American citizen. She received her nursing

84

education in the U.S., and was in Spain when the Civil War broke out in the summer of 1936. She volunteered immediately, and thus came in contact with the Quakers through the International Commission. She accompanied the refugees over the border to France in late 1938 - 39, and settled in Montauban. There, she met José Maria Trias, and together they ran a large canteen with workshops to make clothing and artificial limbs, and they built up a network for taking care of the Spanish refugees.

We took off in Harriet's Peugeot with the three small, lively boys, aged four to seven, to meet Celine in Montauban. She was a small, quiet woman in a worn-out brown tweed suit. She took us to a nursing home, where we found the boys' Spanish mother. The reunion was a sight I will never forget. We were almost as moved as the mother. Tears ran down her cheeks as she embraced her sons. The boys' father came in eventually. His leg had been amputated at the hip, but he was able to walk, thanks to a prothesis from Celine's workshop. It did us good to see how well the people were treated in the home.

Harriet and I had delivered our three small boys. Celine was eager to show us her various workshops and an art exhibit she had put together. The wonderful paintings, sculptures and woodwork were enough to make one think that all Spaniards must be artists. Harriet bought two of the paintings. The time flew by. Dusk was falling, and darkness came quickly in the south. We had to make sure we were home before it got completely dark.

We thanked Celine, and drove off. It was very difficult to see. We were law-abiding, and had only the approved dark blue headlights on the car. Since Harriet did not like to drive in the dark, I offered to take the wheel. But just as I spoke, we hit a dark truck, with no lights whatsoever, parked on the right side of the road. The next thing we knew, we awoke in a double room in Montauban's public hospital. At least we weren't in a huge room with 20 beds! I looked around aghast for Harriet, who had a bandage wound around her head. I had a concussion and various lesions, and had been unconscious for a couple of days. Celine had stayed at our bedside the first three nights.

We remained at the hospital for 14 days, and were truly spoiled by the nuns, doctors and our friends, who made the 100-kilometer journey to Montauban several times. Our nun was always entertaining us with tidbits about the patients in the nearby beds. "Just imagine – he has four passports under his pillow! Definitely fifth column! He has typhoid!" While I was there I finally received a message from my beloved parents and brother in Norway. I had been worrying about them. The day we were to leave, there was an emotional farewell and gala dinner. Then it was back to business.

We had applied for a permit to move about in the free zone when we arrived in Toulouse in the summer of 1940, but the bureaucracy there was hopelessly slow and complicated! So we risked traveling around without papers. Harriet was stopped on the way home from a vacation near Pau, and was taken to a local police station in Toulouse to pay a fine. But the judge took one look at the well-dressed, beautiful American and said, "Was Madame not aware the foreigners are not permitted to travel without special permission, *sauf conduit*?" "Oh, what a *good* idea," Harriet replied with her most charming smile. If he only knew how hard she had been trying to obtain just such a permit for the last six months!

I was up to my ears in debt because of my hospital stays, first in Montauban and later in Toulouse, and had to pay it all off myself. Since I was in private employ, I was not registered with the French social welfare office, and we had no private insurance in Toulouse. But Harriet understood my predicament, and Helga told me that Harriet paid it all for me! Years later, Helga told me that she couldn't understand why she hadn't just taken the money from the Quakers' funds. They should have paid for all expenses incurred when their workers became sick. They had paid all

the expenses for the Americans who had come over.
Harriet was truly an amazing friend!

The Quakers and the Allied Blockade*

We hear from London:

In the beginning of April, the English Quakers, the Society of Friends, made known a declaration which was sent to the British Prime Minister's office, as well as the offices of the Ministers of War and the Economy, and to the press. The document was as follows:

Starvation's tragedy spreads throughout Europe. The Allied blockade has become part of the strategy of both sides. Despite the fact that one's sense of justice inhibits this tactic, Great Britain's politics now prevent the delivery of food to certain European countries.

Hunger is a weapon that affects an entire population, taking no notice of gender, friend or foe, age or youth, but ravages the young to the greatest extent. The food blockade does not only contribute to hunger, it also creates and encourages a heartless attitude in those responsible for the blockade. This results in the end in the destruction of our Christian values, such as charity, empathy, etc. Values our land is fighting for.

If this continues, the world will experience an immeasurable loss of spiritual and moral fiber. We know from the experience of previous wars how difficult it is to convince people who have themselves felt the pangs of hunger and starvation, and who have seen their children experience the same, to contribute to building up a new and better world.

We admit that the food packages can create serious political and technical difficulties, but again, experience from earlier wars prove that it can be done. Just think of Greece.

The Society of Friends believes that finding a solution to this problem is an absolute necessity, in order to enter those European countries that are now shut off by the blockade, in order to bring vital food and clothing. This will keep the children alive and support their future development, even if it depletes our own stores.

* *Gazette Lausanne* 6/5/42 (Alice Resch's translation 1/98)

But war is war. The Germans' occupation of the free zone in southern France in November 1942 ended the deliveries of food and clothing from the U.S. The port in Marseille was now closed to us. Word got around that we had large supplies of American clothing earmarked for the needy. More and more people claimed that they "had a right to" or "hadn't yet received any of" the clothing. We had the feeling that some people – both Frenchmen and foreigners – were just going from one aid organization to the next to see what they could get. The various aid organizations decided to form a committee. Helga was naturally one of its members. In order to stop those who were abusing the system, this committee put together a folder of forms that would contain information on each family and its economic situation. Anyone receiving any help would be required to produce their folder. The responsible party in each organization would note in the folder what the family had received from that organization. That way, we had an opportunity to keep things under control.

One example of how the system worked: A woman came in, and said that she was a widow with seven children to support, and was therefore entitled to our help. I suspected something was not right. When I asked if she had her *Carnet Social* with her, she was obviously surprised. She had assumed that since we were foreigners, we wouldn't know about, or ask for, her folder. I explained that if she didn't have one, she could go to the National Aid Office where she would be issued a *Carnet Social*. Her response was, "Oh, is *that* the folder you mean?!" and she pulled it out of her purse with an embarrassed look. I hid a smile when I saw from the entries on her card that she had been to all the other organizations already, and had saved us for last. Seven children were written in, the eldest born in 1928 and 1929. (This was 1941.) I asked her, "You became a widow in 1931, have you remarried? I see you have had five children since 1932…?" "Nooo," she answered hesitantly, "I live with the children's uncle!" She got the help she asked for.

The Nîmes Committee and the Villages of Puycelci and Penne

Dr. Joseph Weill stopped by on one of his many visits, and Helga told him about some of the problems we were having. This inspired him to gather together as many of the leaders as possible to discuss the problems. Between twenty and thirty representatives from France and abroad met in Nîmes, on November 20, 1940. Helga worked in the true Quaker spirit. She was uninterested in personal glory, and she was highly respected by the other members, who often found their way to her office to seek her advice. She recognized that it was fine to donate food, clothing and money, but it wasn't truly *help*, and didn't make the refugees happy. On the contrary, nothing was as demoralizing as being dependent, and the best way to help one's fellow human beings was to enable them to become self-sufficient. With the help of José Maria Trias she found two deserted villages: Puycelci (which means heaven's mountain in the local dialect) and Penne du Tarn, and she asked: "Why not use them?" The Tarn Prefecture was interested, and gave us permission immediately. Helga informed the others of the plans at the next meeting in Nîmes.

Dr Joseph Weill and The American Unitarian Service Committee also became interested, and donated a considerable sum to the project. Our headquarters in Marseille felt the idea wasn't good. So Toulouse paid out of its own funds. Several dilapidated houses in the villages were purchased for a symbolic sum, restored and given new inhabitants. Carpenters from Lorraine fixed up Puycelci, while Spanish artists and their families took charge of Penne. They were to make wooden toys under the supervision of the Spanish artist Lescarboura. Tools and machinery were purchased for a large, communal workshop in each of the villages, but other than that, the work was based on a cottage-industry model. The project's success surpassed all expectations. The refugees soon had more orders than they could fill, and eventually they were able to be completely self-sufficient.

José Maria Trias settled down with his wife Clara Candiani and their daughter Niouran in a wonderful old house in the town of Puycelci. Clara was famous throughout all of France for her radio programs. When she retired, she was awarded the Legion of Honor. Trias supervised the projects and handled the commercial side of things. Clara was the social consultant. The projects went so well that some of the villages' original inhabitants even moved back. They found work, and got on well with the newcomers.

These villages became tourist attractions. Puycelci is an extremely old, walled-in city high up in the terrain. The area was a center of activity in the Middle Ages as a hiding place for Catholics who had broken away from the church during the Albigensian Inquisition. Penne lies on a slope and has an amazing castle ruin at its highest point. It looks like an arm with a fist reaching toward the heavens.

In a report describing the Toulouse delegation's work from the fall of 1942, I wrote: *For the moment, we have seven people in the surrounding Gresigne forest. They work for us by collecting dry wood in ten-kilo bundles. We pay one franc per bundle to the owner of the forest, and we sell just enough that all the men can be self-sufficient. The rest goes to our various projects.* And in a report from December 14, 1942: *In October, the Prefect invited Penne and Puycelci to participate in an* Exposition Rurale des Pyrénées, *an agricultural exhibition in St. Gaudens, and our exhibit was the highlight! The local committee wrote, "This is what we hope to do here in our own Pyrenees" over our display. It was truly a generous gesture, and was very inspiring for us.*

Our exhibition deserved the praise. The designer from Penne, the Spaniard Lescarboura, had produced a huge board with small figures carved in relief. The figures showed our work in the villages, all the way from chopping down trees to the finished furniture and toys. The carvings also showed the wheat fields at the Branting farm. In honor of the exhibition, we donated an extra 8,000 francs for weaving courses in four Pyrenee villages.

The Branting Farm

In September 1941, the French and Germans gave Helga Holbek permission to pay a private visit to Denmark, accompanied by Madame Chevalley, the president of *Service Social d'Aide aux Emigrés*. She had a layover in Berlin, but there wasn't a single hotel room to be found because it was National Procreation Day, Hitler's idea for creating small Aryan soldiers! That night, Helga experienced her first air raid. The British dropped some bombs on the city, but it was nothing compared to what happened later.

Helga took advantage of the opportunity to visit both the Danish and Swedish aid organizations such as the Quakers and Save the Children, which donated 1.5 million francs from the Branting Fund to the Toulouse delegation. This enabled us to purchase the Branting Farm, which would provide the villages with vegetables, milk, and meat. The Swedish Red Cross donated ten tons of paper bed sheets for the infirmaries in the concentration camps and other places.

The main office in Marseille discovered that the village project was good, and wanted to take over supervision. Who was this unknown Monsieur Trias? Two young Americans: Henry Harvey and Gilbert White were sent up to take charge of things.

Produce from the Branting Farm

Henry settled down in Puycelci, and Gilbert in Gaillac, in order to keep an eye on the Branting Farm and the large warehouses where the reserves of flour, sugar and enriched biscuits were stored along with wine and other things. It turned out that they understood the situation quickly, and worked loyally with both Helga Holbek and José Maria Trias. Their friendships lasted for many years. Gilbert White later became President of Haverford College in Pennsylvania.

When the Marseille office later decided that it was illogical for Toulouse to be supervising the work in villages, they suggested that Montauban – the nearest neighbor – should lead the project. But Henry protested: "The villages are Helga's baby!" And that was that.

Ernest Weilheimer, Richard Weilheimer, Rolf Hess, Hugo Schiller, Hjalmar Maurer, Kurt Walker, Aspet, 1942 (see also page 255)

V. Camp de Gurs and the Aspet Children

I first saw Gurs in the spring of 1941 when I accompanied Toot on her travels to various camps to deliver money that the AFSC had solicited from families and friends in the United States. It was a shock to experience the misery and hopelessness in the filthy barracks. Outside, spring had arrived, but within the barbed wire there was nothing to brighten the bleak existence, only gray sand and mud. I saw the pale inhabitants in their rags behind the fences that separated the *ilots*, or sections, from each other. Men and women were in separate *ilots*. A street two kilometers in length divided the camp in two. The street was paved, and baptized Avenue "Moche", which means ugly, and rhymes with the name of the large Parisian Avenue Hoche.

Here I was a complete outsider. I could see the degradation, the suffering, depression, hunger and cold in the prisoners' eyes and body language. Their clothing was only tattered pieces of cloth. I was tempted to close my eyes and shut out all the impressions. But I continued on, and got a glimpse into one of the barracks where old women sat on their makeshift bed frames, with nothing to do. What *could* they do besides try to keep warm? Reading was out of the question in the dim light. The few electric light bulbs were turned on for only one hour morning and evening. The wind whistled between the boards of the thin walls. There were no windows, only three wooden hatches to air out the room. They told me that when it rained, water leaked through the roof, which was covered only with a thin layer of tarpaper. I saw the latrine: large buckets placed under benches. The only "luxury" was an outdoor row of faucets with running water and a long trough, where they could bathe and drink the clean water from the Pyrenees.

I saw the cemetery - a large, gray, sandy area with makeshift graves. It was constantly being enlarged. I stood and took it all in, sad and ashamed that I had dared to be part of this. Why did these people have to go through all this degradation and suffering, while I was in a position to *observe* it? The anguish was overwhelming.

Later, when I was a passenger on the truck that delivered foodstuffs to the Quaker kitchen, I could see that there had been development and improvement in the camp. The inmates had taken matters into their own hands, and had paved the passages between the barracks so they could keep their feet dry. Small gardens had appeared near the barracks, with flowers and a few vegetables. "Vitrex" windows replaced the small hatches in the barracks, so daylight could get in.

Various organizations were allowed to establish themselves in the camp. A postal service was created, so the prisoners could receive packages and money. The AFSC was the only organization that had official permission to receive monetary donations from private citizens abroad, for relatives in the camps or in the free zones. We were not allowed to distribute money to French families, only to foreigners, as the regular banks were not allowed to do business with them. Millions of francs were passing through our hands. In Toulouse, Toot and her faithful assistant Gärtner had their hands full with all of the transactions.

We were initially responsible for channeling funds to Gurs, Vernet, Ariège, Brens, Noé and Récébédou. Later, Nexon was added to the list. Outside Toot's office, a line of people was always waiting and hoping

Negotiating the mud at Camp de Gurs

for help from family or friends in the U.S. or England. With the money they received, they could support themselves and avoid the concentration camps. The Swiss sent one-kilo packages every month to those who had no money. Madeleine Barot of CIMADE (*Comité InterMouvements Aupres des Evacués*) took over an empty barracks and started social service work: entertainment, a lending library and food distribution. She was thrown out because her activity was deemed "the distribution of propaganda." Madame Jeanne Merle d'Aubigné took over where Madeleine left off, but she suffered the same fate.

CIMADE's history in the camp dated back to the time when it was only for Spaniards. *Secours Suisse* (*Caritas*) and we (the Toulouse Quaker delegation) came in after the camp was once again filled with Jews in October of 1940. In 1943, I was told that both the Protestants and Catholics encouraged conversion, in order to get a little extra food. Their fellow prisoners disapproved of those who converted, calling them "Christians of convenience." Abbé Gros, the Catholic priest, said that occasionally people came to him and asked to be baptized. He told them they were welcome to come to mass or to make an appointment with him to discuss religious matters, but that they should not consider conversion until after the war. He was unwilling to discuss what had taken place in the camp before his time.

Secours Suisse was fortunate to have its own permanent representative, Sister Elsbeth Kasser who did incredible work among the inmates. I met an old, sweet couple, Dr. and Mrs. Mann, who choked back tears as they told me of the first time they saw her - how all these elderly people sat shaking from the cold on their beds in the cold, damp barracks. Then the door opened, and there stood Sister Elsbeth in her white nurse's uniform, her blonde hair like a halo framing her friendly, blue eyes and her smile. It was a revelation! She was a great comfort to many.

Together with CIMADE, O.S.E. (L'Oeuvre de Secours aux Enfants, a Jewish aid organization) and the inmates, we erected a daycare center and established a school for the older children. With the help of money from the American Unitarian Service Committee and the American Joint Jewish Distribution Committee, Dr. Joseph Weill organized regular access to medical and dental services. Approximately fifteen prisoners who were MDs formed a club for doctors. They received a daily meal from us, consisting of vegetables from the vicinity, as well as cooking oil, and rice.

Dr. Eli Weill conducted a physical examination to determine each individual's need for daily food rations. Larger quantities were provided to those who were clearly bloated with hunger, and less for those whose affliction was milder, or who were merely weak. Rabbi Leo Ansbacher founded another international aid organization, which his brother Max and others continued when he fled. They raised funds from among the many wealthy inmates to help the poor and to sponsor cultural events. There were many artists, musicians from the Vienna Philharmonic, actors, and others who provided entertainment including music, plays, revues, and lectures.

Each of the various *ilots* was allowed to take responsibility for its own administration. Chosen from among the inmates, the directors of each *ilot* had an unfortunate tendency to abuse the power they were given. They would punish their fellow prisoners for the least offence. The *ilot*

The children at Aspet, 1942

directors answered to the camp leadership, which meant that many of them were hated and feared by the very people who should have been able to look to them for help and protection. The directors always received extra rations, which in turn meant less for the "civilians."

Food was brought from the supply barracks, and prepared in each *ilot*. The official daily ration was approximately 1,200 calories, but theft was rampant, so the already watery soup with the occasional piece of floating pumpkin became so much thinner. The daily ration for the prisoners in reasonably good health was no more than 700 calories. Helga Holbek was aghast. She managed to coordinate the distribution of food, and to insure that food came to the Quaker kitchen, so that rations could be distributed according to the doctors' evaluations. Both the degree of hunger and the mortality rate declined as a result.

The inmates gradually grew accustomed to this strange life, and after the horrible winters of 1940-41 and 1941-42, everything was organized in a more efficient way. But in the summer of 1942 came the first deportation orders. The *ilot* directors compiled lists of the "chosen" and of course omitted themselves! Panic spread among the prisoners who couldn't understand why they had been forcibly deported from Germany, only to be sent back again. To what? And why? They were worried and frightened, and tried to flee or hide themselves in the camp. But where? The deportation quota had to be filled, and those who

The boys at Aspet, 1942

resisted or hid were hunted down. Woe be it to those who were found. The guards and camp staff were the worst sort of bullies. The poor unfortunates who were caught were beaten and taken to the prison yard, where they stood for hours before they were herded into trucks and driven to the cattle cars waiting for them in Oloron.

Members of the various private aid organizations were allowed to move freely among these poor, frightened people, but what could they do? What help were comforting words? Initially, the workers in our Quaker kitchen were not arrested, but we saw them later on a train, when it stopped in Toulouse on its way to the camp in Rivesaltes. There, Helga was able to get them out, but it caused a dilemma. "We managed to free some, but who will take their places? The quota must be filled!" Helga was devastated after having seen the various "scare" deportations from Gurs in the summer of 1942. In the beginning of 1942 there were still approximately 20,000 inmates left in Gurs. By Christmas time there were approximately 13,000 left, and in March 1943 still another 1,000 were taken away.

The Children are Sent from Camp de Gurs to Aspet

Then there were the children. Our efforts to do something for them were a never-ending and complicated puzzle. I received a huge stack of bureaucratic papers to and from

the Prefects in Pau, Toulouse and Vichy just to get 48
children out of the camp! Finally, in February of 1941,
everything was in order. There were many tearful good-
byes between the children and their parents, who dreaded
letting the children go even though they knew it was for
their best. The children sobbed and could not understand
why their parents "didn't want them anymore." But sending
them away actually saved them from being transported to
certain death in camps in Eastern Europe. They would
never see their parents again, but no one knew that then.

Andrée Salomon and the Cohns - a married couple -
accompanied them to *La Maison des Pupilles de la Nation* in
Aspet, leaving them in good health, but with only travel
documents. Their permanent papers were still not ready.
There they stood, before Monsieur Couvot, who was aghast,
exhausted. The children spoke not one word of French, and
he spoke not one word of German! The enormity of the
responsibility he had taken on began to dawn on him.

Toulouse had counted on the Cohns staying with the
children, and when Mr. Couvot's desperate phone call for
help came, Helga asked if I would go and stay there until
the Cohns came back. I was fairly nervous. I had helped
tame *Larade*, and I had had a sort of responsibility for the
Spanish children with whom I had become good friends,
but at a distance. I had also cared for sick children in my
nursing past. Now to suddenly be responsible for 48
children I did not know! But duty called and Couvot was
certainly happy to see me. He had no idea what to do with
these foreigners, and to tell the truth, neither did I.

It turned out to be a very happy and enriching time for me.
My "bedroom" was a corner of the room where the 19
youngest boys slept; my walls were two sheets hanging on
a clothesline. But I quickly adjusted to this existence,
sleeping like a log, and awaking happy at 6 a.m., to look
out on our "personal Pyrenee," Mount Cagire, which was
still white with snow, glowing in the red morning light.

The days began at 7 a.m. I helped the smallest children to dress, make their beds, and wash themselves. This went quickly, because most of them showered in the basement every evening. All the routine work went as it probably does in most orphanages. We were fairly isolated, and did not come into contact with the French children on account of the quarantine. Couvot was terrified of lice, and the children from Gurs often had "tenants." So we had many de-licing sessions.

Luckily the weather was usually good, so we could be outdoors most of the day. We had neither books nor toys, so we used our imaginations. I was fortunate to have the help of an Austrian Jew, Jules Frey, who had been forcibly relocated to Aspet. He had nothing to do, so when he heard that there was a German daycare center, he came by and asked if he could help. And he did! We got a soccer ball, and he coached the boys. All sorts of outdoor games were organized, and we had wonderful walks along the small mountain paths. We would end up in a village, with a local café. There we could buy homemade war soda, a sort of sweet drink made from fructose, or perhaps a shriveled apple from the previous fall. The children's meals were always well prepared and the portions were large, but the children missed chocolate and candy. They would write to their parents and tell them that there were no potatoes in Gurs. In Germany as in Scandinavia, potatoes had been an integral part of the daily diet, and some of the parents had promised their children this nutritious, tasty treat in Aspet. Still, there was a large vegetable garden, and aside from the absence of potatoes, Southern France was a dream come true as far as preparing meals was concerned.

The children gained weight, unlike the vast majority of children in Southern France. The French were irritated when they discovered that the German children had hidden a large loaf of bread. But it was not because they themselves were hungry, but because they wanted to send the bread to their hungry parents in Gurs!

Frey taught the children songs and they hummed them all day long. When the weather was unpleasant, they gathered in the gymnasium where we had a makeshift school. Soon they were speaking French fluently. The tiny village could not possibly make room for all these foreigners, so not until the fall of 1941 did the children between the ages of 8 and 15 begin to have some formal schooling. And by that time, they were able to understand French.

It was an interesting experience for me to get to know all these different children. I went around and said goodnight to them every evening, and took time for a little chat with each one. They opened up to me, and in that way we became good friends. The evenings were hard for them as they lay there in the dark and felt they were alone in the world. They would tell me about their homes, about the difficult years of flight, the terrifying journey into the unknown, and life in Camp de Gurs. They worried because they knew that their parents were still hungry and living under difficult conditions. But the letters they received from their parents were filled with pleas to take good care of their clothing, to behave themselves and to remember to write often. They were always upbeat. The parents were worried about their children.

One of the more unusual boys was Carl Landau, who took two excursions from Aspet. Carl was allowed to go to Toulouse for his Bar Mitzvah. He told his friend Michael Oppenheimer that he "fled" from Aspet, but in fact he had permission to leave. Children were allowed to travel more freely than adults. Then, in 1942, when he was 14 years old, he received permission to visit his parents in Camp de Gurs. That was the last time he saw them - shortly after they were deported to Auschwitz where they perished in the gas chamber. But of course he didn't know that until many years later.

During the winter of 1942-43 he went to Le Chambon sur Lignon where he was hidden for nearly a year. This Village became famous because of the Protestant Pastor André

The girls at Aspet, 1942

Trocmé. The farmers were all descendants of the Protestant Huguenots, who suffered the most awful persecutions for more than 100 years (from the abolition of the Edict of Nantes in 1685 until the French Revolution in 1789).

Remembering their own persecution, the inhabitants in Le Chambon understood and felt for the Jews and their sufferings under the Germans. Pastor Trocmé and his congregation protected more than 5,000 Jews – hiding them or helping them or over the border to Switzerland during the war.* The people of Le Chambon were like the Danes, who rescued more than 6,000 Jews by sending them over to Sweden, where they were welcomed.

Some of the Aspet children had an Aryan father or mother in Germany. Those parents had been forcibly divorced because they had committed *Rassenschande*, (destroying the purity of the race). A small boy told us that he never wanted to see his father again because he was in the SS. One small girl could not believe that her parents loved her, since they had simply sent her away to Aspet! There were so many hurt feelings and incomprehensible tragedies in these small souls, so it helped them to be able to talk and be tucked into bed at night and to have a goodnight hug.

---

* The full story of Pastor Trocmé and Le Chambon is beautifully told in Philip Hallie's book: *Lest Innocent Blood Be Shed* (New York, Harper & Row, 1979).

The War's Events and Consequences

We followed the war news closely. We tuned in to radio London, and the BBC at every opportunity, even though it was forbidden. Vichy* France did it's best to disrupt the broadcasts with interference. Suddenly, at the end of June 1941, we heard that Germany had broken its friendship pact with the Soviets, and were sending many troops to the Russian steppes. We had been anti-Soviet, but now all our sympathy went to the Russians!

The next shock was worse. December 7, Pearl Harbor! Now we became involved on a more personal level, since this meant that the U.S. was at war with Germany and Japan. What would happen to our Americans?

Helga and Ima Lieven immediately went to the district office to assess the Americans' situation in light of recent events. But they returned no wiser than before; the district office could not tell them anything. They found Howard Kershner playing the harmonica, while Henry and Gilbert demonstrated American folk dancing! *They* certainly weren't worried! We went to a very emotional board meeting in Marseille the week of Christmas. The Americans couldn't decide whether to go home. How would the Germans react? There was enough food, clothing and money for about a year, but Kershner decided that we should send some of it to Marseille, Montauban and Perpignan. These were supplies that Helga had purchased specifically for various programs of the Toulouse delegation, which would have to be reduced considerably.

At the end of January 1942 we had a sad, emotional farewell lunch for our beloved Harriet, who had finally decided to return home while there was still time. We

---

* A resort town on the Allier River, Vichy was the capital of unoccupied France from July 1940 until November 1942. It was the site of German headquarters from 1942 until 1944. As a consequence of French concessions to the Germans, the term "Vichy" became synonomous with "collaboration."

laughed and chatted as usual, but our hearts were heavy. After lunch, Helga, Celine, Toot and I drove with Harriet on snowy, icy roads to Oloron Saint Marie, where we spent the night. Luckily, there was very little traffic, due to the drastic reductions in gasoline rations. We were among the few who were privileged to have gasoline at all.

The next morning, Toot and Celine went to Camp de Gurs, while Helga and I accompanied Harriet on the train as far as Urdos, the last station before the border. From there, Harriet was to continue on through Spain, Portugal, and finally to the U.S. She hung out of her window, waving and waving. The last we saw of her was her profile against the white snow, with the long feather on her chic little hat like a periscope sticking up toward the heavens. Helga and I had some time before the train returned on its way back from the border. We took a walk in the sunshine, admiring Pic d'Ossau, the highest mountain top in the French Pyrenees, and we got a peek at Fort Col de Pourtalet, where Renaud and Aladier were imprisoned until they were deported to Germany in 1943. We spoke of our dear Harriet. "She was our sunshine and champagne," Helga said. We felt the vacuum of her absence.

But wonderful Harriet didn't forget her colleagues and friends! From Portugal, where she had had to wait for a space on the Clipper seaplane which had the first air route between France and the U.S., she sent us the most wonderful packages including our first nylon stockings! She remembered us all in her will when she died in 1971. She was over eighty years old.

We parted in Oloron. I went to Toulouse, while Helga went on to Gurs, where Toot was in the process of dividing money among the prisoners. Helga had finally gotten eight long-promised barracks designated for Quaker work. They were large and well built, on the inside of the barbed wire fence, but at a distance from the rotting barracks where the prisoners lived. We had kitchens and dining areas, as well as living space for the workers, offices, and storage areas.

One of them was turned into a clothing depot. A large field near the Quaker section was turned into a magnificent garden, where all sorts of vegetables were grown and used in the Quaker soup. Helga tried to convince the camp's leader, Monsieur Gruel (otherwise known as "Mr. Cruel") to let us take over the distribution of food to the elderly and ill, and to transfer their tiny rations to our kitchen. Gruel refused, claiming that "It is completely unnecessary, why should they be better off than the others? No one in France today has enough food!" He practically needed a wheelbarrow to cart his stomach around!

The next time Helga visited Vichy, she made a point of seeing the man responsible for all the concentration camps, a *Mr. L'Inspecteur des Camps* André Jean-Faure. She was quite pleased when she returned with permission to take over the rations for the ill, and there was nothing Gruel could do about it. During the winter of 1941 – 42, several hundred people were so weak and swollen with hunger that the doctors were close to giving up on them. The rations were organized better, and after the doctors' visit it was decided that there were to be three rations each day rather than two, which improved the patients' condition somewhat.

Initially, Dr. Joseph Weill put together the rations by deciding what amount of calories each inmate needed. His brother Eli Weill succeeded him, but soon he had to flee. Then there was a young Romanian doctor, Alex Feigenbaum, who lived on a small farm in the village of Gurs together with his wife Sonia. He bicycled to the camp every day, and worked both for O.S.E. and for us. We never saw the final result of the food program, unfortunately, because the summer of 1942 was a true summer of fear: the Jews were now persecuted in the unoccupied zones as well as in those that were occupied.

Deportation and Arrests

In Paris at the end of 1941, the Germans were already hard at work. They raided entire sections of the city for the sole purpose of finding Jews and sending them to the horrible camp in Drancy, and deporting them from there. Now they started in the camps too. When the first deportation came, we witnessed the most heartbreaking scenes. The imprisoned Jews' names were called out, and without consideration for age or sickness, even those who could barely walk were required to pack up what belongings they had. Then they had to stand up straight for hours along the road while everything was checked. It was the middle of July. The sun beat down unmercifully and the earth gave off a dry, burned smell. There stood these old, sick people, wearing their winter clothing, with bags and sacks and baskets – there weren't many suitcases around in the camps. Some fainted from the heat and exhaustion. We workers had permission to speak to the prisoners, but that was absolutely all we were permitted to do. There was unfortunately not much we could have done, in any case. We knew that they were all headed towards certain death; the Jews were to be exterminated. We tried our best to speak with them to keep their fears of the future at bay. It was admirable the way most of them managed to stay calm. Very few gave in to panic or hysteria.

Most of the prisoners had to walk a short distance over the fields from camp Récébédou to the railway station at Port Saint-Simon, but to the weak prisoners it seemed like an eternity. They struggled over the dusty fields, sweating as they lugged their small, yet inconvenient baggage. The tops of the corn stalks had just started to come up, and the small shoots felt like needles to poorly shod feet.

With our two cars, we were permitted to drive those who were in the worst shape, and carry some of the baggage. It was practically impossible to convince the prisoners to give up any of their few belongings. They knew from experience that the chances of having them returned were very small.

We were run off our feet. There were as many guards and police officers with guns as there were prisoners being deported, but we insisted, and eventually the lieutenant gave us permission to help.

I walked beside two sisters, both of them over 70. One was a widow who complained and dreaded what was to come. The other took the first under her arm and tried to comfort her. She spoke partly to her sister and partly to me, telling of their home outside of Heidelberg, where their family had lived for many generations and where they had a happy childhood. A third sister had died at Camp de Gurs in December of 1940. These two were grateful to have each other, and to be permitted to travel together when so many others had been separated.

The one who was trying to comfort her sister knew that they were facing certain death, but she was glad to be there. The quota had to be filled, and she hoped that another, younger person who still had life ahead of him would be spared. She was an amazing woman. After two years in the camp, she still wore a lovely dress with a clean white collar, and a hat. "Yes, keeping yourself well groomed helps you to keep morale up," she said when I commented on her appearance. I looked at all the ragged, miserable people and the men with stubble on their chins. Most of them formerly had good positions and wealth.

The "travelers" were loaded onto cattle cars. There were 50 in each car, which was crowded, but not as bad as the later deportations. Panic started to rise when the baggage was loaded onto a separate car. Suddenly, we heard a scream from one of the cars. A woman had a heart attack and died on the spot. She was taken out and the remaining 49 fought over her food ration.

The camp had sent bread and cheese with the prisoners, and we – together with *Colis Suisse* and *Secours Suisse* – had made individual bags weighing three kilos for each person. One never knew how long the trip would last. We walked around and spoke with the prisoners until the train finally left as evening drew near. We were given letters and messages and addresses for their friends and family who weren't being deported, or who weren't in the camp.

This was the first deportation we experienced. It doesn't sound so bad here, but it made a deep impression on us. As she was driving home in the dark, Mademoiselle Daufy sobbed as if she were being tortured. She had been tireless during that entire day, walking among the prisoners, smiling, talking, and giving comfort. I bicycled home as usual. There were countless deportation trains, and each one got progressively worse.

In Gurs, life had been hell. The camp's organization was falling apart. So when the staff came around to call out the names of those who had been "chosen" for a deportation, many prisoners had disappeared. The young, strong workers wanted to avoid deportation at all costs. Some had bribed the guards but only a very few managed to make it through the barbed wire to freedom. Most of them were found in a search through all the barracks, nooks and crannies and they suffered for trying to escape the inevitable. Those who were caught were forced to stand outdoors in the cold mountain air for 24 hours, until they were put onto buses that took them to the train in Oloron Saint Marie. Helga and the Swiss priest, Abbé Gros, who represented the *Caritas* organization, stayed with them all through the cold night. Helga ordered the Quaker kitchen to cook rice porridge, so that each prisoner was assured a healthy portion before they were taken away.

Helga had become a regular bank. Everyone wanted her to take their jewelry and other valuable belongings, as well as money and papers. They were all constantly writing letters. She was completely exhausted when she came back from Gurs.

It was odd, here in our world all of this was happening, but the outside world knew nothing of it. At Pentecost, I took a wonderful bicycle trip with some friends through the Pyrenees. On the train coming back, we were discussing conditions in the camp, when an elderly gentleman suddenly broke into the conversation. "Gurs," he asked, "just what kind of place is that?" When we explained, he exclaimed, "No, that's not possible. We don't imprison innocent people in this day and age. We are still in a free France! They must be criminals if they have been placed in a camp." We were silent. This man lived right in Pau, but he did not want to understand, and there was no point in arguing with him. But it showed us how little people knew about things that were going on right under their noses.

The Resistance

I got quite a few new foster children during the spring of 1942, because right before Christmas the Vichy police had arrested a group of well-known men. They were placed in the military prison in Toulouse, and later moved to a concentration camp in the south of France. They were released in the summer of 1943 after "serving their time," and most of them fled to the woods to join *le Maquis**, because although they had been released, they knew they were not safe.

Among those who had been arrested was Professor Pierre Bertaux, who later became Prefect in Toulouse. Monsieur Van Hove was the editor of *"Témoignages Chrétiens"* an illegal magazine. Jean Cassou was the head of the Luxembourg Museum in Paris, and Professor Bugnard later became the head of the World Health Organization. The Italian Francesco Nitti was the son of a well-known Italian politician whom Harriet knew from his exile in the States. These and many others met at the resistance's gathering point, Sylvio Trentin's bookstore at rue Languedoc. Harriet took me to meet the Trentin family, and after that I stopped in now and then. That's where I met Magnus Synnestvedt, who later became my husband.

---

* *"Le Maquis"* is the name used by the military wing of the French underground and guerilla fighters against the Germans.

Many of the families were in dire need of help after the arrests, so Callebat suggested that I take some of them under my wing. Some hid in the country, so our only contact was by letter. I am still friends with Madame Baradat who took her two children with her when she went into hiding. They sent me a photo from the country. The children are standing in front of a huge Lorraine cross, painted onto a steel door which had been christened *Croix de Gaulle!* They warned me to be careful about who saw the photo saying: "It can be dangerous for all of us if a collaborator sees it!" I still have it.

Eventually, we discovered that our dear Augustin Callebat was a de Gaulle disciple, there in our building at Bonrepos, which helped explain why he had turned down an important position in Vichy. At the time, we thought that he ought to accept the position, that it would be good for many reasons. He just smiled his secretive smile, and said, "No, I want to have a clean dossier when the war is over." After the war, he was made Secretary General of the *Association des Résistants de* 1940, and I received a nice little thank-you letter, which of course made me very happy.

But my own resistance work was extremely peripheral. Helga once said: "You have to choose if you want to work for the Quakers or for the resistance. We can't risk compromising our work. If you are discovered, it will be the end of us!" One of our secretaries, Jeanne Modigliani, the daughter of the famous painter, quit and went into the resistance completely. She was discovered in 1943, and imprisoned in a camp until the end of the war.

In the end of March 1942, we had a staff meeting in Toulouse, to say farewell to the Kershners. Helga drove Howard and Gertrude Kershner to Pau, and from there, they went on by train to Portugal to await transportation to the U.S. It was very emotional for Helga to part with Kershner. Despite their misunderstandings, she had quite a soft spot for him. It was difficult to find a hotel room in Pau, as was the case everywhere, so Helga stayed in a small closet in the Kershner's double room. That meant of course that she had to go through their room to get to her space. This amused Kershner, who said that this was the first time he felt that he really could keep track of her! Later, we heard that he had spoken very well of her when he arrived in Philadelphia.

Vacation in Switzerland, Spring 1942

We had experienced the first horrible deportations. It was a shock, and none of us felt that we could take a vacation when all of this was happening around us. But Helga said, "We *will* take a couple of weeks off, who knows when an opportunity like this will come again!" The Quaker office in Geneva had offered to arrange travel permits and pay for us to come and stay there. We practically had to force Helga to go first; she worked day and night, while I at least enjoyed some days off on the weekends. Naturally, she combined the trip with several meetings and other work opportunities. I set off, somewhat against my will considering the situation, but it turned out to be a wonderful experience!

I had an invitation to stay with my teacher from the American Hospital in Paris. At the beginning of the war, she left Paris to take a good position in Geneva, where she now lived in a tiny house in the garden of a large property. Talk about being spoiled rotten! There were shops bursting with temptations, and all kinds of food! Marthe took me to a large department store. My jaw hit the floor. "What can we help you ladies with?" I gulped, and answered, "I would like a skein of yarn," as I hesitantly picked one up. "What else?" the saleswoman asked. "Could I take one more?" I asked nervously. The woman looked at me incredulously. "You may take as many as you like!" Marthe explained that I came from France where there was a shortage of everything, even with ration cards. The saleswomen crowded around me and gave me their own ration cards. Yes, they had them in Switzerland, too, although almost everything was available. Oh, if only I had had money! Just think what I could have bought and taken back to my friends in France! Marthe gave me a wonderful red jacket, and I bought several pairs of wool socks to give as gifts.

I rented a bicycle and went to see Neuchâtel, Lausanne and Bern. I stayed with friends along the way, or in small country inns. It was odd to experience Switzerland in wartime, with soldiers everywhere, and mines under bridges, ready to be detonated. Important places were walled-in and guarded, so that they could be closed at a moment's notice. And not a single road sign to be seen anywhere! The country was armed to the teeth, ready for a German invasion, but no one bothered to check out a lone Norwegian tourist.

I took the gondola lift from Lauterbrunnen, past the amazing mountain wall Scheidegg, and on up to Jungfraujoch, which I had wanted to see. Even at 7 a.m. the gondola was crowded with excited mountain climbers. One asked if I would like to accompany him up to the top of Jungfrau. I hadn't planned on climbing that day, but said yes anyway. He lent me a pair of trousers after taking one look at my bare legs, and we were off. The skies were gray and it was a bit windy, so we didn't attempt Jungfrau, and chose Mönch instead. I ran across the glacier. He cried out: "Oh no, you mustn't do that! There are cracks in the ice, and we are at over three thousand meters above sea level, so mind the oxygen level!"

I was given an ice pick and secured with a rope when we reached the starting point for the sharp, narrow ridge that ascended steeply to the summit nearly eight hundred meters away. Then I became seasick! The next thing I saw was the leader's checked stocking. I didn't dare to look down the steep ice on either side of me, and managed to keep my nausea to myself. It started to thunder and lightning so we sought shelter under a piece of rock. We had to throw away our ice picks – they could attract lightning! I never saw the magnificent Alps due to the fog, but I satisfied my urge to reach the summit of a real Alpine mountain.

Marthe gave me a huge package with all sorts of wonderful food to take back to my friends in Toulouse, and accompanied me to the French border, where the Swiss officials confiscated it all saying "foodstuffs must not be taken out of Switzerland!" So Marthe took it all back with her.

More Deportations, Raids, and Escape Attempts

I returned to Toulouse to find that the atmosphere had changed. The routine work was still being done, but we were drowning in deportations. After the first direct transports bound for the north, all the Jews were sent to the huge camp in Rivesaltes, so Helga set up base there. Since there were only a couple thousand people in Noë and Récébédou, each of these camps had only two and three transports, and those who were in reasonable shape were moved quickly. The only ones left behind were those who truly could not survive a transport.

We made sure we were in place to receive the trains traveling from Gurs to Rivesaltes by way of Toulouse. Helga or someone from CIMADE would send us a cryptic telegram – something along the lines of "Happy Birthday" – to signal that a train was on the way. Getting to the train was no easy task, since no one was in a position to give us exact information on when it would be passing, where it would be stopping, how long it would be at the station, or which track it would come in on. We relied on a fair measure of bravado, and we coaxed information out of the French guards by offering them food.

Mr. Gruel, the head of distribution in Gurs, had promised Helga that the Quaker helpers were safe, so you can imagine our horror when we discovered that half of our helpers, including Hedwig Würtzburger our head cook, had been placed in the camp. They stayed calm, but were white as ghosts and scared to death. They all knew they were most likely headed for certain death.

One child from Aspet had been given permission to visit his parents in Gurs. This inspired me to write to Monsieur Coste, the Director of the Office for Aliens – a very frustrating man to deal with – and ask for permission for a group of children from Aspet to visit *their* parents, at Rivesaltes. These children hadn't seen their parents since February of 1941, and I thought it best to have the paperwork in order before attempting to organize the trip. The permit took ages to come through, like everything else.

One day, Mr. Couvot called, shaken, and told us that at 6 a.m., the gendarmes had come with a list, and had taken five children to be sent to Rivesaltes! I raced over to Coste, who just smiled his crooked smile and said: "It is an order, and besides – you yourself asked a while ago for permission for fifteen children to go to Rivesaltes! We can't separate children from their parents, after all!" They were already on their way, and it was my fault. Helga was very upset, and went to Vichy immediately to protest. She got them to agree that no children in Quaker or *Secours Suisse* institutions were to be touched, regardless of religion or nationality. She waved the letter confirming the agreement under Coste's nose, and went to Rivesaltes and brought the children back with her.

Those who worked at Rivesaltes did excellent work, especially Andrée Salomon from O.S.E. who managed to get through the war unscathed. She always managed to be somewhere else when someone was looking for her. She had good coworkers as well: Yvette Samuel, Margot Cohn, Solange Sitlenok and Dora Wertzberg, all of whom were untiring in their efforts to help and hide people who the Germans and their cohorts were searching for. There were many others, like Madeleine Barot from CIMADE, and our own Mary Elmes and Helga, who had managed to talk the administrators at Rivesaltes out of sending our workers off to the camps. We got our dear cook, Hedwig Würtzburger back, as well as some of the others who had been sent away. Hedwig worshiped Helga, and in November of 1943, when Gurs was closed, she came to Toulouse to be Helga's housekeeper in her new apartment.

A few managed to escape from Rivesaltes. The barbed wire wasn't electrified. The French guards were easily bribed. Many opposed the persecution of the Jews, and looked the other way as the inmates made escape attempts. Cars waited, hidden on the other side of the barbed wire, ready to drive the escapees to safety. Unfortunately, after November 1942 the French guards were replaced with Germans.

Mary Elmes managed to smuggle four children out of the camp in the trunk of her car. Andrée got a group of twelve out. They were on their way to a checkpoint when she came along smiling cheerfully, and said, "Children this way!" and led them neatly out of the convoy. The authority in her voice made the guards think that her activities were just part of the whole plan. She led the flock down a side street, where a truck from O.S.E. was waiting and quickly put the children on board. Andrée climbed in beside the driver, and they drove right out through the main gate where she just waved her "permit" at the guards as usual. The guards recognized her and the car, and didn't bother to check her papers, and the children were saved.

We often witnessed heartbreaking scenes at the office in Toulouse. The Jews knew that their names were on Coste's infamous list. They didn't dare to sleep in their homes, so they spent the nights out in the fields or with Aryan friends. They moved toward the Spanish border as best they could. Some of them actually made it over, because they could afford to "buy" guides. This of course meant that some dishonest individuals took advantage of the situation, and charged a fortune to guide those who were desperate. The Jews had to pay them in advance, and the crooks were paid again afterwards, when they delivered the Jews right into the Germans' hands.

There was one especially sad story. The police inspector had given us a strong recommendation for a young man named Vogel, whom we hired to keep an eye on our vehicles and the Spaniards. He was a good-looking refugee from the north, usually dressed in rags. Eventually he started showing up in one new suit after another. They were purchased on the black market, but not with money he earned from us. During the sad autumn of 1942, a Jewish woman began scolding Helga. She claimed that the Quakers had tricked her into paying fifty thousand francs to go to the border, and she had ended up in the clutches of the gendarmes. By some miracle, she had managed to escape, and now she wanted her fifty thousand francs back! Helga was speechless in horror. Could someone affiliated with the Quakers really have done this? Fifty thousand francs was a fortune. She calmed the woman down and got her to tell who her contact had been. It turned out to be Vogel. We had jokingly called him a police spy, because the superintendent had recommended him: to keep an eye on us, as it turned out. Helga went immediately to the superintendent, and told him the story. We got rid of Vogel right away, but his protectors higher up kept him from having to face any repercussions.

People came to us and asked us to hide them, or at least their children and they would find hiding places for themselves. All the organizations' colonies in Toulouse were filled to bursting with Jewish children. The private organizations felt a strong sense of solidarity. When the situation got too hot for them, we took over some of their work.

The Archbishop of Toulouse, Jules-Gèrard Saliège (who later became a Cardinal) was not afraid to speak up against the persecution of the Jews. Both the convent and monastery opened their doors and filled their homes with frightened, persecuted people who sought a place to hide. It was not always easy to have them as houseguests. Strangely enough, they were not able to grasp that it was important, both for them and for their hosts that they lay low.

One day, the Jesuit priest Roger Braun turned up with a copy of a pastoral letter written by Archbishop Saliège. It was read aloud from the pulpits of all the churches in the city on August 22:

Bretheren:

There is a Christian morality; and a human ethic, which require us to heed certain duties and rights. They are part of human nature. They come from God. They can be abused, but not abolished. That children, men, women, mothers and fathers, are treated like animals, that family members are separated from each other and sent to unknown destinations, are sad spectacles which we must witness.

Why does the right to asylum no longer exist in our churches? Why have we been overcome? The Lord have mercy on us!

Holy Mother of God, pray for France! Frightful scenes have been played out in our parish, in Noë and in Récébédoux. Jews are men and women. Foreigners are men and women. …They are our brothers like so many others. A Christian cannot forget this!

France, beloved homeland! France, whose children, true to tradition, bear respect for humanity in their very fiber, chivalrous, generous France, I cannot believe that you bear responsibility for all of these terrible events.

With my affectionate devotion,

Jules-Gèrard Saliège
Archbishop of Toulouse

Young men were the most difficult to hide so they took to the woods, and joined *le Maquis*. The Jesuit priest at rue des Fleurs hid many young men and helped them on their way when they were ready to move on. René Kapel, the O.S.E. worker and Rabbi in the camp, lived on rue des Fleurs until the Germans became interested in his activities. Père Godard had turned his house into a workshop for orphaned boys from the streets. He found craftsmen who took the boys on as apprentices, so that they would eventually be able to support themselves. But the Germans became suspicious, and in 1943 Père Godard and René Kapel were forced to flee. They came to us, shaved their beards and obtained civilian clothing. Suddenly, they were transformed into normal young men, and they went underground. In 1984, I met Rabbi Kapel in Israel, and heard what had happened to him after he left us. He had been caught, taken to a camp in Frésnes near Paris, and was included in the last deportation on August 18, 1944, just two days before the liberation! Fortunately, he managed to escape from the cattle car.

Abbé Lagarde was the most amazing priest with whom we worked. He had an unattractive bright red face with a huge potato nose that was always dripping, thin unruly gray hair, intense eyes behind his glasses, and a *soutane* so old and worn that it barely held together. We invited him to lunch many times. He had been a prisoner of war in Germany for one year, and was one of the first allowed to return home to France, only to end up in another prison camp where he continued his work, speaking up for France and encouraging the soldiers to flee. He preached down-to-earth, practical Christianity.

The Germans eventually tired of him, and sent him back. He then turned up in Toulouse, and went immediately to Camp de Noë, where his priest's garb was his passport, and there he stayed! He lived alongside the prisoners, in order to help and comfort them, until the director, Monsieur Mathieu, took notice of him, and asked what he was doing there every day. "I live here!" was the response. Mathieu was not especially pleased with the idea of someone in the camp who might report on the prisoners' miserable conditions, and all the corruption surrounding the distribution of food. So the Abbé was thrown out. He went to Camp de Gurs and Récébédou. Then he went to Monseigneur Saliège and reported on what he had seen.

The report was sent on to the Pope, who made one million francs available to the camps in southern France, to be administered by our previous host, Monseigneur de Courréges, one of the Bishops in Toulouse.

But Abbé Lagarde was the heart and soul of this work, and he managed to help many people out of the camps and into good homes for the elderly. He was constantly on the lookout for new hiding places, especially for adults. Père Braun from the *Comité Catholique*, who had just become a Jesuit priest, was one of his allies. He devoted himself to helping the Jews, and did wonderful work. He liked to stop by our office for a chat, but he also gave practical help when the need arose. He became a dear friend.*

Hiding the Jewish Children

Once the persecution and raids had begun, we were constantly on the run with children and our foster parents risked imprisonment and deportation. A desperate mother, Madame Sperber, came to my office, where she begged me to take care of her fourteen-year-old son and four-year-old daughter. My heart sank. It was late afternoon on a day that had been especially difficult. Where in the world could I place these children at the last minute? All of our hiding places were already full.

Madame Sperber's husband had been sent to Rivesaltes by the French Civilian Corps that cooperated with the Germans. By a lucky coincidence, the mother and children had not been home, but it was now impossible for them to live there. She could stay with friends, but she didn't dare have the children with her, since the smallest indiscretion would give them away. Something had to be done. I asked the mother and her son to wait in the back room of the office, while I drove the little girl down to *Les Petites Soeurs*

---

* In 1984 Alice wrote about visiting Yad Vashem: "I suddenly had an urge to look behind me. There was a portrait of a kind, white-haired priest with shining eyes and a small smile. It was Père Braun just as I had known him forty years earlier!"

des Pauvres, an order of nuns who had an orphanage. Fortunately she spoke French well, so she would cause no problems. But the boy was a big, strong 14-year-old, with red hair and down on his chin, and a deep, masculine voice. He could have easily been mistaken for an 18-year-old, but he had to be hidden somehow. After an emotional farewell, I drove the young man the 25 kilometers to Levignac, where Sister Louise of *Les Souers de St. Vincent de Paul* ran a home for orphaned boys between the ages of 5 and 12. Sister Louise greeted my passenger pleasantly enough, but when she saw me, her expression changed drastically!

She asked the boy to wait in the car, and took me out in the courtyard, where the children ran around playing like little chicks. "Look at my tiny, thin boys," she said. "He would be like a cuckoo in a sparrow's nest! I wish I could take him to repay the Quakers for all their help, but it just won't work. Wait here in the parlor for a bit," and the tiny nun disappeared into the chapel. The waiting room of a convent is just about the most boring place one can imagine. They all seem to be narrow, whitewashed, with a few ugly chairs, a crucifix hanging on one wall, plaster copies of Notre Dame de Lourdes in one corner and Saint Thérèse de Lisieux in the other. There I sat, freezing in my thin summer dress. I waited and waited, looking at the crucifix and the saints. I must admit that I prayed to all of them for a solution to the problem at hand!

Finally, Sister Louise came back. "I've just been in the chapel praying as hard as I could to the holy Mother of God for help, and it never fails!" While she was praying, Brother Jean from the Trappist order came in, before bicycling home. She implored him to take the boy with him. He couldn't decide that alone, but insisted that I should bring the boy out and speak with the Father Secretary. I thanked Sister Louise for her help, found my passenger. He looked as if he wanted to apologize for being alive. I comforted him with the news that help was in sight.

I would have enjoyed the drive along the narrow, hilly roads through the meadows if I hadn't been so nervous. The sun was low in the sky; the shadows were lengthening. But in the clear September air the light seemed to heighten the colors of the green trees, the yellow meadows, and the few whitewashed farm buildings along the way. It was my absolute favorite time of the day. It always reminded me of the intense painter Vlaminck. Suddenly, at the crest of a hill, the monastery of *La Trappe de Saint Marie* appeared, looking just like the castle in the Norwegian tale of Soria Moria, with the setting sun shining white in the distance, surrounded by large trees and wide-open meadows.

We drove up, and were let in. The boy remained in the car, and I took a seat in the parlor, which looked just as it should, except Saint Benedict was in the corner instead of Saint Theresa. The impressive Father Secretary entered the room. He had visited our office and shown an interest in our work. I explained why I was there. "But my dear child, you can't possibly expect us to hide all the Jews in France! We can't take children. This isn't an orphanage. There are only grown men here." I pointed out that the boy *looked* like a grown man, and we discussed the situation for a while. Oh, how desperate I was! I couldn't take him back to my hotel room and try again the next day. I was so worried and tired and scared that the tears started to roll down my face. The monk was dismayed. "Oh, no, Mademoiselle, you mustn't cry, I shall see what I can do." He gathered his robe around his bare legs and disappeared up a spiral staircase.

Finally, he returned with his arms hidden in the folds of his monk's garb. "We will take him – the Abbot has given permission." I could have hugged him! But I limited myself to thanking him warmly, and started to get the boy from the car. But, man of the world and aristocrat that he was, he was now ready for some polite conversation. "You understand," he said, "Jews are completely safe here with us. We have the local police force in the palm of our hand. We make sure their larders are well stocked from our large farm, so it is in their interest to keep quiet about our activities. Occasionally, we have visits from unwanted guests, but we have such a good view of the surrounding area, we always see them coming, and we have plenty of time to hide the Jews living with us. All we ask is total discretion. Do you think the boy can manage that?" "I certainly hope he understands that," I said, and drove home with the gift of a wonderful loaf of white bread! (See letters from Al Sperber, page 251.)

VI. Escapes and Escape Attempts

A nice Polish family, the Korytowskys, had paid us regular visits since the summer of 1940. The husband was a scientist, and his wife was the loveliest, most modest person I'd ever seen. They had a sweet ten-year-old son. After the police visited their home, without finding them, they decided to try to get over the border to Spain. They took the local train to Boussens, and the bus to St. Girons in the Ariège. From there, they continued on foot, like any other family out for a walk without any sort of baggage. Then they ran into a German patrol.

The boy had fallen a bit behind and when he saw what was happening he detoured onto a small path. His parents were taken in, and we never heard from them again. But the boy managed to get back to Toulouse. He came up to the office and told us what had happened. We gave him to our good friend, the resistance man Ninau de Bonnefoi, who was Mayor in the tiny village of Auriac and one of our reliable sources for false identity papers. He took "Pierrot" in and treated him as if he were his own son. From that time until the liberation, we worked almost daily, hiding both adults and children and securing false identity papers and ration cards. But all of this was done on the sly, even among those of us in the office. We were a neutral, non-political organization after all, and foreigners to boot. We had to be very, very careful not to compromise our work in the camps and for the French children.

One morning, a red-haired girl scout suddenly appeared, accompanied by a nine-year-old boy scout. "I'm here to deliver the boy, Edouard Seidler, to Miss Resch with the Quakers in Toulouse," she said. I drove him out to *Chateau de Larade*, which was filled to overflowing, but they made room for Edouard, too. The police had come to the mother's house, but luckily she had good friends who had warned her, so she made sure she wasn't at home when they turned up. A neighbor had her five-year-old daughter Lisette, and Edouard was sent to us by the Jewish aid organization in Agen.

A week later, a beautiful woman named Mademoiselle Gilberte Marty came in to the office. All the clients had been taken care of so we were alone. She said, "I am Madame Hélène Seidler, Edouard's mother." She had been out to *Larade* to see him. At first, Edouard had thrown himself into her arms and begged, sobbing, to go home with her, but she had explained to him that they no longer had a home, and from now on he must call her Aunt Gilberte. She told him that she had had to go into hiding, but that she had found work in Toulouse in order to visit him every other Sunday. The little boy dried his tears, smiled, and changed his tune from "it's so awful here" to "it is wonderful here, can't Lisette come too, I'll take good care of her!" Edouard never complained again after that day, and he never let on that his "Aunt Gilberte" was his dear mother. Not even the other children at *Larade* knew the truth. Lisette joined him there, and he did indeed take good care of her and raise her! It was truly moving.

Gilberte was Czech, cultured and pleasant and not afraid of work. She had come to Paris in 1939 with her two children. She found a job in a clothing factory, and learned the trade. In June of 1940, she was evacuated to Agen, where she became supervisor in a similar factory, and made a good home for the three of them. She was doing well until the persecution of the Jews began. She made friends quickly wherever she was, and had no problem acquiring false French papers and a job in Toulouse. This time it was a waitressing job in a questionable establishment on the rue Payras, but it was a wonderful hiding place!

In the beginning, she lived with *la Patronne*, a large, good-natured woman who also took in all sorts of men as boarders. Gilberte discovered that this was a regular meeting place for the resistance, so she knew she would be safe. There was a complete radio set-up in the bedroom closet, behind the sheets and pillowcases. The men of the resistance often met in the Bistro. But German soldiers had also adopted it as a meeting place, and Gilberte amused herself by listening in on their conversations, both in German and in Czech. She and I spent a lot of time together. We ended up involved in the people-smuggling business. It was unavoidable, but we risked the Quakers' work in southern France in this manner, so we spoke very little with one another about what we were doing. *"What we don't know, we can't tell anyone!"* We were very lucky. We made it through without being discovered.

Switzerland took in many, many refugees. The adults had to have a permit from the government in Bern or they were sent back immediately, risking German capture and deportation. But children under the age of sixteen were admitted without any difficulty. Several organizations smuggled refugees. The members of *"Cirquit Garél"*, and *"Cirquit Andrée"* moved illegally back and forth over the border. In Bern, they could get the necessary papers to help the refugees get into the country.

Hélène Seidler/Gilberte Marty returned to the office in Toulouse. Her husband was interned in the concentration camp at Theresienstadt. She had no news of him, no way of knowing how he was. She no longer felt that *Chateau de Larade* was safe enough for her two children. She asked if I knew of any way to get them to Switzerland where she had relatives. Around the same time, the orphanage in Aspet had two children whose parents had been deported to camps in Eastern Europe, and they asked if we could help these two children over the border.

I contacted "Cirquit Andrée" and shortly after received a message that I could come. I told the others at the office that I was going on a week's winter vacation in the Jura Mountains. Then I collected the four children, Martin, age 12, and Bernard, age 8 from Aspet, and Hélène's two children Edouard, age 10, and little Lisette, age 5. We left on a Sunday at the end of January 1943, together with a French couple who really were going on a vacation, in Savoyen.

The children and I arrived around noon at the tiny village of Annemasse right on the border near Geneva. We got through the eye of the needle by the station. There were Italian guards at the border, good looking, dark-eyed boys, who smiled and laughed, and were very gallant. They were more interested in a pretty face, and couldn't comprehend the French papers. We were heading for a tiny Hotel de la Gare, right above the station, where we were to meet "Anne Marie." We went into a café with simple painted chairs and tables, where many people were sitting quietly with a book or magazine, but no one turned a page. They had a frightened look about them, and it was pretty clear that a lot of them were candidates for the border. I spoke to the woman working at the bar. She smiled understandingly, and showed us to a room with two double beds – one for the boys, and one for Lisette and me. We ate some of the food we had packed, and waited.

We heard a knock at the door, and a tall, dark woman in a skiing outfit came in to the room. She looked at me suspiciously. "Are you going over the border? I wasn't expecting any more today, the quota is filled!" My heart sank; hadn't Andrée's message reached her? "I can only be here five days at a stretch, otherwise I have to register. Do you have money? It costs 5,000 francs per person. I have to pay off the toll officers and guards so they'll look the other way." I knew full well that it would cost money; those who accompanied refugees across the border were known for their high prices. But I didn't have enough. We volunteers in the Quaker program had 3,000 francs per month for lodging, food, and other basic expenses. So 5,000 francs per person was quite a sum. In desperation I said: "I have 15,000 francs and a gold cigarette case." "Give me 10,000 francs," she said. I did, and she disappeared.

We stayed indoors and out of sight, except for a short walk to get some air after dark. The less visible we were the better. But Monday passed, and all of Tuesday and we wondered if Anne Marie had forgotten us. The two oldest children, Martin and Edouard, understood the seriousness of the situation and were very well behaved. They helped out with the two youngest as best they could. But little Lisette was lively. She teased the boys constantly, especially Bernard, who was somewhat slow. I ventured down to the café in hope of catching sight of Anne Marie, but to no avail. Now and then, some of the silent guests disappeared. Finally, Anne Marie turned up with a satisfied look on her face, but she ignored me completely. Nobody said anything, but apparently the mission had been accomplished satisfactorily.

Finally, just before lunch, she said, "Now it's our turn." She started off on her bicycle, and we followed, trying to look like we were behaving normally. She explained that when we came to the house where the road divided, she would go to the left, and the children were to take the road on the right, down to a bridge. There was a barrier there. They were to run as fast as they could and crawl underneath the barrier. Then they would be in Switzerland.

I gave the children a farewell hug, and sent them off. I could hear my heart pounding. I waited a bit. When I thought they must be over the border, I decided to start back. Then I saw to my horror that Edouard and the two youngest were running back, with a French border official on their heels. He gave up the chase when he saw me.

Anne Marie had long disappeared. It turned out that the French and Swiss toll officers had been standing on either side of the barrier, chatting. Martin, who was the eldest, and a quick thinker, ran like the wind and was under the barrier before the French guard had time to react, and he was safe! The three others had stopped in fear, and run back. The officer was on salary and got paid no matter what, so he didn't bother to chase them. We found Anne Marie. She was very upset; nothing like this had ever happened to her before. "We shall try again!" she announced.

After lunch, we went to another small village, Ville la Grande. Anne Marie bicycled, and we followed on foot. We saw Anne Marie laughing and talking with some Italian Alp border guards. Should we turn back? We chose to go on as planned, nonchalantly, and thank God, the soldiers just smiled and laughed, and greeted us pleasantly! Perhaps it helped to be a blonde Norwegian? The children were to go into a bistro on the outskirts, order a soft drink, and ask for someone called W.C. Anne Marie came in shortly afterwards, and distracted the woman working at the bar with conversation. She watched the children disappear out a garden door. They were to go down through the garden, over a low stone wall, and then they would be in Switzerland.

I made my way to the train station, and got in the long line for tickets. There was just enough time to catch the train back to Toulouse. I looked out of the window, on to the square. Suddenly – I thought I would faint – there was Edouard running with his tongue hanging out of his mouth, the two youngest bringing up the rear. What had happened? They went through the garden and ran down to the low stone wall. But there had been a gendarme in the tiny outdoor toilet in the lower part of the garden, and he finished his business and came out just as they were approaching the wall. "Stop! What are you doing here?" he had yelled. "Oh, we were just going over to buy some cigarettes!" Edouard had stammered. But it didn't work.

"Get back where you came from!" the guard commanded, and threatened them, saying that they would be shot if they were discovered by the Italians.

I sent up a small prayer of thanks for the delayed train, which meant that I wasn't already on my way to Toulouse. What would have happened to the children if I had been gone? But I began to wonder if I would ever manage to get these children into Switzerland. The situation seemed hopeless. But Anne Marie turned up again. She clenched her jaw and announced that these children *would* get into Switzerland, even if she had to carry them there herself!

In the end, she almost had to make good on her promise. We took the train to Gaillard, where there was a creek that was no problem for adults to cross, but was a bit difficult for small children. On the other side was a steep slope, and on top of the slope, a barbed wire fence with a big hole in it. There were no toll officials, and the Italian border guards were in the local café, having a drink or flirting with the barmaid. So we helped the children over, they crawled up the slope and through the hole in the fence. I was completely exhausted from the stress, and had lost three kilos!

Before long, the Germans, who had now occupied southern France, discovered that too many refugees were getting into Switzerland. They sent home the Italian border guards. The situation at the border changed drastically, and it became nearly impossible to get over. Some time later, Andrée came to our office in Toulouse, and told us of a Jewish girl scout who accompanied fifteen children to the border. She had excellent "Aryan" papers, but it didn't help. They met a German patrol, and were stopped. "Where are you going?" the Germans demanded. She mentioned the name of a children's colony in the Jura Mountains. "We will accompany you," the Germans announced. When they arrived at the colony, the woman in charge was asked if she was expecting a group of children. "Yeeesss, but not today, and not these children," she answered. The Germans took the children with them, and they were never heard from again. They were most likely sent to the gas chambers in Eastern Europe. The young Jewish girl was later found in a ditch. She had been shot and mistreated.

Choosing 500 Jewish Children to Emigrate to the U.S.A.

The situation calmed down somewhat during the autumn of 1942. Approximately 20,000 Jews were deported from Germany to southern France and the rest were more or less hidden. But there was one big problem: all the remaining, "parentless" Jewish children. Approximately 6,000 of them were in the western part of "unoccupied" France alone. The United States was not eager to take them. To begin with, it was agreed that the AFSC and the *Union General des Israelites de France* (or U.G.I.F.) would jointly take care of 1,000 children.

Canada was also willing to take 1,000 children, but they wanted to see how the experiment turned out first. Santo Domingo was willing to take 500. Russell Ritchie, my colleague from Marseille, was to choose five hundred children in the southern part of France, and I was to choose five hundred in the southwest. He and I met in September of 1942 in Montpellier to confer with the heads of U.G.I.F. We stayed up until 4 a.m. discussing the matter. Later, I heard that the police had been at the hotel. "Who were these strange Americans who suddenly had a pow-wow in Montpellier, only to disappear in the middle of the night in different directions?" But it turned out well.

So I traveled around in my part of the country for six weeks, together with Dr. Ratner from O.S.E. and the fashionable Parisian doctor Dr. Robert Worms, to choose five hundred "suitable" children to be sent to the United States. Dr. Ratner was a well-known Russian journalist, with a fantastic sense of humor. His funny stories helped us through the cold, early-morning hours on the train!

Dr. Worms found life in Paris too difficult. His family had lived in France for hundreds of years. They belonged to Parisian society, and never gave much thought to their Jewishness. Both he and his father had fought in the

Dr. Ratner, Mr. Jablonsky, Madame Reine,
Felix Chevrier, Alice, Dr. Worms

First World War. They were French, just like all other Frenchmen, but like so many others, his life was struck by tragedy. It was quite a shock to discover themselves outcasts, who risked losing everything in a raid. He managed to get into the free zone, where he offered his services to O.S.E.

In Limoges, we visited many colonies for Jewish children, such as Hte. Vienne and Creuse. All of them had nearly twice as many children as they officially had room for, and all of them had hiding places ready, in preparation for raids. We visited villages and cities, where the local aid organizations or social workers showed us children who lived with private families, or with nuns in religious institutions. The problem was the same everywhere: how to choose five hundred children from among several thousand? The Americans had set an age limit of fourteen years, but how were we to prove the children's ages when they lacked papers? They stipulated that the children must be in good health and that both parents had to be dead or deported, with no possibility of discovering what had happened to them.

In the beginning, we spoke with and listened to the children's stories, but that took much too long. Dr. Ratner

135

and I examined those who were found suitable, and sent them on to Dr. Worms for a complete check-up.

We soon agreed on four different categories:

1) The German children from *Kristallnacht* in 1938 who were sent to Madame Edouard de Rothschild's colonies near Paris, and later evacuated to the south of France when the war started,

2) Those who came to Holland and Belgium as refugees from Germany together with their parents after 1933, and who then fled to southern France in May and June of 1940,

3) Those who were sent to concentration camps in southern France from Baden and the Palatinate in 1940, and

4) Those "uncategorized" children who were helped over the line of demarcation by friendly neighbors, and then abandoned to the social services in the south, when their parents were taken in raids in Paris.

Many children were so small that they barely knew their own names, let alone the names or addresses of their parents. So we had plenty of difficulties. For example, one tall boy was born "after January 1, 1929" so he was not yet fourteen, but I had to really watch my step. If the boy was "especially suitable" they might not make a fuss about his real age. But I had a responsibility to both the AFSC and the U.S.A., so I had to be firm, and there were more than enough to choose from. We "adjusted" the facts only with the "uncategorized" children, never with the ones from the children's colonies.

The children were surprisingly calm when they told about their parents and their horrible experiences. Both Dr. Ratner and I often had problems controlling our own emotions as we heard their stories. I wondered if their reasoning was really as adult as it seemed, or if they were simply numb from shock. A small blond boy came in with a serious expression on his face, and said: "My name is – I can't remember my name, unfortunately – and here are my papers." He opened up a file filled with papers. "This is the key to my suitcase." He had the key on a string around his neck. For the last few months, he and his parents had lived in Camp de Milles near Marseille, a sort of waiting station for immigrants who had been granted permits to emigrate to North or South America, and who were now waiting for French exits visas. But promises were broken. The parents were arrested, and the little boy ended up in the colony at Masgélièr. He made it on to our list.

At *Chateau de Chabannes*, we met a twelve-year-old Polish girl called Chajas, and her funny little two-year-old brother who came from a small village in Creuse. One day their parents were taken away. The mother managed to put the boy in his sister's arms saying: "Now you will have to be both a mother and a father to him. Help him to believe that people are good! He must not learn to hate, that is the root of all evil!" When the two children came to *Chabannes*, the first thing Chajas said was, "I must learn something or other, because I have to take care of my little brother." She was put into a leather workshop.

When we arrived, we were told that soldiers had been there a week before. All the older children had run to hiding places out in the woods, but unfortunately a couple of them were caught, so the institution was marked by sorrow and fear. The small children had been left alone.

Back on my old stomping grounds around Indre, we visited farms and other private homes where the now-parentless children had been taken in. But we didn't find any children for our list, simply because the families had become so attached to "their" children that they didn't want to let them go. This was wonderful for the children, and many families were even eager to have more children. We slogged on, traveling on the bitterly cold local trains that always seemed to depart at 4 a.m. We had to arrive at each new place with plenty of time to start work at 9 a.m. We shook with the cold, until Dr. Ratner awoke after a few hours of snoring. Then he warmed us up again with a new round of stories. There was always a line in front of the social services office wherever we were. The work became routine, but the choices were always difficult.

A new type of candidate appeared: adults who perceived a wonderful opportunity to get to the United States by offering to be responsible for groups of children. They asked to speak to me, the "American" in private. They told me their sad stories, and their special qualifications for such a job. I hated to disappoint them, but it would have taken months to acquire the necessary papers, and the AFSC in Marseille had already chosen group leaders.

Then, in the middle of our work, Marseille was on the line. Our quota was to be cut in half. As if it wasn't difficult enough already to choose from among all the candidates! It turned out that the American Secretary of State, Cordel Hull, had criticized the French Prime Minister Pierre Laval in a radio address, for having permitted the raids and deportation of Jews and other political "undesirables." This had naturally insulted the Prime Minister and he sought revenge by reducing the quota of child-immigrants from a thousand to five hundred. "The rest can stay where they are!"

Although our quota had been reduced from 500 to 250, we decided to continue as if nothing had changed. Who knew? Maybe those we chose would get out after all. We stopped in Montauban and in Moissac, where there was a large institution for older children. I enjoyed showing my companion the famous convent garden in Moissac. And finally, Toulouse! It was wonderful to sleep in my own bed for a few nights. Celine Rott and Mademoiselle Cahen from O.S.E. had organized our visit and had the children waiting in the office, so the process went smoothly.

We could start the last leg, the trip in the Pyrenees. I borrowed the Peugeot, secured the valuable gasoline coupons, and we started off early on a morning in November, headed directly for Pau. We felt like tourists, enjoying crisp mountain air, wonderful autumn colors. We got a flat tire as soon as we arrived in Pau. The tube inside the tire had been punctured, and it couldn't be repaired. It was completely impossible to get hold of a new inner tube in these difficult times, and after two and a half years of hard use, our tires were worn out. We took our chances, and drove on eastward without a spare. We found ourselves in narrow mountain valleys with hidden villages, where many refugees had been forcibly placed. The number of young men surprised us. They were hoping to get into Spain, then on to the free French troops in North Africa. But the snow in the mountains made the trip dangerous this late in the year. Naturally, we stopped in at Aspet, where we added two children to our list. I would have loved to give them all the chance, but it just wasn't possible.

We reached the interesting medieval castle *Chateau de la Hille*. It was a true castle, not just one of large country homes or mansions. This institution was mainly for French and Spanish children suffering from malnutrition, and persecuted Jewish children were in the minority. At Perpignan, Mary Elmes had a small group of "suitable" children. At our last stop was Monpellier, we heard the wonderful news that the Allies had landed in North Africa! We were of course thrilled, but we wondered if they would land on the Riviera, where there were still no German troops.

My two traveling companions and I took a last look over our lists: we had one list with 500 children, and one list with 250. We talked to the heads of U.G.I.F. and said an emotional farewell after our difficult and rewarding six weeks together. The AFSC office had arranged for transporation to Portugal, and the O.S.E. had the first one hundred children ready to leave on November 12.

On November 8, 1942, when American and British forces landed on the beaches of Morocco and Algeria, we began to hope that Hitler might be turned back. But soon it was apparent that the Germans would occupy all of Southern France. They were expected at any moment. We heard that the borders were closed and there would no longer be any exit or entry permits. I still hoped that these hundred children would be able to depart. But Helga insisted on my returning to Toulouse. I arrived on November 11, at 3 a.m. What a sigh! First of all, it was raining cats and dogs, and the entire square in front of the railway station was packed with tanks and huge trucks, all flying the Nazi flag. A large truck with radio transmitting equipment was buzzing unpleasantly, and every once in a while; orders were issued through a megaphone. The entire area was lit up with floodlights, and there were soldiers everywhere, sitting, standing, even lying in the deluge.

I wandered down to the Hotel Capoul where we had our rooms. The lobby was full of Germans. The owner and some of the staff were clearly nervous. The owner told me that the *Wehrmacht* had taken over the hotel, and my room had been emptied. Luckily, the maid said "No, Mademoiselle's room had been so full of belongings that they had decided to empty Mademoiselle Holbek's room instead, and put all of her things into Mademoiselle Resch's room!" Thank God, I thought to myself, I at least have a bed, instead of a chair in the lobby, or even out in the rain! By the time Helga got back, a solution would no doubt present itself. I spent the rest of the night packing our things. Strangely enough, when Helga, Toot and Celine returned, rooms became available for them, too, and we all stayed there for the rest of the winter. It was the best winter we had, because the Germans made sure the heat and water functioned. When the hotel ran out of coal and wood, we reaped the benefits of their ability to get more. But we had to make sure to lock our doors at night. Many nights we heard a careful knock, followed by "Open up, Fraülein." They gave up when they got no response.

The Germans arrived in Marseille on November 11 as well; all our emigration work had been for nothing. The children were sent home again. The only ones we sent to the U.S.

were the 150 children who went over during the autumn of 1941 and the spring of 1942.

It was back to the grindstone for me. But the winter turned out nicely even so. Sylvio Trentin introduced me to a handsome older gentleman, Magnus Synnestvedt. His father was Norwegian and his mother was French. He had a duplex apartment in a new building, full of the most wonderful things, and it was always a pleasure to visit. We took much pleasure in each other's company, attending concerts, movies and the theater, and we had small, strange dinners that he made from ingredients that generally weren't available at that time. He was a widower, without any commitments other than his two adult daughters. The first time I was at his apartment, I had to laugh. There were stacks of used plates on the kitchen floor. He had just taken a clean plate from the cupboard every time he needed one! I rolled up my sleeves and got working. We married a year later. Sylvio Trentin had to go underground in the end of November. The Germans were after him. He and his family returned to Italy right after Mussolini's fall.

We celebrated our third festive Christmas with the children at *Chateau de Larade*. The AFSC had sent over fifty tons of clothing in the autumn of 1942, to be distributed among the inmates in the concentration camps as well as to others in need. *Secours Suisse* had received a large shipment of toys from Switzerland, which they gave to our children. The holiday was a happy one for the children, who were thrilled with their new clothes. We gathered for dinner at the office on New Year's Eve. Gilbert White and Russell Ritchie came from Gaillac where they were still in charge of our large warehouse. They now had responsibility for all the clothing from America. 1942 had come to an end.

The Free Zone Occupied, Registering Valuables

During all the months of raids and deportations, we had an extra accountant and secretary whose only job was to sort and copy all the information, take care of registration, and carefully pack all goods, small and large, that the frightened people had entrusted to us in anticipation of deportation. Jewelry and other items of value, and envelopes with money: everything was to be sent to the International Red Cross in Geneva. We kept all kinds of packing materials. Everything could turn out to be useful at some time or other. All valuable items were packed in metal containers that had come from Hungary with dried food. They were buried in Pastor Mayou's garden outside of Toulouse until the end of the war. The International Red Cross took care of tracing the survivors or their descendants. But when the Germans occupied the free zone, the borders were blocked and all packages in and out were checked carefully and even confiscated. Decades later, I spoke with one of my Aspet children, who told me that she had received her mother's ring and some old letters and photographs through the International Red Cross. Perhaps they had gone through our hands.

We continued to distribute clothing to needy individuals in the concentration camps and childrens' colonies. Since I knew my Aspet children and their needs so well, I personally picked out garments for them from our *Vestiaire*. Several bags of clothing were prepared and the children were expecting a party. So I dressed in my best rags, complete with high-heeled pumps and the nylons Harriet had given me, and caught the train for St. Gaudens. I should have been there just in time to get on the charcoal bus up the valley. But it was market day, and the bus was full of farmers homeward bound with their purchases, so it hadn't bothered to wait for the train. There wasn't another vehicle to be found, so I started off on foot for the longest fifteen kilometers I'd walked in my life! And how the children laughed when I finally showed up, wet and mussed, with my suitcase on my head, stockings and shoes in hand, and bloody feet. The hilly gravel roads did not agree with my high heels.

The children had been fearful. I had promised to come, and had let them down by not arriving on time. Then when I did turn up, the party began. They put on a little play, they sang and danced, and afterwards came the main event – the distribution and trying-on of the "new" clothing. But when Helga saw clothing I had appropriated for the children, I got an earful. "You would think that only *your* projects are important! You must not play favorites!" I countered with my usual argument, that since we had responsibility for these children, we had to do our best for them. The difference between Helga and me was that she was able to see the big picture, while I concentrated on my individual assignments.

I was quite worried about the Aspet children. The prefecture in Toulouse, who kept an eye on the foreign children, had recommended the institution. But their papers all had the word "JUIF" (Jew) stamped in red. The Jewish children at *Larade* had managed to avoid this. Gradually, we simply smuggled the children away from Aspet. We claimed that the colony was too far away and gave Coste a fictional list of people who were willing to take the children into their homes. The youngest came to *Larade*, where we erased the "JUIF" mark from their papers. Others went to the institution in Moissac, and yet others to Aveyron, far from Coste's clutches!

Attempts to Disband the Quaker Organization

New things were happening all the time. All the Americans in what had previously been the free zone were arrested and placed in large empty hotels in Lourdes. On their way back from distributing clothing in Gurs, Helga and Toot stopped in Lourdes, where they managed to persuade a German officer to let them see their friends. All were very depressed, because they heard that they were to be sent to Germany, but they were certainly happy to see Helga and Toot.

The Americans had everything they needed from the American Red Cross, but they were prisoners, and had to be content with a short walk once a day under the watchful eyes of German soldiers. One evening while I was turning the dials on my radio, I heard a German voice, saying, *"America criticizes us for having sent their diplomats and countrymen from Vichy-France to concentration camps. This is not true; they have been placed in comfortable hotels in one of our largest spa areas!"* One year later, these Americans* were exchanged for German prisoners of war in the U.S.A.

Then our own Mary Elmes in Perpignan was arrested, and placed in the military prison in Toulouse. Helga tried to arrange her release, but to no avail. Nothing could be done at the Prefecture; they said she would have to talk to the Gestapo. So Helga and Ima Lieven went to the Gestapo office at 2 rue de Maignan. The doorman who announced them was thrown out with a thundering RRRRAUSSSS! They jumped. At least they were allowed to visit Mary and the other prisoners and to send them packages with a few necessities. Later, they were all transferred to the Frèsnes prison outside of Paris. Mary managed to talk her way out after only a few months. She arrived in our office, as attractive and well groomed as always, as if she just made a journey like any other. What a party we had!

On February 10 we had a real scare. Our "best friend" in the Prefecture, Monsieur Coste, asked me to come over because he had an important message. I took Toot along, and Coste received us with his usual crooked smile. "Yes, I've just received a message from Vichy informing me that you are now disbanded! An American organization cannot exist here now that the Germans have occupied this area as well." I replied: "That's no problem. We are now a French organization, *Secours Quaker*. May we see that message?"

---

* Nine American Quaker representatives, including Gilbert White, Russell Richie and Rose Thorndike were interned in Baden-Baden, Germany, where they remained until the prisoner exchange.

"Hmmm, we got the news on the telephone, but I felt it was best that you be informed immediately."

We raced back to the office. Luckily, Helga returned to hear the whole story. If *le Bulletin Officiel* published news of disbanding the Quakers, there would be nothing we could do, so we had to avoid *that* at all costs. We sent a telegram to Professor Cornil (the head of *Secours Quaker* since November) in Marseille, and Helga and Toot took the night train to Vichy. But Cornil didn't turn up. It turned out that neither Cornil nor Vichy had been informed. Coste had simply been trying to get rid of us. He called around to the various camps, and told them that the Quaker work was over. In Gurs, the keys to our warehouses were turned over to *Secours Nationale*, and we were effectively shut out.

Helga and Toot arranged for Prime Minister Laval to sign a statement postponing the disbanding. In Toulouse, we had been given five days to shut down and turn over everything to *Secours Nationale*. But it was not to be. And Coste had to eat his words. I have no idea what transpired between him and Vichy, but he certainly wasn't any happier with us!

Helga went to Gurs to protect our interests, and was denied admission! Coste had "forgotten" to let Gruel know that we weren't shut down after all. Our two allies, Löser and Danziger, *waren geflitzt* (had escaped). So the prisoners were in the process of doing exactly what they wished with our supplies and new groups of people were awaiting deportation. Helga spent many hours at the station in Oloron Ste. Marie, unable to enter the camp, watching one truck after another disappear into the goods station. She was depressed and discouraged when she returned to Toulouse. The story of Coste and the Quakers turned out all right, and a few weeks later Helga returned to Camp de Gurs where she ran into Gruel. "Oh, how nice to see you," he said, "It's been so long!" The crook! What a mess she found! There had been no supervision for weeks, and much was gone.

On February 27, I wrote in my diary: "Yesterday, our dear Thérèse Dauty was arrested." She was the wonderful woman I had met the first time I accompanied the prisoners from Récébédou to the deportation trains at Port St. Simon. She ended up working with Abbé Lagarde and Père Braun from the *Comité Catholique*, and she was a great help when we needed to find hiding places. She was transferred to Frèsnes and released along with Mary Elmes, but the experience had made a deep impression on her. Our friendship lasted until her death in 1967.

We heard through the grapevine that very same day that a deportation train with about two hundred people would stop for half an hour at the main train station at Gare Matabiau. We got in without difficulty, bringing pans of porridge and bottles of water. Then we saw the long row of locked cars with closer to one thousand men, not two hundred. We saw faces we knew, both from Gurs and Toulouse – silent, worried. We didn't have enough food! The German guards didn't pay any attention to us, so we at least managed to distribute what we did have.

One day later, Coste called us – to our surprise and trepidation – and asked if we wanted to feed a convoy headed for the camps at St. Denis and Compiègne, north of Paris. Had Coste suddenly developed empathy? What a difference between this convoy and the one from Gurs the day before! The men were in good humor, in third-class cars, leaning out of the open windows to gossip with us and they already had plenty of food. They all seemed to be British, white and black, old and young, who had taken their chances and stayed in France. They didn't understand how the Germans had found them, in the "free" zone – which was of course no longer free. They were well treated compared to the Jews.

Life in Camp de Gurs

I took over Helga's duties at Camp de Gurs in April of 1943. We weren't allowed to have a permanent Quaker representative in residence, so Helga had been there for various periods since December of 1940. She heard about a fellow called "P", a prisoner who was a favorite of Gruel. He was a spy who had gotten himself installed in our living quarters and stole! Madame Dupréz, the Red Cross Representative kept the keys to the clothing barracks, but it was a simple enough matter to get into the warehouses. Huge amounts of clothing and other supplies were spirited away in empty latrine buckets. We heard the most unbelievable story from our head cook, Frau Würtzburger, who had to stand by helpless and witness the whole escapade. Then "P" was fired and Madame Dupréz refused to return the keys saying: "Monsieur Gruel entrusted them to me!" But Helga made a scene that "la Dupréz" didn't forget for quite some time. From that time on, she was exceedingly polite, and all the dramatic episodes were over.

The 2,000 inhabitants made apartments for themselves in the barracks, using wool blankets for walls, and making furniture from bed frames, To my amazement I saw that the same class divisions one could find on the outside had sprung up inside the camp, and those who were better off paid the poor to be their maids, housecleaners, and hairdressers. Some who were given clothes from our supplies continued to use their old rags because they were saving the new items for the end of the war!

The Quaker rations started up again, with only 400 recipients, as opposed to the many thousand before the deportations began. We had to make sure that the food was eaten in the barracks that served as a canteen. Many people wanted to take their rations home with them, but we knew that they would be sold, or traded for a pack of black market cigarettes. It was comical to see how angry they were when we wouldn't let them leave before they had eaten everything! Fortunately, the large vegetable garden was thief-proof and the soil was wonderfully fertile. The summer I was there, we harvested over ten tons of various vegetables and the loveliest flowers on a hectare of earth. Gathering flowers was an important job. Together with the gardeners, we picked them and made bouquets for the hospital, the canteen and our own common room, which was also our dining room. We also took flowers when we visited prisoners. We also had a whole row of rabbit cages. They and the doves were taken care of by a Spaniard whose name was Sabino, but he was never called anything other than *Lapino* (rabbit). We always had enough meat for canteens and private use.

We had two responsible women working in the *vestiaire* or clothing barracks. The steady stream of "customers" also took up quite a bit of my time. They were not always easy to please, and came to me to exchange what they'd been given. It was amazing what one could do with the clothing on the black market. Once, I ran into the wife of one of the guards, wearing a nice American dress I had given to a prisoner. The guards went in and out of the camp, and made a bundle on the black market. What could we do? Only keep our archive in order, so we knew who had received what. When someone said: *"Ich bin drei jahre im Lager – und ich habe nie was bekommen, ich habe nichts anzuziehen!"* (I've been in the camp for three years, but have gotten nothing. I have nothing to wear!) we just took a look at our card catalogue. But nothing could be done about the black market, so I adopted my own philosophy: that they might as well trade for something they really wanted. But they had no luck when they came back for more.

From time to time we invited the camp's inhabitants to a private meal in the Quaker salon. All the furniture was made in the workshop of a Jewish organization that also made shoes and clothing. The inhabitants seemed to appreciate the meals with us, even though they were far from luxurious. Helga forbade the use of food acquired on the black market, but our dear Frau Würtzburger always managed to make the best of the rations. The vegetables from the garden were extra good, and we could buy good Jurancon wine at a reasonable price. Once, a guest said with tears in his eyes that this was the first time in three years he had actually sat down at a table set with porcelain and real silverware. Both Helga and I brought our own possessions to the table.

The six months in Camp de Gurs were an interesting experience for me. It was a self-contained society, full of all sorts of people with good and bad characteristics. Everything was magnified, in both directions, no doubt as a result of the years of suffering. Some of these people I thought of as saints, others - especially among the leaders of the camp - as something completely different. Some of the inhabitants and representatives of various organizations became my friends for life. It wasn't difficult to be popular, but perhaps that was because I represented an organization that provided something everyone needed – namely, food. But it was exciting for me to meet so many interesting people and to hear their stories.

Two who became good friends were the O.S.E. workers, Dora Wertzberg and Ruth Lambert. They lived and worked in a barracks right next to ours, so we saw a lot of each other. We often ate meals together, and put on a social evening for the inhabitants. Sometimes we danced to music from London! It was actually strictly forbidden to dance in Pétain 's France, but our barracks were isolated from the rest of the camp.

Occasionally, other aid organizations would entertain us. One of the most memorable parties was at the home of the Swiss Abbé Gros. He wandered, illegally, over to Switzerland now and then, and came back fat with goodies hidden under his robes: chocolate, real coffee, cigarettes, nylons, yarn for darning and things we had almost forgotten existed! Abbé Gros invented party games and pranks and stories, but he was a good priest as well, and could be very serious when the situation called for it. Ruth wanted to invite him to dinner, along with Dr. Joseph Weill. "Then we'll be treated to an interesting discussion of religion!" Abbé Gros said: "You know how I enjoy Dr. Weill's company, dear Ruth, but I can't measure up in a deep, philosophical discussion with him. I am a simple priest who feels secure in his faith."

Our dear Abbé had too many escapes on his conscience. The Gestapo got interested in his activities, so one day he wandered over the border for the last time, and took Ruth Lambert with him. She was also quite vulnerable. Dr. Weill had already fled to Switzerland. Both he and Abbé Gros had good contacts with the various organizations in southern France that helped to arrange escapes.

Sometimes, I was invited to an evening meal at Max Ansbacher's office. He served as rabbi after his brother fled. It was the first time I had ever been present at the Sabbath ritual. CIMADE had arranged for Swiss entrance visas for Max and Siegfried, but Max refused to leave as long as there were people in the camp who needed his help. When the camp closed, he was transferred to *Centre de la Meyze* in Haute Vienne. But he was at great risk of being arrested, so one day, he went to the Centre's head, said adieu, and informed them that he would now flee. The leader couldn't believe his ears!*

But that summer of 1943 in Camp de Gurs was something special. On the surface, it was like being on vacation. Things were going badly for Hitler and better for the Allies. We wondered where the invasion everyone was talking about would take place. Would it be in Norway? The Riviera? The Atlantic coast? Some said Rommel was hiding in Toulouse; others said the Côte d'Azure. The sun was shining, and everyone was relaxed. Even the horrible, brutal Gruel, and his little shrimp of an assistant, Hess, became almost human, allowing the inhabitants to walk freely through the entire camp between the hours of 8 a.m. and 10 p.m. Once a month, the "privileged" were even allowed "out," to circulate in an area of up to five

---

* Many years after the war, Max and his new wife Bella visited Helga and Alice in Copenhagen. They asked him if the story was true, and he blushed and said that that was more or less the way it happened.

kilometers from the camp. It was a wonderful to sit under trees, wander in the high grass, and be out in the green countryside. Those with money could sit at a sidewalk café in one of the nearby villages or take a dip in the river Gave d'Oloron, in the fresh water from the Pyrenees.

Once, on my way home to the Quaker section, I passed a woman near the barracks wall. She was dressed only in her bra and panties, with her hair loose. "I see you're enjoying the good weather," I commented. "Oh yes," she said, "I've never been so happy! I have a place to sleep, and food at regular intervals and I don't have to cook! I don't have to work, there are books in the library, and I have no sorrows or worries!" She had fled from her butcher shop in Paris when there was no meat there to sell anymore. It did me good to talk to her.

Despite the seemingly relaxed atmosphere, an unavoidable unrest was bubbling under the surface. Around France, young men – both Frenchmen and foreigners – were being taken into the S.T.O., or *Service de Travail Obligatorie* (Forced Labor Service). The last thousand were sent off from Camp de Gurs that very spring. I don't know what Gruel was thinking, but we knew that he was a laughingstock in London, and he was terrified, not knowing what his own fate would be. We heard rumors that he had received a "coffin" in the mail from the resistance, as had the infamous Dr. Cuvigny, head of the infirmaries. He tried to flatter the inhabitants, and he was a very model of politeness to the remaining aid organizations, while sending countless prisoners off to their fate on the convoys. When Gurs was closed, he was transferred to the penal camp, Camp de Vernet, and given the position of head doctor. We heard rumors that he was shot by the resistance on liberation day in August 1944.

The Germans were still building the Atlantic Wall, and had started to expand on the Côte d'Azur. The allies were on their way up through Italy, getting closer and closer to France. But the resistance was ready. One dark night, the boys from *le Maquis* came down from the Pyrenees with two big trucks. They overpowered the guards, stormed the entrance and released the men who had been collected to be sent to *Organisation Todt**. They broke into a large barracks and took all the weapons, and disappeared before anyone had time to react! Gruel and the others slept peacefully during the entire episode. Perhaps they knew what was going on. They acted pretty innocent the next morning. But he was fired, and the Germans and the Vichy police questioned all of us. Of course we knew nothing.

There were fewer and fewer people in the camp. Our friend, Gilbert Lesage organized several small centers around France for women and children, with good barracks and better food and without barbed wire. But something strange happened: They didn't want to go! The devil they knew was better than the devil they didn't know, and Gurs didn't look so bad after all.

---

* A giant industrial firm which used conscripted labor to support the German war effort.

Camp de Gurs, by Sigismund Koloszvary

VII. Fates from Camp de Gurs

Sigismund and Matyi Koloszvary

Both Helga and I became attached to the little Hungarian painter Sigismund Koloszvary and his wife Matyi. They came to Paris when they were quite young, following the dream of all artists, and they quickly became part of the international artistic milieu. When the organized attacks on Jews began in Paris in 1942, their friends advised them to relocate to the unoccupied zone, and helped them on their way. But they were the world's most impractical and naive people, even according to themselves, and they walked right into the arms of a gendarme. Because they had gone over the demarcation line (separating the occupied zone from "free" or unoccupied France) illegally, and weren't able to come up with a good enough reason for the gendarme to look the other way, they were sent to Camp de Gurs. "Don't be nervous, it will only be for 48 hours, just until you get your permit to live in the free zone," the gendarme comforted them. And there they were, once again on the wrong side of the barbed wire. Kolos wrote of his flight from Paris and his time in Camp de Gurs in an unpublished manuscript, *"Ce n'est que Pour 48 Heures"* which he dedicated to Helga and me.

One of their first experiences was witnessing a deportation. Since Hungary was a "friendly" nation as far as Germany was concerned, and they were Hungarians, they were exempt. That winter they learned what it meant to be cold and hungry but they were so modest that no one discovered them, to give them an extra meal now and then. Then Elsbeth Kasser, the head of *Secours Suisse*, asked Kolos to draw a caricature of the Swiss work, and with that, his fortune was made. Soon he was asked to draw caricatures of everyone, from the camp head on down. He was given half an empty barracks as a studio, along with drawing equipment and paper. Kolos said one day that he prostituted his art: "...for an insignificant material gain, I put together embellished drawings of my contemporaries, or made horrible caricatures that make them laugh." It was a huge honor for us when he showed us his *real* paintings. Their beauty was very moving, pure imagination. "I am a painter-poet," he told us.

In June of 1943, a privileged few were permitted to leave the grounds each month, so we took Kolos and Matyi, Dora Wertzberg, and our doctor Alex Feigenbaum and his wife Sonia for a swim in the river Gave d'Oloron. There, we ran into the other Hungarian artist, Victor Tulman, and his fiancée, the dancer Hella Bacmeister Tarnov. We had a wonderful afternoon, and ended up at the home of Dora and (my egg and pork farmer) Monsieur Candeau for a meal. Everyone was carefree, unconcerned about what the future might hold. We headed home in the evening sun, blue around our mouths and on our fingers from all the blackberries. We struggled up the steep Dognen hill, stopped for a moment at Alex and Sonia's farm for an aperitif, and then ran as fast as we could to make it back through the camp gates before 8 p.m.

The Germans required those men who were able to work to go to *Organisation Todt*, to fortify the Côte d'Azur, but someone always managed to disappear on the trip from Camp de Gurs. We were helping thousands of starving French children, so we didn't involve ourselves in this traffic. Still, there's an exception to every rule, and on one occasion we did give it a try ourselves.

156

Helga had connections with Madeleine Barot from CIMADE, who was in charge of the courier traffic to Switzerland. Abbé Gros and Dr. Joseph Weill worked there, trying to convince the

Camp de Gurs, by Sigismund Koloszvary

Swiss authorities to grant entry permits to people like the Koloszvarys and the Feigenbaums. The approved lists were then smuggled back. As soon as they received their permits, it was important to get them moving. My job was to photograph them for their identity cards, and to go to Pau to acquire the false cards from a young man with the code-name Joe Hammer. He made wonderful documents.

The Feigenbaum's lived outside the camp and were able to take care of themselves, but the helpless, impractical Koloszvarys' were another story. Helga was exhausted from all her work, and had been instructed to go to Ax-les-Thermes to rest. She had put in a request for the special permit, since Ax now fell within the forbidden 30-kilometer belt along the Pyrenees, but it took a long time. Then one day, our friend Père Godard, the Jesuit priest, offered to pay for half her gasoline if Helga would drive le Père Provincial and two other Jesuit priests the next time she went to Gurs. Helga forgot all about her need for rest, and decided that this was fate! *"Grynene!"* The word means "the grits" or "groats," and was used as a code for human beings who were to be smuggled.

Helga dropped her priests off at *le Centre Ouvrier de Nabas*, at Rivehaute, 14 kilometers southwest of Camp de Gurs where the Jesuit director Etienne Thouvenin de Villarèt was a go-between for many of those headed for Spain. We planned that the *Grynene* would leave on Monday morning, as soon as the inmates were allowed to move freely throughout the grounds. They were to go through a small, secret gate that the guards used as a shortcut through the barbed wire 100 meters away from our barracks. It was usually unlocked. Then they would go through the forest, and wait at a bridge that connected Gurs with the tiny village of Hôpital St. Blaise and Helga would drive the back road in order to avoid passing the camp once more. Kolos' and Matyi's faces were white as chalk all Sunday with dread, so it was obvious that something was up. Sunday night I put on the darkest clothing I had and sneaked over the long empty stretch to the gate. All of France was in blackout; only Camp de Gurs was illuminated. There was a light on a long pole with a bright bulb 20 meters from the gate and I saw to my dismay that it was shut. The grass around it was tall, and the guard was in his little hut, some distance away guarding the prisoners' barracks, not ours. With a lot of hard work, I managed to peel off the steel wire and open the gate a crack.

Around 8 a.m. Monday morning, the *Grynene* wandered past the various guards who smiled at them and said good morning. Everyone knew Kolos and his caricatures, and they all let him pass. But ten minutes later, they were back. The gate had been fastened again! The guard hadn't seen them because he was patrolling along the barbed wire on the outside of the barracks. But dealing with the steel wire in broad daylight put *that* exit out of the question. I got on my bicycle and hurried off to Nabas, where Helga was waiting with the Jesuits, and reached her just as she was about to leave for Hôpital St.-Blaise. Helga was just as disappointed as I was, and wasn't able to think of a solution so she drove off, keeping to back roads. Later, she told me that she had felt inspired. She recalled that one of the officers in the camp owed her a coupon for five liters of gasoline that she had once loaned him. When I got back from Nabas, crestfallen, I found a letter on my desk from

Helga: "Everything's fine, bring the papers to the field past St. Goin." I had all the counterfeit papers for the *Grynene*. I got back on my bicycle and headed for Geus and St. Goin.

I found them sitting under an apple tree just past Géronce. And there they told me the unlikely story. It turned out that on the way back to their own barracks in *Ilot* A, they had run into Madame Dupréz from the Red Cross. "Why do you look so sad?" she had asked. "Oh, we were so hoping for a swim in this wonderful weather," Matyi replied, thinking fast. "I can arrange that for you," Madame Dupréz assured them, and she went to the assistant director, Hess, and got a special permit for them. Then they went back to my office, to wait for me to return from Nabas. When Helga found them there, she already had her five liters of gasoline. "Of course you must use your permit," she told them, "this is important – walk in the direction of Oloron, I'll be back to pick you up after we've eaten lunch with the Mayor of Oloron!" Finally, they were successfully placed among all the priests, and off they marched, so fast that I only saw the cloud of dust in their path as they turned the corner! I bicycled back at a comfortable speed. In the next few days, it was hinted that we had helped the Kolos' escape, but it was Madame Dupréz who had obtained the permission to leave camp – she was able to influence Gruel, the director. A couple of days later, on August 31, 1943, a letter came to say that all was well.

Helga had gotten a permit to enter Switzerland – it was stamped in her passport. She wanted to get some more money to subsidize the Quakers' work, and to purchase more food from her faithful supplier, Vafiades the Greek. She also wanted to visit our good Quaker friends in Geneva, Ross and Marjorie McClelland* who were our go-betweens with the US.

---

* For more on Marjorie McClelland and her work with Spanish Civil War refugees in France (including photographs of Helga and Ima) see the AFSC web site: www.afsc.org/about/hist/spainfed.htm

Helga took Kolos and Matyi along with her to Chambéry and left them temporarily in the care of O.S.E. Then she continued on to Annemasse to speak with the Italian border guards about official entry and exit visas to Switzerland from France. They took her passport, and said that she should come back the next day. But that night the Germans took over all border patrols, and the Italians burned all the papers in their possession – including Helga's passport – before they were either taken prisoner or managed to flee. There was no option left to her, she had to go back and forth illegally. She took Kolos and Matyi by the hand, one on each side, and got over the border at the place Abbé Gros had shown her, near St. Cergue, just past Annemasse. But they were met in Switzerland by two border guards, and sent to a camp for temporary detention. The other inmates were delighted to see Helga!

"Oh Miss Holbek, Miss Holbek," echoed around her, as they all asked her to do this and that. Imagine their surprise when she just laughed and said, "I'm just as much a prisoner here as all of you!" She was upset to find herself so helpless, unable to get through to speak to the right person. A day later, they were taken for questioning by the Swiss authorities, one at a time. When Helga came back to the school that was serving as the camp, she looked for the *Grynene*, but couldn't find them anywhere. The guards wouldn't help her – they knew "absolutely nothing." Finally, she ran into a friend who had also come from Gurs. He had heard that they were to be sent back to France! Helga's heart sank. She had ripped up their false identity papers once they were safely in Switzerland, because the Swiss would not take in Frenchmen. How had the misunderstanding come about? We knew that the Swiss authorities had officially accepted Kolos and Matyi. Helga was miserable!

When Colonel Henriot himself came to collect Helga three days later, the directors and guards were clearly impressed. The Colonel apologized for the inconvenience and pointed out that she had made her way over the border illegally, without papers. Helga was now free in Geneva, where she managed to collect 100,000 Swedish kroner for our work with French children. But she was still worried about *Grynene*, so she hurried back to France. This time she crossed the border like a V.I.P., thanks to the new passport she had acquired in Switzerland. The toll officers opened a hole in the barbed wire, and said, "Run about 400 meters in that direction, then you'll be safe." "Ha," she thought, "Me, run on my fat legs, wearing six sets of new underwear?" But fear of the German patrols who shot first and asked questions later, drove her on toward the steep fields. Finally she reached the road, and sank down out of breath at the edge of the ditch.

As she was still trying to find out what had happened to *Grynene*, a charcoal-fueled bus came along. She flagged it down and asked for a ride to Annecy where she knew a priest. With his help, she found out that Kolos and Matyi were in the prison where he worked. He helped her get permission to visit them, even though it was past visiting hours. Helga was dismayed when she saw that they had lost quite a bit of weight, and she saw Kolos without his beard for the first time. They were pale and worried, because they had heard that their names were on a list of prisoners to be deported to Germany or Poland the next day. It was very moving to see how their eyes lit up with hope when they saw Helga. But she wondered what she could possibly do for them in an unfamiliar city surrounded by strangers.

She pulled herself together and found the Prefecture. Although it was lunchtime on a Saturday, and the offices were empty, she managed to locate the Secretary General, holding the deportation list in his hand! He listened to her story of Kolos and Matyi. Then she told him about a young man whom she had met in Geneva at the home of Ross and Marjorie McClelland. He had told her that his father was the Hungarian minister in Vichy, and that if she ever needed help, she was to call him up immediately and say that "Mr. Thomsen" had sent her.

"If you can prove that your friends are under the protection of the Hungarian minister, I can cross them off the list, but I have to know by 12 noon today." During the war it practically took an act of state to make a call from town to town, and especially to the capital, Vichy. Helga was on pins and needles. The connection didn't go through. Time was passing – it was 11:30, then 11:45. When there were only five minutes left, the Secretary General got ready to leave. "I'm sorry, but there's nothing I can do," he said. Then the telephone rang!

"Congratulations," he said when he hung up, and crossed the two names off the list. But that meant that *Grynene* would be sent back to Camp de Gurs. Helga couldn't let that happen. The Secretary General recommended that she contact a young female attorney who might be able to help her by keeping them in the prison at Annecy. Later, they told Helga of their "return trip." Together with five unhappy men, they had been driven to the border in a police car and escorted through the barbed wire. Swiss border patrol told them: "Get out of here, and don't try to come back!" as they headed over the border. The five young men disappeared, and there they sat, Kolos and Matyi, alone in the grass not knowing how to avoid the Germans. A shepherd stood at the top of a hill, looking down at them. They asked him where it was safe to go, and he pointed with his staff and said, "There are Germans everywhere!" They ran off in the direction he had pointed, when suddenly a French soldier appeared from behind a bush.

"Out for a stroll?" the guard asked them. "Yes, we're on our honeymoon," Kolos answered wryly. "Can I see your papers?" "We have none, we are Jewish refugees on our way to Switzerland, but we got so frightened by all the Germans," Kolos burst out. "You are lying! You've been sent back from Switzerland, follow me!" the soldier insisted. "Oh, let them go," they heard the shepherd say. "I can't – I've got my family to think about, I have to follow orders!" the soldier replied. "You miserable mutt, I'll remember this," the shepherd said in disgust. So they went with the soldier back to the prison in Annecy.

Helga, in the meantime, had made a fuss over the fact that *Grynene* had been sent back to France, since the Swiss authorities actually had given them permission to enter the country. It took several weeks to apply for new visas and acquire new false identity papers. O.S.E. had managed to get them permission to live in Nice, and after they had spent a month in prison Kolos got into a work camp, while Matyi was placed in a women's camp near Annecy.

Permission was finally granted – this time in writing – and Helga went all the way across France to find her *Grynene*. She got to Chambéry, where she was told that the Koloszvarys had a permit to live in Nice, so she went there to find them. At the station in Chambéry people were milling around everywhere, because a train had been sabotaged. After a long while, another train showed up, and it was stormed by the waiting crowd. Helga was lucky – she got into a car, and was shoved along the corridor and practically thrown into a crowded compartment where she found our dear friend and colleague from O.S.E. in Camp de Gurs, the young Dora Wertzberg!

"What an odd coincidence," they said at the same time, "Where are you heading?" Helga said she was on her way to Nice to see the Koloszvarys. "But they're not in Nice," Dora told her, and explained that they were near Annecy. Helga got off at the first stop, and managed to get on a train going in the opposite direction. It was late in the evening and pitch black when she finally got to the little station Dora had told her about. She started off down the country road, repeating, "Never afraid of the power of darkness! The stars will light the way" and "Our Father, I pray, I will not shudder!" And before she knew it, she was lying in the ditch, laughing at herself. But it all worked out, and a few days later Helga accompanied Kolos and Matyi to the station. They got their tickets, false papers and the Swiss entry permit. The attorney pointed out the young man with dark glasses who would make sure they got over the border. They finally made it over without any difficulties, and lived in Switzerland until the end of the war. This was the only escape in which Helga played an active role. For her, the Quaker work always came first.

The Koloszvarys came back to Paris in the autumn of 1945, and we met at Deux Magots for a drink. "We're getting divorced," they told me. Kolos had fallen in love with a very young and very beautiful Swiss dancer. They were married, and had a wonderful son. But those two and Matyi stuck together, and became an inseparable trio, though they didn't live together.

Helga and I often discussed how odd it was that we helped certain people and not others. We saw such misery at the station in Toulouse: cattle cars with the words "Eight horses end to end" written on the outside, filled with hundreds of suffering people, who were sent to German concentration camps and to gas chambers. All we could do was to offer them buckets of boiled rice and water and small food packages, and accept their written last words which they smuggled to us through the cracks in the walls of the cars as we walked along the trains with the Germans at our heels. It makes you believe in fate.

Alex and Sonia Feigenbaum

It didn't go unnoticed that the Koloszvarys hadn't returned to Camp de Gurs that evening. Gruel wasn't at home, but Hess, the assistant director, was furious; there had been far too many escapes during the previous month. "All the aid organizations ought to be closed down!" He was also furious that Kolos could abuse his permit in that fashion. They were only supposed to go for a swim! What if they had drowned? This would be discussed at the next general meeting of all the organizations! I didn't admit to knowing anything; I had been working all afternoon, blue-eyed and innocent. Dupréz smiled craftily and patted my hand when we met. I knew nothing about her request for the permit for them to go for a swim. But we *had* misused it. How does one's conscience deal with that? Well, at least they avoided deportation.

I dreaded the meeting of the organizations, with the furious Hess. Luckily, Gruel came back and led the meeting, and the disappearance wasn't mentioned.

I had the feeling that I was alone in the camp. Just before the Koloszvarys disappeared, Dora Werzberg had gone to eastern France to get her father and 17-year-old sister over to Switzerland, and the Jewish organization had moved from Montpelliér to Chambéry.

Abbé Gros had arranged a position in Camp de Gurs for the young Romanian doctor, Alex Feigenbaum and his wife Sonia who had originally come to Paris as students. The Feigenbaums were Jews but since Romania was a German ally they were allowed to live outside the camp, on a farm in the village of Gurs. Alex bicycled to the camp every day to work, and they had secured false French papers (as Dr. Alex and Madame Simone Ferry) to be on the safe side. As the Germans pulled back from Russia, it was less and less certain how long the Romanians, and especially the Jewish Romanians, would be left alone. So Alex and Sonia went to Chambéry, to wait. Their names and the Kolosvarys' were on the same list of those permitted to enter Switzerland. On September 15, I had six prisoners to dinner. While we were relaxing and chatting, two young girls suddenly appeared with a letter for me.

> *Dear Alice, I would like to see you this evening if possible, do what you can to make yourself available, but if it's not possible, come to our house tomorrow morning.*

> *Affectionately Sonia F.*

The guard at the north gate had been given it by a woman who asked that it be delivered to me. I put it in my pocket, and returned to the lively conversation. Finally, at 10 p.m., the guests had to return to their respective *ilots*. What had happened? Were Alex and Sonia back?

I bicycled furiously toward Gurs in the pitch-black night. I managed to keep on the right side - there wasn't any traffic, after all. But even so, a shadow suddenly appeared right in front of me. I steered over towards the middle of the road, then POW! We crashed, and both ended up lying in the road. We pulled ourselves to our feet, so at least we had not broken any bones. My strong Peugeot bicycle had survived the crash, but my opponent's front wheel was now in a figure eight. He apologized profusely for having been on the wrong side of the road, but he had not been able to see his hand in front of his face in the darkness. We parted on good terms, and I eventually got to Alex and Sonia. Alex's face was pale with nervousness, but Sonia was calm as usual. Alex disinfected all my scratches and cuts.

But what had happened? They reached St. Cergues together with Dora and found the place where they were to crawl through the barbed wire, when they suddenly became aware of Germans behind them, and they ran back! They found Dora, who said that the people they had seen were Swiss, not Germans. It was easy to confuse them because their uniforms were the same color. They tried once more, and poor Alex was truly a hero, because he was practically in a coma from fear. Sonia didn't share his fear; she had no desire to spend the rest of the war in a camp.

They got over safely, and reported to the border guard, an unpleasant fellow who yelled and complained about foreigners who were streaming into Switzerland. Did they have any papers? No, but they had been granted an entry permit through Abbé Gros from Bern. "Oh, that Abbé Gros who always sticks his nose in things that don't concern him," the guard said. They pointed out that their names were on the list of approved persons, and asked the guard to call Bern or O.S.E. in Geneva. But he refused. If they didn't have any papers as proof, they could just go back to where they came from! *Allez vous!* And back through the barbed wire they went.

In Chambéry they were given new French papers. They had been told to rip up the first ones before they tried to get into Switzerland. Alex and Sonia went back to their farm in Gurs pretending that they had been on a vacation. But the farm wife met them there and said, "Oh, no, you can't live here any longer. Two days after you left, the police came asking about the doctor. He was supposed to go to the reprisal-*ilot*, and be sent on to *Organisation Todt*."

I was their last hope. I suggested that they take the first bus to Pau and the express train to Toulouse, where they could go to the Quaker office. I would be in Toulouse myself in a few days, and we would figure something out then. When I got there, I found them in a back room in the office, pale and discouraged. Helga was still occupied with the Koloszvarys, and the others felt that Alex and Sonia were my problem.

I called Mother Dolores at the *La Motte* convent at Muret. She was willing to take Sonia, but unfortunately couldn't take Alex. I didn't sleep that night, worrying about how I would deal with this problem. Suddenly, the answer came: Magnus Synnestvedt, of course! He had visited me several times while I worked at Camp de Gurs. He was never granted a permit to enter the camp, but we swam in the river and ate black-market dinners in the tiny village restaurants in the area. And he proposed marriage every time! I called him the next morning, to ask if he could put up a couple of friends for a bit. "Of course, I'd be happy to help!" he answered. I could practically hear how happy he was! And not a single question about who or why.

At that moment I decided: "You are truly a good guy, dear Magnus, I'll marry you!" He lived in a wonderful two-story apartment, where there was plenty of room for Alex and Sonia. They could sleep in the upstairs bedroom, and he would sleep in the high-ceilinged atelier living room. It was quite an experience to see the look on their faces when they first entered that beautiful apartment, filled with the most wonderful antiques. Their jaws just dropped! They had pictured something along the lines of a bicycle workshop with a ladder up to a sort of shelf! Sonia took over the housekeeping duties and Magnus had a wonderful time. They stayed there for a couple of months. Alex, or Dr. Ferry as he was now called, worked for us in the office at Boulevard Bonrepos, and eventually they found a place of their own.

My Marriage to Magnus Synnestvedt

Once I had accepted, there was no longer any reason to wait, so we were married on November 27, 1943. The ceremony at City Hall was followed by a reception at the office, where we served champagne and received friends and clients who wanted to offer their congratulations. The whole office was decorated beautifully with flowers.

We also had an unforgettable ceremony in the reformed church filled with flowers. Our friend Pastor Dombre gave a simple, yet spellbinding speech. He spoke of my parents, our country, our work and the responsibility of establishing a new home, and our duty to let as many as possible enjoy its comforts, in spite of – and because of – the sorrows and suffering that surrounded us. I was so moved by his words that the tears ran down my face, and my grandmother's lace handkerchief was transformed into a wet rag. The speech also moved Magnus. He was musical, and had arranged for the organist to play Norwegian psalms and folksongs including "Når bruri gjeng yver dørstokki" (When the Bride Steps over the Threshold), arranged for organ by David Monrad Johansen, who we later learned was a Nazi sympathizer.

At 5 p.m., a fantastic feast was served in the office, thanks to our good friends of means. They had sent delicacies of all kinds, such as foie gras, guinea hens, and wine. And the bride? I was well dressed in a black, tailored suit made out of Magnus' former tuxedo. On my head, an elegant black hat, from our American clothing supply. I had Helga's real silk blouse from before the war, and nylon stockings sent by

Harriet from America. Thus, Miss Resch became Madame Synnestvedt. The "honeymoon" ended abruptly five days later, when Celine, who had taken over my work temporarily, broke her right arm. So it was back to the grindstone. But we had a marvelous Christmas vacation.

Magnus was a Doctor of Law, but never a practicing attorney. He put his money in strange inventions, and was the eternal optimist, always sure that *this time* his fortune was right around the corner! Together with two good friends, he developed a wonderful motor which used charcoal as well as gasoline, and could run a car. One friend owned large forests in Les Landes, and a large lumberyard in Toulouse. Magnus took care of all of the paperwork. The third friend, the inventor, was never completely satisfied, and always had a new idea to improve the motor. When it was finally good enough, the war was over, and gasoline was again available, so no one had any need for "the world's best charcoal-driven motor." The only ones to benefit were the big trucks that commuted between the lumberyard in Toulouse and the forests in Les Landes.

The friend who owned the forest lived at a vineyard on the border between Les Landes and Gurs. Magnus and I were invited to his romantic little "castle" for Christmas. We drove a charcoal-powered truck both ways and spent a lovely week, taking long walks in the forest to see the oven that made the charcoal. I noticed with interest all the small containers collecting sap from the trees. The smell of pine forest was enchanting, and a welcome treat for us city folks.

Our friend had bought an old Basque house for his daughter when she became a widow. The original owners were dead, and without heirs. Only one piece of furniture, a huge old wardrobe, was left behind. When the workmen who were renovating the house lifted the wardrobe to throw it out, they heard something rattling inside. They opened it, but found nothing, so they suggested to the new owner that perhaps there was a secret compartment. When they broke it apart, they found the traditional French stocking filled with a fortune in gold *Louis d'ors*. Since the previous owners had had no heirs, the find fell to the new owner who announced, "Here we have a true dowry for my daughter." The workers were given a reward for their find, and the rest was taken to the castle. This could only happen in France!

Christmas Eve was magnificent. There were thirty of us: the family, including the aforementioned daughter with her children and various servants and their wives. They slaughtered a poor pig, and I saw geese and ducks on a long spit over the fire. Wonderful things were prepared on a huge oak table in the middle of the room. There was goose with foie gras, vegetables, and wines from the family's own production. During a pause between courses we drank the house's own armagnac, *Le trou Normand*, to make room for more. Fruit and cake topped it all off. We sat at the table until 11:45 p.m. and then we all made our way to the small village church for the lovely service where children acted out the Christmas story.

We got to bed late that evening. The big bedroom was warm and inviting, with a fire in the fireplace. Even the bed had been warmed up, using a "munk" which is a contraption made of four runners (like those from a sleigh), joined at the edges. From a metal tray hung on chains, glowing coals sent warmth out to all four corners of the bed. The eventful week came to a close. We decided to accept a ride on a truck back to Toulouse on New Year's Eve.

Sonia and Alex had gotten a new apartment which we had arranged to borrow. When we arrived, we heard conversation and laughter but we decided to proceed cautiously to see who was there. We opened the door. The room was filled with people we didn't know, wandering back and forth between the kitchen and the living room, talking and laughing. Suddenly, Alex appeared before us, his arms filled with bottles. "Oh, so sorry – we'll be on our way immediately" he said. But we suggested that instead of leaving, he invite us to the party! We were introduced to everyone, and had a wonderful New Year's Eve. We ate and danced until dawn. 1944 was upon us.

Our home

Magnus and I got busy enjoying his beautiful home, which was now my home, too. It was filled with wonderful old furniture, paintings and antiques. But oh, how we shivered that last cold winter of the war. The radiators were cold and there were no fireplaces or wood burning stoves. Everything was rationed. The only source of heat was the pilot light on the stovetop, two hours every morning and evening. We moved two easy chairs out to the kitchen, and let the gas burn away full blast for the full time allowed. There we sat, wrapped up in coats and blankets, staring at the lone flame. The effect was mostly visual!

Luckily, spring comes early to the south of France, so we thawed out again. Guests began to descend on us. We were all eager bridge players. Food was our biggest problem, but it was a problem for everyone, so people brought their own food to a gathering. We all enjoyed the sight of the table filled with everyone's contribution, and Magnus's porcelain, silverware, and fine Czech crystal. Fortunately, flowers were not rationed!

Once, we invited everyone to a surprise *Suppe à la Magnus*. Magnus had managed to get four kilos of awful, small crabs, the kind that bites your toes on the beach. I shuddered when I saw them. Magnus rinsed them, and cooked them with boiling water for two hours. Then he crushed the crabs to powder and put them back into the broth and cooked them another two hours with all sorts of strange spices. The guests arrived at 8 p.m., and the soup was brought to the table in a lovely tureen. Eight pairs of eyes were lit up in anticipation, wondering what was in store for them. The hot soup smelled fantastic and we, who had become accustomed to so little, lifted the spoons to our mouths in awe and respect.

Oh! Groans and gasps for air! It was so hot and strong; smoke came out of my mouth. But my gosh it went down quickly; I don't think there was a single drop left. The guests ate the food they had brought with them. We couldn't offer them bread, because there was no more flour. The bakers were resorting to cornmeal and as a result the bread was lemon-yellow and tough, and it turned green in the evening. Two things made us especially popular among our friends. Magnus owned a huge armagnac bottle. Thanks to his childhood friend with the lumberyard and castle, we had taken the empty bottle along with us on our charcoal-powered trip and re-filled it with armagnac.

The other was tobacco. Magnus knew everyone, and was an entertaining guest everywhere he went. He had friends in Lot et Garonne, where tobacco was grown. The government had a monopoly, but there wasn't a single plantation owner who didn't have his own private corner where he grew his own tobacco, or who bribed the government controllers. We spent occasional weekends with them, and always carried an empty backpack to fill with the finest tobacco when we returned. Magnus had the proper tools and necessary expertise, so it actually turned into the finest, purest tobacco!

Women weren't allowed any tobacco during the war. Men were allotted four packs of 20 cigarettes each per month. Magnus came home the first of each month with his four packages: "Here you are, two for you, and two for me," he said generously. But it was of course great sport to try to get hold of black-market tobacco. Never had so many women taken up smoking as during those war years.

Yes, we had a wonderful home life, despite all the restrictions, little food and no heat, and the curfew from 9 p.m. to 5 a.m. every day. There were lots of strange things, like the coffee made of burned barley (and even that was rationed). But there were always four or five real coffee beans at the top of the little monthly package. Magnus and I picked them out carefully and saved them for months. A couple of friends came over for bridge, and we brought out the coffee maker which consisted of two glass chambers connected by a glass pipe. We poured warm water in the lower chamber, enough for four small mocha cups, and the precious ground coffee beans were put into the upper chamber. A small flame was ignited, and we watched, silent as mice as the water boiled, rose through the glass pipe, sprayed over the coffee beans, and disappeared down through a filter. The water in the lower chamber became more and more coffee-colored. Then – the chamber broke! The precious drops, saved up for months, ran out onto the felt of the bridge table! We were devastated, but we laughed anyway!

Magnus had a large map of Russia on the back of the kitchen door, and we monitored the Germans' progress in the battle for Stalingrad, and the difficult retreat to the west. We thought the war would soon be at an end. If the Gestapo were to stop by, we didn't think they would discover the map, full of blue and red tacks and lines. The door opened toward a wall, so there was no room to hide a person.

Someone from the Gestapo actually lived on the fifth floor. He had thrown out an architect and taken over his lovely apartment. He didn't really seem to know what to do, and he didn't bother the nice old Jewish lady who lived below. We didn't see much of him, but we had an extra key to his place "just in case." As the war was going badly he became more and more nervous, and tried to commit suicide. Magnus just happened to go up to have a chat with him, and smelled gas! He found the man on the floor, shut off the gas and opened the windows. Luckily the man was still alive. We got a doctor, and put him to bed at our place. Later, we got him out in the country and the son of the owner of the building moved in to prevent someone else from the Gestapo from having it.

Victor David Tulman Toldy and Hella Bacmeister Tarnov Tulman

Victor and Hella came to play quite a large role in my life. Victor was a Hungarian Jew, who looked positively Aryan, with his blond hair and blue eyes and a small nose. His book Va t'en describes his restless life as a poor child, sent from one Jewish family to the other, and how he managed to complete his rabbinical education. He had a beautiful, trained voice, and was engaged at the Dresden Opera. He was also a dyed-in-the-wool communist, and in 1936 he joined the International Brigade in the Spanish Civil War and befriended the Frenchman Andre Malraux.

Victor ended up in the Ministry of Propaganda in Barcelona. But with Franco's victory in February 1939, Victor and the government troops were sent back to France and they were put behind barbed wire on the beach at St. Cyprien. The soldiers dug themselves down into the sand and made a roof out of wool blankets. Later, they constructed primitive barracks. Huge Senegalese soldiers guarded the camp and ruined all of the prisoners' belongings. "One shoe for you, one for me, one arm for you, one for me," they would say, as they ripped apart the prisoner's shirts. The most upsetting thing for Victor was when his photo of Picasso with a personal dedication was ripped in two. "Half for you, and half for me!" said the guard.

In the summer, most of them were transferred to Camp de Gurs where Victor became quite popular. He laughed and joked all day long. He got an orchestra together, and arranged open-air concerts where he sang solos or duets with the Italian tenor Toffoni. Whenever one of the Jews died and was to be buried, Victor volunteered to perform the funeral; after all he was a rabbi. Most Spaniards were sent to work camps, where they worked for the French war industry. But Victor, as a Jew and a Hungarian, remained at Gurs, where he had many long, hard years. He told of being so hungry that he hallucinated; a piece of wood looked like bread to him, and he leaned over to eat it.

In September 1939, when the war broke out, all the Germans in France were arrested and incarcerated, Jews and Gentiles alike. That is how Hella Bacmeister, alias Tarnov, ended up in Camp de Gurs. Hella was German and Aryan, and had trained as a dancer. But she wanted something more. One day, she saw a Javanese troupe perform. Hella was fascinated. This gave the very soul a different means of expression than western dance forms.

She asked the Javanese to take her on as a student and, to her parents' dismay, spent ten years in France with the dancer, his Dutch wife and the rest of the troupe. She learned the form and the culture behind the dance, but her teacher said that she must find her own expression; she would never be oriental. If she were to dance as they did, it would only be imitation. Despite this, she became his prize pupil and an assistant to the teacher and his wife. She had no money, but she had found the means of expression for which she had been searching.

When the war came, Hella was arrested and ended up in Camp de Gurs, where she met the positive, easy-going, child-like Victor, who soon became the man in her life. The camp loved Hella because she would do anything she possibly could for her fellow prisoners in her quiet, discreet manner. When the French capitulated, the Germans came to Gurs and announced that anyone with German citizenship could return to *das Reich*. Many (including German Jews) took advantage of the opportunity but Hella was among those who preferred the hard life in the camp to Hitler's Germany. In October 1940, when Jews from Baden and Westphalia were sent en masse to the concentration camps in southern France, Hella worked tirelessly to help the newcomers who were old or ill, until she became ill herself.

She became postmaster in *Ilot* L, one of the women's sections. I met her every day on the long street between the various *ilots* but at first she was so shy that it was difficult to make contact with her. It was no problem getting Victor's attention! He had been appointed head of the waterworks, and could move freely. He was no longer especially popular with his fellow inmates because his loud manner (most likely a front for an innate shyness) could be tiring in the long run. But we became friends. He could be extremely entertaining, and he didn't take himself too seriously. Once when Victor had guard duty, I invited Hella to dinner in the Quaker barracks. We set the table with our own silverware and porcelain, with flowers and vegetables from the Quaker garden. That's when she told me about her life.

Many managed to escape that summer. The administration was starting to get nervous because of the German army's faltering progress, so prisoners were allowed to go down to the river to swim. I had a good connection to a "work center" in Nabas, some distance from Gurs, which was led by a young Catholic priest. I had arranged with him for Victor to join a convoy over the Pyrenees. His post gave him the right to go down to a small electrical station near the Dogne Bridge, from which he could have kept on going, but he declined. Perhaps he just didn't want to leave Hella. Those two belonged together. But then there was a raid, and Victor was caught. After a month in the reprisal-*ilot*, from which escape was impossible, he was sent to Camp Malaval in Marseille to work for *Organisation Todt*. Hella was inconsolable, so she sought out the Quaker barracks more than ever. When Victor was sent to Marseille he asked me to take care of Hella for him.

The camp was closed down that autumn and the last prisoners were spread out to various camps throughout southern France. The sites were no longer called concentration camps, but *centres d'hébergements*, or hostels. Hella was sent to one of the camps in Hautes Alpes, near Gap and she wrote to me:

September 9, 1943

Dear Miss Resch,

I often think of our warm parting, because there were only cold showers awaiting us here. The journey was very tiring, and we were soaked when we finally arrived …and some of the women found themselves behind barbed wire once again. The nurse Olly Maag managed to get out at night, and went to the Germans to inform them that many of the women in Aspres were being poorly treated, and were just waiting to be saved by their countrymen! The next morning, Olly came back, riding in a car with a German officer, who interrogated all the women thoroughly. Three women ended up volunteering to work for the Germans … I just can't understand their idiocy and lack of convictions. But when one looks around, up into the mountains, one forgets the ugly factories that we live in, where the walls and mattresses are full of unpleasant small animals. … Here there are huge amounts of nuts and fruit and potatoes at reasonable prices. The food is better than in Gurs, although there's not enough of it here, either. There are many Spanish families, and the children play happily in the courtyard. … In Aspres, there is just about everything one needs - even three cafés! It takes about half an hour to get into the village. It's very beautiful; the mountains always seem to be changing. I want to draw them, even though the wind is freezing cold and gives us red and swollen hands! I am so grateful for the wonderful wool blanket, and have already begun to make use of the knitting needles, even though all inspiration disappeared when the Germans turned up. But I am looking forward to being able to gossip with you. I fear there are more difficult times in store, for us as well as for so very many others! My main pleasure is the mail - I hope for good news from Dr. Tulman. Then all will be easier to bear. I await the further progress of world history, and look forward to being reunited with that wonderful person.

With warm regards and sincere friendship,

Yours,
Hella Bacmiester Tarnov

In the beginning of 1944, I made my first trip to Paris since the occupation, to attend a Quaker General Assembly. I was thrilled! I loved Paris, and I wanted to feel the city's pulse in times of trouble, not only in times of plenty. The Paris Quakers had been quietly working for refugees from Hitler's Germany since 1933, and continued to do so under the guise of working for poor foreign students, and in the prisons. The official leader was Henry van Etten, an interesting idealist and a real Quaker. Ellinor Cohu represented the Marseille office.

It was peculiar to experience Paris during the occupation. Naturally there were "Fritz's" everywhere. Due to the gasoline shortage, there were almost no buses or private cars and the only taxis were bicycles with an extra seat on wheels. A few motor-driven vehicles ran on charcoal. The Metro was the only relatively reliable means to get around. It was always packed, and during air raid alarms it stopped wherever it was, even between two stations. You risked being trapped under ground for hours. We heard anti-aircraft artillery several times, but there were no bombings during my stay.

I stayed with my dear, Norwegian friend Elisabeth Eydoux. In my spare time, I visited various friends and heard many stories about how difficult things were under the occupation. But the greatest experience was meeting Hella Bacmeister Tarnov. I went to see her at the Hotel Strassbourg, which was exclusively for the "gray mice". That was what the German female employees were called, and I was mistakenly thought to be one of them! There was no way I was going to put up with that, so I dragged Hella out and insisted that we not speak German. Luckily her French was excellent.

Elisabeth kindly invited Hella home for a cup of tea. How she appreciated that! It was the first time she had set foot in a real home since before the war. I asked if she would dance for us. Elisabeth dug out an old blue taffeta evening dress and an Indian shawl, and Hella danced "Maria Leben" so beautifully that Elisabeth and I were enthralled. The pleasant living room with all the bookcases and the comfortable chairs just disappeared. There wasn't even any music, but Hella's dance transported us to Palestine in the time of Christ. Late that evening, when I finally accompanied Hella through the darkened streets to the Metro, the last thing she asked of me was that I take care of Victor. She was on her way to Germany the next day.

I suppose I let her down. Years later I wondered why on earth I hadn't hid her too, as I did so many others, especially then, when it was so easy to get false identification papers and ration cards. She hoped to get a job and come back to France to be near Victor, and I just automatically assumed that she, as an "Aryan," would manage. We hid Jews and resistance people, not anyone else.

After fourteen days in Paris, I returned to my work in Toulouse. On April 12, I was sitting in my office quietly dictating some letters, and I didn't even look up when someone came in through the door. But then I heard my name, and I looked up and there was Hella's beloved Victor Tulman Toldy! I sent my secretary away so that I could hear what had happened! I had sent Victor a package and written a letter because Hella begged me to. I didn't like him as much as Hella did, but she loved him more than life itself, so I reasoned that he must be a good person. And there he was, standing before me, poor fellow. There wasn't much left of the jolly, fat, loud fellow from Gurs, with his long hair, sky blue pants and a short-sleeved shirt, and a big smile that showed all his white teeth. Now he was thin and pale, with short hair and a grey, worn suit.

It turned out that the Gestapo had heard about his relationship to Hella, and he had been accused of *Rassenschande* (mixing of the races). Victor swore that there was nothing between them, and was sent back to the camp. The situation was investigated further. He was called in a second time, and had to answer a thousand questions: Why had Hella visited him in Marseille? They knew he had been outside the camp (he had bribed the French guard, and a friend had answered for him at roll). But Victor stuck to his story. Again he was sent back, and told that the interrogation would continue the next day. Then Victor fled. Just outside the camp was a small bar, where prisoners were occasionally allowed to go. The French guard looked the other way. A young woman who ran the bar acted as an unofficial post office for some prisoners, so their letters weren't censored. She also washed some clothes for them and did a few errands. Victor went to the bar. He didn't know anyone else in Marseille. He sat in a corner with a glass on the table in front of him, worried and depressed. He had a little money, but no papers.

The barmaid asked him why he seemed so sad, and he told her the whole story. "Oh, don't worry, we'll deal with that," she said, and called out to a man in police uniform: "August, get papers for our friend here!" She hid Victor in a room over the bar for a few days, until August came back with the documents. When Victor left, he was Otto Müller from Strassbourg. The only person he could turn to was me, so he headed toward Toulouse. What could I do? My heart sank, but he looked so helpless and unhappy that I finally said, "All right, I'll try to help you over to Spain, but first you have to go straight home. Our housekeeper will remember you from Camp de Gurs. I'll be there at lunchtime. But don't show yourself here in this office!" I contacted Paul, one of the students who helped out as a waiter in the Quaker canteen. He wasn't particularly reliable, disappearing for days at a time, until he finally admitted that he was a liaison officer in the resistance. I asked him to take Victor in the next convoy over the Pyrenees, in three days and it was arranged. Meanwhile, Victor stayed with us.

The next day, Paul came by with the sad news: there had been a horrible accident with the last convoy that had gone by way of Perpignan. The guide was shot and most of the others had been taken prisoner. Paul's best friend Jacques had disappeared. The next convoy was postponed for a week, so Victor had to stay with us. He was easy to have

180

in the house, very discreet, and he helped in the kitchen. He was thrilled to lose himself in my husband's huge music library. They got along like a house on fire. Victor was especially happy in the evenings, when he beat us all at chess. Soon his hair started to curl again and his smile was back! He kept us spellbound with all his outrageous stories.

In the meantime, my friend Herzog (who lived with his wife in Toulouse under the assumed names of Monsieur and Madame Pierre Mansuy) got a good set of forged papers for Victor. We gave him the new name of Victor Carrere, a French identity, and a Spanish birthright. I gave him my Norwegian backpack and boots from the Quakers, and three days worth of food. Finally, Paul arrived and told us to take Victor to the five o'clock train to Pau the following Friday. He was to stand by the flower stand holding a copy of the magazine *Pariser Tageblatt* in his left hand. Paul promised to take care of him from there.

On Thursday, Jacques came to the office and told us of his amazing flight from the Germans after the last convoy had been stopped at Perpignan. Jacques rested in one of the offices and slept at Helga's that night. He was to go with the same convoy as Victor the next day. On Friday afternoon I accompanied Victor to the station and instructed him to stand by the flower stand. I waited at a distance. I just had to see him safely on to the train. It got to be 4:50, then 4:55, then finally 5:00: no sign of either Paul or Jacques. Victor was still in front of the flower stand with the German magazine in his hand and the train left! I had no idea what was going on, and neither did he. Victor had trusted me completely. I had to send him home alone while I went back up to the office, where I told Helga the whole story. Could she make any sense of it? She knew all about Jacques, after all. Helga just shook her head. The convoy had left at 5 *a.m.*, not 5 *p.m.*! I was miserable. I had ruined Victor's opportunity to get over to Spain! I didn't have the courage to tell him. I couldn't destroy his faith in my ability to deal with the situation. So I just told him that something unexpected had come up at the last minute.

I felt better about the whole episode when I heard that the Germans had been getting more and more aggressive and had started patrolling all the way along the mountains with dogs. Several of those on the convoy had been shot, and the rest were sent to the "camp of fear" Camp de Vernet. I didn't tell Victor this either, but I started to listen to his talk about his lucky stars.

But what was I to do with him? He wouldn't stand a chance if the Gestapo paid us a visit in our apartment, where there were no doors between the rooms. They were already a little suspicious of our last name with all those *stvdt* consonants – was it Polish? They had deported the Jewish architect and appropriated his beautiful apartment right over us, and a French Nazi had thrown out a Jewish family to get the apartment on the first floor. But the wife of the building's caretaker was our sworn friend because we delivered a few Quaker packages to her child, and she told the Germans that we were Norwegian-French and Quakers. The part about being Quakers helped. The Germans remembered that the Quakers had helped feed them after the First World War. We were left alone, but for how long?

We had quite a few nighttime bombings during that period. The airport and factories were of course targets. Victor went down to the bomb shelter with us once. It was pitch black except for all the flashes from the bombs, and a few flashlights pointed right at our faces to see who we were! This made Victor very nervous, so he decided that he would rather die in the apartment than go through the flashlight trauma again.

We were accustomed to having guests, and resumed our social life. Victor had to keep out of sight when we entertained, and often ended up sitting in the bathroom with some sheet music while we played bridge with our friends. There was always the chance that the Gestapo would surprise us with a visit, so I suggested that Victor could crawl out of our fifth floor bathroom window and reach an iron hook that held the electric wires that ran down the side of the house. It was about 30 centimeters long and strong enough to support a person's weight if he stood on it. Victor shuddered and announced that he'd rather fall into the Gestapo's clutches. But every morning I sighed with relief when I awoke and realized that we had made it through another night unscathed.

The group stopped sending people over the mountains after the last incident, so I contacted the Zionist group led by our friend Chaineau. They smuggled young Jewish men to Palestine, where they enlisted in the army. We had to provide pictures and all sorts of information. A week later, they told us that 43-year-old Victor was too old! It was a real shame, because that convoy with fifty boys made it safely over. They came together in Toulouse, ate in our student canteen, and hung around for a couple of days until they finally were on their way. I feared I would never manage to get Victor out!

I told Sonia Feigenbaum the whole story. She passed it on to Henriette Léon, *Chef Régionale du Service Sociale de la Resistance*. Victor, who had started out as a secret, was now known to half of Toulouse! Henriette told Sonia that the man at the grocery store would be able to help. The grocer, Victor, and I sat on a bench by the *Canal du Midi*, waiting and looking around. A round little guy arrived on the nicest bicycle I'd ever seen. He said that since Mademoiselle Estelle (one of Henriette's many names) was involved, Monsieur would be taken care of, despite the fact that he was neither American nor French. The leader would come down to Toulouse in a few days, with instructions. He told me to telephone a number and ask to speak to *le Patron*, and he would come. I called three times, but never spoke with *le Patron*.

Finally, one day we were told to go to the station, and buy a ticket on the 2 p.m. train to Tarbes. The grocer himself would be there. We did as we were told, but the grocer came at the last minute only to tell us that the mountain guide hadn't shown up and the trip had to be postponed. My heart sank. Victor had been staying with us for five weeks and at this rate, he would be with us until the end of the war! He was pleasant and fun to be around, but the whole thing was getting a bit tiring. Sonia, who was very understanding, set up a meeting with a fellow named Jean Cazaux, the treasurer for the regional resistance group. He knew of a room for people who were "passing through" at the rue de la Bourse. After dinner we packed up Victor's few belongings in a small suitcase and a backpack, and headed off through narrow streets. A black cat ran across the street and Victor jumped. "That means good luck – it came from the right," I said. We turned into a long, narrow, dark entrance, felt our way to the staircase, and made our way up to the third floor where Madame Prévost lived. We rang the bell, and a Hindu woman opened the door. She was very polite and invited us into a salon, and asked what she could do for us. We told her that we had heard that she had a room to rent. She seemed a little surprised, and asked us where we had heard this. We told her that a young man, a friend of her son's, had told us.

"I'm afraid you are mistaken," she said. "As you can see, there is no room for rent here. There is only the kitchen, and my own bedroom in back of that curtain." I didn't mention the door I had seen at the end of the hallway. "The room you are looking for must be in number 11. People come here now and then asking for a room, and I send them all to number 11."

There was no use insisting. Maybe she hadn't gotten the message about us. We had to be careful. I didn't mention any names, just in case all was not as it should be. But when we were outside again on the stairs, I sat down and laughed harder than I'd laughed in quite some time. *Everything* having to do with Victor went wrong. When we got out on the street again, we looked around, and saw that there *wasn't* any number 11. "I knew it wouldn't work when I saw that cat run across the street," Victor said darkly, and we straggled back the same way we had come.

The next morning, Sonia appeared like a puff of air before I had left for the office, and asked if I'd gotten rid of Victor. She didn't understand what I was talking about when I just laughed and shook my head. I told her the whole story, cat and all. She went immediately to talk to Cazaux, and came back to the canteen at lunchtime: Cazaux had been held up, and got to Madame Prévost ten minutes after we had been there, but everything was okay now. We could go back that evening.

So Victor went to the rue de la Bourse. I visited him every day, and took him food. Henriette Léon got lots of ration cards, both for Victor and Madame Prévost. Her son had a grand piano in the attic, which Victor was allowed to use, so he kept his voice in shape; he even had some private students. The Germans kept their distance from those narrow, scary streets. The Italian tenor Toffoni (who had been at Camp de Gurs) was one of the first people Victor met in Madame Prévost's home, which was also a meeting place for the resistance. He was a saboteur, and was always armed with some horrible thing or other.

I kept up my telephone contact with the grocer. There *had* to be a way to get Victor to safety! But the grocer had one spell of bad luck after the other. When we had last seen him at the station, his mountain guide had been captured and shot by the Gestapo. His associate kept saying that he was coming to Toulouse, but he never appeared. Then several Americans from the north were supposed to arrive. The convoy was set up and cancelled because the guides didn't come. It was a tense time. When we got a new message to be at the station for the train at 5 p.m., we didn't get very excited. We just assumed it would be a false alarm once again. But this time the grocer was there and it looked like things would work out. The grocer pointed out two well-dressed Frenchmen and a young man wearing a checked jacket, all of whom were taking the same route to freedom. He explained that Victor was to travel to St. Gaudens, where he would meet a chauffeur with bright red hair, freckles and two missing front teeth. He would drive them to a village, where they would start their march before dawn. He told Victor they were to keep away from each other on the trip. I said goodbye, and Victor was finally on his way to Spain! It was the beginning of June.

Now there was nothing to do except wait to hear how the trip had gone. I had awful nightmares where I heard Victor yelling my name and crying that the Gestapo was after both of us. It was a relief to wake up and realize that it had only been a bad dream. So when the telephone rang one day and I heard Victor's voice on the other end, I practically fainted. I bicycled to rue de la Bourse faster than ever before. "Don't be angry with me Alice, just hear what I have to say first," he begged in a pitiful voice that sounded like he had a cold.

The five of them had left as planned. But fate had decided that a bridge at Boussens would be blown up just before they got there, so they had to walk some kilometers to get to a footbridge, and continue on a train that was waiting on the other side. This took time, and the train got to St. Gaudens just before 10 p.m., not 9 p.m. as planned. Due to the curfew, there was no chauffeur or truck waiting, and there they stood. "Well, I guess it's up to us to get ourselves out of this one," one of them said to the others. "It will look much too suspicious if we all walk around together at this time of night." The three well-dressed men disappeared up the street, and the young nervous man in the checked jacket asked Victor what to do. Victor was scared, but he decided that they should stick together. They spent the night behind the station, sleeping in shifts while the other kept watch. It was raining, so Victor lost his voice and caught a nasty cold.

When morning finally came, and with it, the first train back to Toulouse, Victor decided to take it, instead of hoping that the truck would show up to see if the passengers were there. Later, I heard that the three well-dressed Frenchmen had managed to get over the mountains, but here was Victor, back again. I just told him what I thought about his turning back. He was so unhappy; I said that we would try again. But Victor insisted that he wasn't *meant* to get to Spain, that his lucky star had stopped all his attempts, so now he had decided he should stay right where he was. He still had the 10,000 francs he was going to use to get over the mountains, to live on for a while.

On June 6, 1944, I went to see him to celebrate the invasion of Normandy. "Do you see now that I was right?" Victor said. "Wouldn't it have been a shame if I'd left?" He stayed on with Madame Prévost, and lots of resistance people and saboteurs, so he started talking as if he was one of them. But he didn't even dare to go out of the house, except after dark, and then only along the back streets, when he came to us to eat. Toulouse was liberated on August 19, with shooting and fighting in the streets and Germans fleeing as quickly as they could in panic. Victor came – by the main streets this time – and ate dinner with us, and was crowing with pride, as though he personally was responsible for the liberation! He came back a few days later to tell us that he had been made a lieutenant in the resistance, known as the *Forces Francais de l'Interieure* or FFI.

He had been given an awful khaki-colored French uniform made of homespun material, and he had sewn a thin gold stripe on the arm. He was so proud, but he looked just dreadful. Thanks to his friends from Madame Prévost's, and his participation in the Spanish Civil War, he was given the rank of second lieutenant. He was asked to organize entertainment for the troops, in the Royan district near Bordeaux.

And Hella? She was forced by the Germans to return to *das Reich*. She kept writing to me asking for news of Victor. In April 1944, she was living with her mother in Greifenhagen near Stettin, and had gathered together her birth certificate, school reports, French identity papers, and written proof that she had lived in France for so many years, to apply for a French work permit. But because she had been out of France for more than two years, permission was denied. She had to work in the fields for ten hours every day and she fell into bed exhausted every evening. She was so sad and disappointed that she stayed in her room when she wasn't working, alone with her thoughts and prayers, waiting for the mail to arrive. She was so cut off from everything that she didn't even see that spring was on the way. She just waited for the end of the horrible war so that she could be reunited with her Victor.

I didn't hear anything from Hella until the autumn of 1945. In the meantime, Germany had been destroyed. Then, a letter arrived:

> It's been two years now since Victor was transferred from Camp de Gurs to Marseille, and soon it will be two years since we last saw each other during those days in February. But for me, these years have bound me even more to him, and I hope that I will one day be deserving of his name …I long so for him and long to be able to work with him for art, sacred art. … What about Victor's voice? The future? Write, write!

And then on June 24, 1946.

> Victor has been here for three days! Now I know that we belong to each other for all eternity! Nothing can separate us now. I've gotten a position as a translator through Victor's connections. I work for French industry and the Chamber of Commerce here in Baden-Baden – here, it should be easier to acquire a permit to be with him. All my papers – including those from Gurs – have been sent to Freiburg, where they and I will be treated as "Opfer des dritten Reiches." (Victim of the Third Reich) I'll try to get a permit for a short visit to France, and once there, I will apply to stay. … My art, my dancing, is maturing inside of me – I long to take it up again. And what about you, Alice? Oh, if only I were able to express my gratitude for everything you've done for my Victor! He is alive! I am so grateful, so grateful, so grateful! Victor writes such wonderful letters – he was also overjoyed to find out that I was in one piece, though not so strong. Perhaps

because he himself looked so well, so strong – his breath of life and his voice are completely back to normal again!

I asked my friend Pierre Berteaux, the head Prefect in Toulouse, for an entry permit for Hella, using all the supporting documentation she had sent me. Finally, in February 1947, Hella was granted permission to visit Paris and Toulouse, but she had to leave again on February 21. When Victor called to ask if I could help I said: "I'll see what I can do. After all, she has permission from the Prefecture to visit." She did come, and luckily I knew the right people in the Prefecture, so I was able to get her a *Carte d'Identité des priviligiés* (an identity card that lasted for 10 years). Now, finally, she could start her new life with Victor.

Victor had gone to Paris after the war was over, and settled down as best he could. He sang at Jewish weddings, and as a cantor in the synagogue. Hella converted to Judaism and they were married in 1953 and had a little girl, Caroline Paloma. But unfortunately nothing ever came of Hella's dance. She had to make a living. She met a Dutch woman who taught her an interesting form of massage, and she built up a first-class clientele.

As always, Victor was a big talker. He boasted of being a communist and criticized France, though he really meant no harm by it. But his words reached the ears of someone they weren't meant for, and eventually he was thrown out. They went to Israel, which he didn't like. He just dreamed of France. Hella returned to Paris where she arranged to have his expulsion annulled. He moved back, and lived and worked in France peacefully thereafter.

Barracks at Camp de Gurs by Otto Berendt, 1941

VIII. Camp de Gurs is Closed

*I*n 1943, when Helga finally came back from her eventful trip to Switzerland, she had spent her time well. She corresponded with our American colleagues in Baden-Baden, and met with Ross and Marjorie McClelland in Geneva. She also proposed joining our southern delegations with the little French Quaker group in Paris and moving the head office there. Everyone liked the idea. We had been sending financial assistance to the Paris Quakers for some time, and we had given them one of our trucks. They wanted us to change our name: we were neither Quakers nor Americans, nor French. Professor Cornil in Marseille, who had been the official *Secours Quaker* head in southern France, stepped down, and Ellinor Cohu moved up to the Paris office.

Unfortunately, the cooperation with the Paris group was not without problems. Henry van Etten, the pleasant administrator in Paris, was an intellectual idealist and a true Quaker who had had written several books on Quakerism. He was arrested by the Germans and taken to the Fresnes prison where he met a German soldier who was also a Quaker, who was willing to vouch for him. He was lucky – he was released after only one and a half days!

The Paris office said that we were no longer to work for the Jews and others who were persecuted, so that Henry would have an easier time looking the Germans in the eye. There were many well-meaning and kind workers in the Paris group, but one office administrator - a recently converted Quaker - was power-hungry and jealous and the rest of the group was afraid of him. Once, we in the south pointed out something he had done that none of us liked. Quakers try to reach all decisions by consensus. His response was that we in the south had run things by ourselves for so long that we were having trouble adjusting to leadership again! We had to live with our consciences, of course.

Back at Gurs, we were in the process of closing up shop. I managed to pack *seven tons* of wares in less than a week! All our men were *"geflitzt"* (disappeared) or sent to *Arbeitsdienst* (work duty), so my only help was our head cook, Frau Putzmeier, Hedwig Würzburger, and her young assistant, Jenny Scheibe. I worked till steam came out of my ears. Helga had directed that everything that didn't belong specifically to the camp was to go to Toulouse. Luckily, all the clothing had been distributed, but an entire floor in the clothing depot was covered with potatoes and onions. So I put together cartons, carried furniture, filled sacks and wrote addresses and numbers. Frau Würzburger made sure I was allowed to work in peace. She just nodded and smiled at everything I said, then turned around and did exactly as she pleased. But finally – after months of waiting – we were assigned a train car to transport everything to Toulouse. Frau Würzburger laughed later when she told of those days. "Don't get too close to Fraülein Resch, she's dangerous!"

I left on October 1, in the Peugeot weighed down with things that couldn't stay in the warehouse too long. I drove slowly down toward Avenue Moche for the last time. There were still quite a few people left, people I had come to love, and to whom I wanted to say goodbye. The barrier was raised, and the Gurs chapter in my life came to a close.

Outside our Home

Earlier I described our wonderful home life. Out-of-doors was another matter. Even in the tiniest villages, the German Wehrmacht soldiers and SS outnumbered the original inhabitants. Two big regiments of SS were stationed in and around Toulouse. They took over all the best locations, and turned them into things like a Soldiers' Home, and a Soldiers' Café. White fences closed off the sidewalks, and they placed grillwork in front of sidewalk restaurants, so they were christened "Monkey Cages." Rumpled, empty-faced guards stood in front of the doors and entrances on wooden pedestals, to the amusement of the natives. There were German signs and huge vulgar posters everywhere, with propaganda for the noble German race, or against the "Jews, Churchill and Roosevelt." The signs were either ignored, or vandalized during the night. Huge "V's" for victory were painted on them. There were explosions in German hotels and in cinemas showing German films. After these episodes, there were sure to be raids directed at Jews and communists. Some men were taken hostage when the sabotage got completely out of hand.

There were still northbound deportation convoys, under the supervision of German military police and the Gestapo. As

Gurs camp recalled

From our Correspondent
Paris

A memorial has been erected on the site of a former concentration camp at Gurs, a small village in the Pyrenees not far from France's border with Spain. Mr Asher Ben-Natan, the Israeli Ambassador, and Mr Helmuth Ruete, the West German Ambassador, were among those who attended the unveiling ceremony.

The Gurs camp was originally set up in 1939 as a reception centre for former refugee members of the Spanish Government forces fighting against the insurgents led by General Franco in the Spanish civil war. These included a considerable number of Jews who had fought in the International Brigade on the Government side.

In 1940 some 12,000 Austrian and German Jewish refugees were interned in the camp by the French authorities, bringing its population up to 20,000—men, women and children.

The inmates were kept on a starvation diet by the Vichy French authorities responsible for running the camp until deported to Auschwitz in 1942 and 1943, where few survived the gas chambers.

193

Quakers, we were allowed to go to the station with food rations and bottles of water. Hostages were taken from all sorts of groups. The Mayor of Toulouse was one of them, as was our friend the Belgian Consul and Monseigneur de Solage. Our ugly duckling, Abbé Lagarde, was taken, and one of Toulouse's most well-known nerve specialists, Dr. Lyon. The Jewish welfare office was disbanded, and little Mademoiselle Cahen was sent off, wearing Harriet's old leather coat. She never returned.

Helga could visit them all in the prison in Caserne Cafferelli that served as a collection point. Once she came back laughing from a visit there. The director of the prison and two armed German soldiers had followed her around the entire time as she spoke with the prisoners. Then Dr. Lyon, whom she knew from her years in Toulouse, came and gave her a huge hug and a big smacking kiss on each cheek! Helga felt a small paper "bullet" pressed into her hand, right under the Germans' noses. It was a farewell letter to his wife. Dr. Lyon was one of the few fortunate ones who survived and returned, and one of the first things he did was to come up to the office and ask Helga's forgiveness for his sudden show of affection.

We were all at the station when these "hostages" departed. The Germans' machine guns followed our progress as we made our way along the platform. There were many cars with frightened Jews from Toulouse, as well as political prisoners from St. Michel and Fourgolle, and there was the third-class car with the hostages. Even the Germans were impressed by Monseigneur de Solage, and stepped back in respect. He was young, tall, one of the most attractive men I'd ever seen and so modest! "Oh, Miss Holbek," he said, "I had the pleasure of meeting you at Christmas at *Notre Dame de Lamotte*." The Monseigneur spoke calmly to all, and behaved as if he were on the way to a weekend jaunt rather than deportation into the unknown.

For the hostages, the deportation meant death. But both Bishop de Solage and Abbé Lagarde survived the camp at

Bergen-Belsen. Little Abbé Lagarde came back looking like a skeleton, and more full of the milk of human kindness than ever! He had seen so much horror, but he felt that the only way we could prevent this from happening again would be if people would concentrate on loving each other rather than focusing on revenge.

The Gestapo had been to see the elderly brave Archbishop as well. Monseigneur Saliège had protested officially against the persecution of the Jews (see pg. 119). Now he was paralyzed in most of his body, and he was difficult to understand, so he usually had a young priest with him who could interpret and translate. Helga, Mademoiselle Dauty and I met with him in his office. Celine went to him once to ask him to intervene on behalf of a Jew. She was animated when she came back: he had blessed her. To Helga he said, "Oh, Mademoiselle, from here down it is only dead meat," and smiled. "But from here up, there is life!" And he pointed from his eyes up to his forehead. He smiled contentedly as Helga kissed his ring.

When the Gestapo arrived, he transformed himself into a shaking old fool, practically impossible to understand as he asked for his shawl. The Gestapo reacted with surprise: was this the famous Archbishop of Toulouse? They wouldn't waste time on this feeble old man. When they were gone, the sparkle came back into the old man's eyes. "We fooled them this time," he said to his nurse.

Bombs fell in France starting in 1943. We soon learned the difference between British and American planes. The British came at night and focused on a certain target, while the Americans' "blanket bombing" came during the day. Toulouse itself was not bombed, but the factories and an airport in the area were hit. *Chateau de Larade* was on the outskirts of town, near a factory, so we had to close it down and evacuate the children. The "foster parents" were once again an enormous help, and took our children into their homes. Mr. Merello, the last head of Larade, disappeared without a trace, but turned up at the office with a smile on his face after the liberation. He was the commandant of a Spanish resistance group, and was proud of the four gold stripes on his smart uniform!

Many children were evacuated from Toulouse because of the bombing. Placing the Jewish children was therefore made easier. They could be mixed in with the others, but they had to be "French". They needed French ration cards, issued to French names. Mr. Herzog (alias Pierre Mansuy) was an expert forger, both for children and adults, and I made use of his services many times. His work was scrupulously exact, and completely correct. There were so many small, important details that had to be taken into account. For example: before a certain date, the stamp would be for 13 francs, but after that date the stamp would show 15 francs.

It was my job to distribute the new identity and ration cards. I brought the necessary photo equipment and information to a bistro where we met for a drink, and returned some days later to pick up the result. This was an easy task as far as the adults were concerned, but it was harder to explain to the children that they suddenly had a new name. Still, they adapted remarkably well. Once I visited a family who had taken in Jewish children. I asked a lovely four-year-old girl what her name was. She looked at me seriously for a bit before she decided that I didn't mean her any harm, and asked carefully, "My *real* name?"

The BBC regularly sent out mysterious coded warnings, like "The goose arrived yesterday." Somewhere, someone understood what was really being said, and the grapevine spread the word as to what was happening – a bombing, for example. We were used to the air-raid sirens, so we didn't bother to seek shelter, but slept on. One evening, the sirens were followed by the sound of anti-aircraft artillery. This was the real thing! Magnus was convinced that the town itself would not be hit. The nocturnal raids were British, and they usually hit their mark. We all got dressed quickly, but we trusted Magnus' prognosis, and didn't bother to seek cover. Instead, we hung out the bathroom window and witnessed the most amazing fireworks! The heavens were illuminated by an incredible show of light and color. We saw huge fireballs hanging in the air, lighting up the entire city so that we could count the roofs around us. There were towers of light where the bombs hit. The anti-aircraft artillery projectiles shot up in the air like golden pearls on a string. The shooting got closer, and then it retreated into the distance. Now and then the entire building shook from the force of the air pressure. Once, we were all blown back into the room with the force. We had opened all the windows so that the pressure from the blasts wouldn't shatter them.

We started to laugh. In a strange involuntary reaction, we were shaking like leaves with our teeth chattering so loudly we could hear it! The attack lasted about 45 minutes, and then it was quiet. We went up on the roof, where we could see fires over the entire horizon. It seemed that all the factories and the airport were in flames. The sirens of fire trucks and ambulances howled in the streets. People were out on the streets, but we went into the kitchen and made ourselves a nighttime snack, and we had a large snifter of armagnac! It was my first bombing.

Magnus and I spent an interesting weekend at the home of our friends the Bonnefoi's in the village of Auriac. Ninau was in hiding in Paris, so his wife Lily ran their large store. There were SS soldiers everywhere; lots of officers lived in *le Chateau* and quite a few tanks were hidden under the trees in the park, covered with leaves. There were many guests, all from the resistance, but there was room for everyone. The daughter of the house, 18-year-old Marthou, was a southern beauty who attracted a lot of attention from the Germans. But she knew how to put them in their place, with a charming smile. After the war, she was awarded a medal for her fearless work as a liaison officer between the heads of the resistance in Toulouse, and *le Maquis* in Les Montagnes Noires. It was no mean task to bicycle from

197

one occupied village to another, her bag full of documents and even weapons. Luckily, she was never caught.

Winding Down

In the spring of 1944 we started the last food project for children with extreme cases of malnutrition. The demarcation line was a thing of the past, and we could travel between Toulouse and Paris much more easily. Helga had made such a trip in the autumn of 1943, to visit the Danish Ambassador Mr. Seedorff. The conversation turned naturally to the desperate food situation in southern France. The main crop was wine grapes, which the Germans appropriated (the French who were used to a liter of wine per day were given one liter of wine a week) and the only other cultivated food was feed corn. The Germans took both the corn and the animals it was intended to feed.

Ambassador Seedorff started a collection among the Danish colony in France, and raised enough to buy ten tons of Danish bacon. This was handed over to Helga Holbek personally, for her work with undernourished children. Mr. Busck-Nielsen, the young Danish attaché, later said that they had received 210,000 francs, and the embassy had contributed over half of that amount. Busck-Nielsen was sent to the border between Denmark and Germany to collect the shipment. By some miracle he managed to get the goods car coupled to a passenger train, and proceeded to "sit on the flesh" all the way down to make sure it got where it was going.

We cleared out a large warehouse in the office at Boulevard Bonrepos, and gave 250 children a solid meal every weekday, with Danish bacon as the basis. A medical examination determined which children were especially undernourished, but something always went a bit wrong. The children were given water with a splash of red wine mixed in to drink with their meal. We had our own supply of wine in Gaillac, and the children's drink was mixed in large containers. One day, a couple of the students who were helping with the meal made a mistake, and poured undiluted red wine into the containers! What a spectacle! The alcohol hit the small, thin bodies like a ton of bricks. The dining room full of intoxicated children was a scene right from Brueghel! The children laughed and chatted. They were up on the tables, under the tables, the benches were tipped over and the "porcelain," which was luckily aluminum, crashed to the floor everywhere. The youngest started to cry. The whole mess just got worse and worse. It was incredibly funny. We laughed more than was good for us! Practically the entire office staff had to come to our aid before we were able to restore some sort of order. The drinks were checked carefully after that.

We knew from the BBC that train stations, bridges and other important transportation points would be bombed, so we had spread our supplies out to various places to be on the safe side. The camp work had been greatly reduced. Récébédou and Gurs were closed. Vernet had been taken over by the Germans, and the new horrible police officer Marty had appropriated our supplies in Camp de Vernet.

We continued our work in Noé, where there were approximately 600 elderly and sick people. Serheilac and la Meyze in Haute Vienne, and Douadic in Indre were full of evacuees. But we soon stopped sending supplies to them because the food situation there was quite good, and sabotage was making travel so difficult. Finally, in the end of March, Helga succeeded in getting Hedwig Würtzburger released, and she came to be Helga's housekeeper at a little rented house on with a lovely garden full of grapes, figs and plums. But after the occupation of southern France, the Germans came in droves to Toulouse. The locals evacuated Helga's neighborhood. It was closed off with barbed wire, and the Germans moved into all the attractive private houses. Right across the street from Helga's house, there was a large building with German offices and guards who paced in front of the doors around the clock. The most horrible screams could be heard

199

coming from the torture chambers in the basement of Gestapo headquarters a block away. The street was later renamed rue des Martyrs.

Thus Frau Würtzburger, a Jew from Gurs, landed in the middle of the enemy camp! Naturally, her false papers were perfect, and without the Star of David. She dreaded every time that she had to show them to the guards at the barbed wire gate whenever she needed to go to the office . But the guards got to know her after a while, and smiled and chatted. She mostly remained indoors, taking care of Helga as if she were a valuable treasure. She simply adored Helga, who had saved her from deportation, and Helga enjoyed her cozy home, despite the surroundings.

One day Frau Würtzburger got a real scare when the doorbell rang and she looked out the window and saw two Germans standing below! She couldn't speak French, but luckily the Germans couldn't, either. They said they had come to appropriate the house! Würtzburger hoped that she was saying *"Oui Monsieur"* and *"Non Monsieur, Secours Quaker!"* in the right places. "Ah, Quaker," they said, and discovered the *Secours Quaker* calling card on the door. They bowed, and didn't even ask to come in. Frau Würtzburger collapsed into bed, weak with relief!

Jacques and Paul

We had asked for volunteers to help serve in the canteen, and Pastor Dombre recommended two young students warmly. Jacques and Paul "had little money, and need the good meal they will get." Jacques was 22, tall, blond and blue-eyed, with a huge blond beard. Paul was 20, tall, also blond and blue-eyed, but he stuttered terribly! These two worked hard at their tasks, and became very popular, but then they disappeared for a couple of days. One day they came up to the office to see me. They explained that a group of American soldiers would be attempting to cross the Pyrenees the next day, but the Gestapo had discovered their usual hiding place, and now two men needed a place to stay for the night. I suggested the reformed church, but they just laughed: that was the hiding place that had been discovered! So I said I'd think it over. I consulted with Magnus, who was more than willing. When the boys came up after lunch I said that they could bring the soldiers over to us for the night. The two Americans, with French work clothes over their uniforms, turned up alone. We put a mattress on the floor. One slept there, the other on the couch.

They were both thin, tall, friendly boys, who were thrilled that we spoke English! They had been shot down over Normandy after having bombed Paris. They showed us all sorts of gadgets, among other things a handkerchief with a map of France printed on it. As soon as the *couvre feu* (curfew) was lifted the next morning, they were on their way over the Pyrenees.

Helga noticed that Jacques and Paul were somewhat irregular in their serving duties in the canteen, and called them up to her office. She told them that either they had to accept that they were there to help, or else they could just forget it, because we needed to have reliable help. Then they told Helga their story:

For two years, they had regularly been directing traffic over the Pyrenees. They went to Paris and collected "passengers" and took them up to the mountains, where a local guide took them over. Helga smiled "ok, come and go as you please, we'll manage! But remember, we who work here know nothing!" And Jacques and Paul continued to come and go. If an extra day passed when we expected them back, we became restless like nervous cats wondering what had become of their kittens. I realized that the boys had spoken to Helga, and she knew what was going on. Eventually, of course, everyone knew, at least unofficially. But to our credit, no-one ever spoke of it until after the liberation, except for Helga and me. But we were best friends, and talked about everything under the sun.

One day I asked Paul if he could take one of my friends over the Pyrenees (see Chapter VII). He agreed, but he looked nervous. Jacques was out on a trip alone, and had not yet returned. "We're supposed to be leaving in two days, but Jacques hasn't come back yet. I'm afraid he's been caught this time!" It turned out he was right. The convoy wasn't able to depart as planned. The guide had been captured and shot near Perpignan, so they had to lay low for a while. Then Jacques turned up at the office again, without his beard. He didn't go to the canteen, but ate with us and told us his story. It turned out that during all those years of involvement in the convoys, he had also been a liaison officer, linking several resistance men. He was affiliated with the *Forces Francaises de l'Interieur* (FFI). He had been sent to Toulouse to collect some papers and was on the way back, when the Gestapo caught him! They handcuffed him, and tightened their hold at the least movement. His thumbs were jammed against each other in a very painful way. He was taken to the headquarters in Biarritz, accompanied by two German soldiers and a French civilian employed by the Gestapo. The Frenchman had been a classmate of Jacques in Versailles, so they knew each other. Jacques couldn't help himself, he said (in French), "I suppose you're proud now that you're doing the Boche's dirty work." The boy turned bright red, and hit Jacques squarely in the face. "That was almost the worst part of the entire nightmare," Jacques told us.

In Biarritz he was tortured. They wanted him to tell who his superior was. Exhausted, he was put into an isolation cell, where he hatched out a plan. The alternative was suicide. He knew he would be able to kill himself by standing at the head of the iron bedstead, then falling back, keeping his body stiff as a board toward the iron bar at the foot. The fall would break his neck. The next time he was taken for questioning, he screamed more than strictly necessary, and shouted that he would tell them everything and show them everything if they would take him back to Toulouse. He gave them a fictional name that was supposedly his superior, "a typical little, dark Frenchman in his forties." His tormentors took the bait, and Jacques was transported to the prison in Toulouse.

The next day, he brought his torturers to the café at the Place Esquirol, telling them that this was the gathering place for the members of his group. He didn't have the handcuffs on now, but had a German soldier on each side. This in itself wasn't particularly odd: many French civilians in the Gestapo's employ would sit with Germans in the café. It wasn't even odd for Jacques' friends to be seen with "Germans" who turned out to be Englishmen and Americans in disguise! Jacques sat with his wrists together. This was a signal they had developed to show that all was not well. It showed that he was a prisoner, and that the Germans were real this time. His friends around him in the café understood, and didn't acknowledge that they recognized him.

Jacques kept up a conversation with his captors as they sat there at the sidewalk café, but of course no small dark middle-aged man showed up. One of the Germans was a long-jawed man of around 45 years. "You have a son my age, don't you?" Jacques asked him. "Yes," the guard said, and woke up a bit. "He's in Russia," Jacques said. The German was clearly surprised at how much Jacques knew. "Well," Jacques continued, "he's dead now!" The man's jaw dropped, and his face turned white. Was Jacques psychic? "But how on earth can you possibly know that?" the German asked. Jacques was thrilled that his improvised conversation was serving its purpose. "Oh, I know all sorts of things; I have a good information network here. I'm sure he was a good patriot who loved and died for his country," Jacques went on. The German was a bit comforted, hearing a Frenchman admit this. "He was just as good a patriot as I am, I'm sure. I am willing to die for my country." After a bit, he asked: "If I tried to escape now, would you shoot me?" "Yes," the answer came without hesitation. "Would you not even think about the fact that I am just as good a patriot as your boy? And just pretend to shoot? Shoot to the side, for example…" "No," he answered.

Time was passing, and the Germans decided that it was time to take Jacques back to prison. They walked up to the streetcar stop. Every nerve in Jacques' body was tense; he saw the streetcar approach, estimated the timing, and offered a cigarette to each of the Germans. For one instant, their attention was focused on lighting their cigarettes. The streetcar came up to them, and like lightening, Jacques was over on the other side and the streetcar was between them. His guards had to wait until the trolley drove the last few meters and stopped before they could go after him, so he got a head start. They were heavier and slower than Jacques, and even though they fired off quite a few bullets, he wasn't hit. He turned down the first little side street, and was gone. He had friends everywhere, so it was easy to borrow some clothes, shave off his beard, and come back to us for some food.

Helga offered him a place to stay for the night, but this time it wasn't necessary. A young Russian medical student arrived with new identity papers, and took Jacques with him. He was going to drive to one of the first stations outside of town, and catch the train the next morning in order to join de Gaulle. But the Germans had tightened security in the Pyrenees during those spring months. Very few made it over the mountains; one guide after another had been caught and shot. The Germans had made it quite clear that hiding allied soldiers and taking them over the mountains was punishable by death. Jacques was in a convoy with about 40 people, about half of whom were allied pilots who had been shot down, or had been on special resistance missions. The rest were like Jacques - men who simply had to get out.

A horrible mayor in a small mountain village above Luchon reported the convoy to the Germans. (Groups often spent the night there, and the locals usually slaughtered an animal on the sly in order to give them a decent meal.)

The next morning when they were on their way into the mountains, they were surprised by a strong troop of German mountain soldiers. Several were shot, and the rest were taken prisoner. We knew nothing of Jacques, and Paul was pale and tired. He knew Jacques well enough to be certain that he had tried to escape, but was afraid he had been shot, since he hadn't heard anything.

Paul took over Jacques' role as a liaison officer. He slept at Helga's place every time he came through Toulouse, and became a good friend of Hedwig Würzburger, who was silent as a tomb about his activities. They chatted and understood each other perfectly, despite the fact that Frau Würzburger didn't speak a word of French, and Paul not a word of German, and he stuttered in the bargain. Paul wasn't even his real name!

Time passed. The entire country rejoiced on June 6, 1944, when the Allies finally landed at Normandy. *Now* it wouldn't be long before the end of the war! But the Germans just got worse and worse, deporting any remaining Jews, Spaniards, and Frenchmen that they could get their hands on. On June 15, the entire population of the camp at Vernet was transported. With our usual permission from the Gestapo, we were at the station with our buckets of rice porridge and our bottles of water. We went up and down the line of cars, followed by two Germans who pointed machine guns at our backs. We were *strictly forbidden* to speak with the prisoners. The doors to the cattle cars were opened about 10 centimeters, just enough to slip in the food and bottles. Suddenly, we saw Jacques' smiling face in one of these cracks! We couldn't believe it. Thank God, he was alive, and would no doubt manage to take care of himself. He managed to whisper his father's name and address to us, and asked us to let him know that all was well. All was well? Here were eighty men stuffed into a locked car! Jacques, the man with nine lives, showed up some weeks later in Toulouse. He stayed the night with Helga, and then went on to *le Maquis*.

That deportation transport arrived at Compiègne, only to be sent on immediately to Germany, where they were anticipating the allied invasion. Again, eighty men were cooped up in an overheated, locked cattle car with the words "40 men or eight horses end to end" printed on the outside. They suffered terribly, and decided to try to escape. All of them had been forced to surrender all knives and other sharp objects, and they had been warned that if any tools were found, all the car's occupants would be shot. Someone had nonetheless managed to sneak in a knife, a bucket and a ladle. The ladle was transformed into a crowbar and saw, and with the knife, they managed to loosen some planks on the floor. One man crept out first, and unlocked the door. Some of the occupants rolled out along the sides of the car, others jumped down onto the tracks. They warned each other: "just make sure you keep a bit to the side, because the last car has an iron hook hanging down underneath, and it will kill you if it hits you". And Jacques made it through unscathed once again.

He had lived at Versailles during the first years of the war, and had joined the resistance in Toulouse. For two years he traveled around with paratroopers. Things got too hot after a while, and he had to move. One of the proudest moments of his life was when he told his father of his work in the resistance, because his father clapped him on the shoulder and said that he also had been working with the resistance for some time! Jacques had had at least eight aliases, but I never learned his real name, because after that I never saw Jacques or Paul again.

The Convent La Motte

Ima Lieven took over as leader of the aid work in Marseille after the head office moved to Paris. Helga and I took care of her work at Camp de Noé, but the Germans revoked our driving permit in the spring of 1944. So if we needed to get to Noé, we had to bicycle. The 32 kilometers were nothing for me; I was always bicycling everywhere, but Helga hadn't been on a bicycle since she was a small girl in Denmark.

One day she wanted to go to Noé, and we pedaled away together. Poor thing, she was completely exhausted when we arrived around noon, and we had a tiring afternoon. The inmates surrounded her asking all sorts of questions and favors. The Quaker kitchen and the supplies had to be checked, and on and on. It was

Ima Lieven, 1940

nearly 7 p.m. by the time we were finally ready to head back. Oh, what a tiring trip that was! The road was good and flat, but we had a strong wind in our faces: "*Le Vent d'Autan*," the equivalent of the *Mistral* in Provence. It was totally dark, and we lost almost an hour when I had a puncture. We couldn't reach Toulouse before the strict curfew went into effect at 10 p.m. We got to Muret, where all the beds were taken by the occupation troops, so we hoped that *La Motte*, the convent seven kilometers west of Muret, could take us.

The Mother Superior was born Dolores Salazar in Argentina, where her father was one of the richest men and her mother was Irish. Her upbringing was broad. She learned several languages, became an accomplished pianist, was beautiful and intelligent, and married an English aristocrat. She was widowed early, and took the veil. Later, the Pope asked her to found the convent in La Motte. She had a wonderful sense of humor. I remember once when Helga and I arrived at the convent in the middle of the day. We heard the sound of a piano and children's songs from an empty warehouse, and went in to have a look. There she was, singing and playing for the small children. When she saw us, she switched over to a lively South American tango.

She was our good friend, and we had a standing invitation to come out and rest whenever we needed it but she was aghast. "Don't you two know that there is a curfew from

10:00 p.m? The Germans are very strict, you could have been shot!" We each got a room in one of the guesthouses, a warm bath, and dinner in bed!

Mother Superior entertained us with frightening stories about the Germans' latest projects. A farmer had been shot in Lamasquere, a village two kilometers north. And just a few days earlier, a grotesque thing had happened in Muret: a worker from Toulouse had been visiting his family nearby and tried to get home after 10 p.m without being discovered. He was speeding down the main street in Muret, when a German soldier shouted at him to stop. He didn't stop, and the German shot him. He fell to the ground, screaming in pain. But who could risk his life to go out to help? Finally, the guard on that street dared to go see to him. He was a little uneasy, because the man could be armed or from le Maquis. The Germans were terrified of the resistance, but the German got the man to his feet, and together they started toward a house. Then another guard appeared, and saw the two men, helping one another. He shot and killed both of them!

The convent experienced many strange things during the occupation. One evening there was a small truck at the gate with some wounded boys from le Maquis. They were of course taken in, nursed and hidden until they could be smuggled to a private clinic in Toulouse. The resistance came to regard La Motte as a good stop for those heading over the Pyrenees to Spain, then on to de Gaulle and the free French troops. When we came on a weekend visit, there were always such "guests." Everyone was received in the same loving, calm manner, even if Mother Superior admitted after the war that she was very worried about what would happen if the Germans discovered what sort of guests she had.

One time she was truly nervous. Two officials from the Vichy government suddenly had to disappear when it was discovered that they were in fact working for the resistance. When they turned up at La Motte, of course they were welcomed in the usual manner. They left their suitcases in the lobby while rooms were made up for them, and they accompanied Mother Superior on a walk in the park. A young nun came running.

"There are Germans at the gate, lots of them!" she said. There happened to be a small chapel in the park, built of stone, like a grotto. Mother Superior took her guests in among the coffins, and went calmly to meet the Germans. "We are sorry, but we will have to search the convent, there are rumors that you are hiding terrorists." "Here in a peaceful convent? All right, come in." She said she prayed as never before as she politely showed the Germans around to win time. She took them into the lobby where the two suitcases were. "What is that?" they demanded. "Oh, two of our young nuns have just returned from a mission – they are in the refectory now," she answered. "Shall I open them?" one of the soldiers asked his superior. "No, let the sisters' bags be," he answered.

She showed them the beautiful little chapel right across from the lobby, and the children's wing, with ten or twelve lively small ones. She picked up one little boy from a bed, smiled and said: "Made in Germany!" This made them laugh, and the tense atmosphere lifted. Two of the officers began to converse in English. When he was able to do so without being noticed by the others, one of them said out of the side of his mouth, "Don't be afraid." One officer said he had studied in Oxford and liked to practice his English. The other, the one who had whispered that she shouldn't be afraid, might have been a real Englishman; there were many of them disguised as Germans!

They toured the entire establishment, and thanks to her stalling, there was nothing suspicious for them to find. The Germans apologized for disturbing the convent, and took their leave politely. But Mother Superior went into the chapel and sent up a prayer of thanks. When she had finished the story, she suddenly added, "These *damn* Germans!" and then, "Oh dear, me, a little nun, using such an ugly word!" And she laughed merrily. My last visit to the Convent was in the summer of 1986. I stood sadly at the grave of Mother Dolores Salazar, my heart full of gratitude for all her kindness and understanding.

D-Day, June 6, 1944. In Toulouse, we heard more and more air-raid sirens. American planes were flying over southern France in broad daylight amidst warnings to evacuate the city near train stations, factories and airports. Finally, on June 6, we woke up to the news of the invasion of Normandy. The entire city celebrated! The newspapers that were controlled by the Nazis reported the invasion as "yet another failed commando raid, just like Dieppe and Nantes. The Allies don't have a chance!" Nonetheless, the German tank divisions hidden in southern France were sent north immediately. Progress was slow, because le Maquis made as much trouble for them as possible. The Germans sought revenge by destroying and burning the villages along the way. The village of Oradour suffered the most. Its church ruins were left to stand as a monument to the German barbarism.

The Last Deportation

Unfortunately, not all the Germans left the South of France. They were expecting an invasion on the Côte d'Azur. They arrested more and more people, both young and old, sending them to forced work detail, work camps and concentration camps. The last deportation occurred on Sunday, July 30, only months before the liberation.

A social worker from the Caffarelli prison woke me early to say that there was yet another long train at the station. I moved more quickly than I'd ever done before with no other transportation than my legs. Helga, Celine, Toot, Gärtner and I hoped the train would stay long enough for us to get there with our water bottles and cooked rice.

I ran up to the kitchen and put on a 30-liter pan to boil water for the children. Then I ran over the square to fetch two messengers with their trolleys. It was such a bother not to have a permit to use a car! Two Spanish helpers were already lighting a fire under two enormous containers to cook the rice. Others were filling water bottles. After the first deportations, we had asked the priests in the town to announce from their pulpits that people could bring us all the empty bottles they could do without. The rice was distributed into empty vegetable containers. One of the messengers took a supply of water along with some boxes of dry crackers, in his wheelbarrow.

Up at the station, I had a brainstorm. German soldiers were everywhere, patrolling alongside the cattle cars. A young officer who seemed to be their leader was sitting calmly on a pile of boards. He was most likely bored, keeping an eye on all the "dangerous" people on the train. I went over to him with my best smile and started to chat. I mentioned our special permission from the Gestapo to bring water and a bit of food to the prisoners, and wondered aloud if it really would cause such a problem if we were to drive these supplies to the train. Would he be willing to arrange that for us? And he was!

I had to take two soldiers with me. (He couldn't risk that we would kill a lone soldier, so he sent two.) We got out our little Austin with the trailer, and loaded the rice. It was easier than a wheelbarrow over those uneven bricks! But how people stared! Many knew the Quakers, and here we were, driving with *Germans* in the car! We distributed the rice, and drove back for more. They discovered that we weren't so dangerous after all, so I came back with just the one soldier. Two big cookers were now going full blast. My soldier meandered around in the courtyard, commenting that this was a strange way to run the operation. I was furious, and scolded him in German. Here we were; *we* were the ones doing all the work, all he had to do was stay out of the way until we were finished, and keep his mouth shut. The look on his face made my day. He slunk out, and waited in the car until the rice was ready. I was a little apprehensive. I had scolded one of *them*. But he became

211

meek as a lamb, and helped me to lift all the heavy containers into the cars. He didn't leave my side until the curfew drew near. The moral of the story is: yell at a Boche, and you've got him in the palm of your hand!

The deportations were always horrible experiences. They never became routine, even after we had been through many of them. We were the only ones permitted to get close to the long trains with our water bottles and buckets of rice and crackers. When we got there that morning of July 30, the prisoners - including many women with small children - were still on the platform, surrounded by huge soldiers. One woman had a four-month-old baby in her arms; two others looked like they could give birth at any moment. We weren't allowed to approach them until they had boarded the cattle cars. The sun beat down already early in the morning, and some fainted from the heat, or had heart attacks. Helga sent me to a pharmacist to get nitroglycerine.

I was afraid that the train would leave the station before we had given them food and water, but it was still there when curfew time came. The departure was delayed because the track had been sabotaged at Castelnaudary. They were expecting a train with 600 men from the camp at St. Sulpice, so we cooked rice for 1,600 people. The poor men were exhausted and weak, and herded into the cars in "our" train. They could barely sit. We walked along the train with our food and bottles, and a soldier pointing his bayonet more or less at our backs, so it was more difficult than usual to accept the small letters the prisoners tried to smuggle to us. Once again I was impressed by the way most of the prisoners remained calm. Or perhaps they were just struck dumb with terror.

The train stayed at the station until Monday morning, and then began its odyssey around France. It was called the "Ghost Train." Some said that the Allies in the Rhone valley had liberated the prisoners, or that they had been set free by le Maquis. The train had supposedly been seen in the south of France on August 18, or in Paris on August 25. The last rumor was that it reached Germany by way of Strassbourg.

That same Sunday, Magnus and I were to visit our friend Madame de Sévérac in St. Felix de Lauragais. Because I was caught up with the transport, Magnus went alone, and got home again right after I did. I had gone to bed, wanting more than anything just to put my head under the pillow and to empty my mind of all the horrible experiences and thoughts of what would happen to all those terrified and unhappy people. I was extremely grateful that I didn't have to talk about it, because Magnus had all sorts of things to tell from his day.

Madame de Sévérac had a big house where she hosted the General Assembly of the FFI. The successful landing at Normandy was naturally a topic of discussion. Her guest room had been taken over by German officers, including a doctor. A friendly, quiet and cultivated man, he was an exception, because he wasn't a member of the Nazi party. He was even invited to join the family now and then! That Sunday, the daughter of the house, Magali, decided to invite the doctor in after the General Assembly's members had left. Suddenly, in perfect French, the doctor proposed a toast to the daughter of the house: *La patronne du Maquis.* "*Merci*," smiled Magali graciously. August 19 came, and the Germans disappeared as quickly as they could. Madame de Sévérac offered to hide the German doctor if he wished. He was quite touched, and said that although he had always loved France, he was still a German, and he had to accept its fate with the others. But he would never forget his intermezzo in St. Felix de Lauragais.

In southern France, we were waiting anxiously for the allies to land at the Côte d'Azur, and in Toulouse, the resistance was preparing for a coup. French Nazi sympathizers were guarding 30 political prisoners in a large room in the hospital Hotel Dieu. They had to be rescued. The preparations took several weeks. One person was responsible for the "kidnapping," but finding 30 safe hiding places was a big task. They needed places where the wounded would receive the necessary care. The job fell to Henriette Léon, Jaqueline Braun, Sonia Feigenbaum and others.

One afternoon in July, Magnus and I were at a pleasant reception with everyone from the resistance. Jacqueline came panting in the late afternoon. Sonia had just gotten out of a tight spot, and was afraid that Jean Cazaux had been captured! She didn't have any details. This news broke up the party. I got on my bicycle right away and hurried out to where Sonia and Alex lived. Alex was on his way out as I got there. "Has Sonia come home?" Alex got very angry. "I've always said that she – a Jew – should stay away from these resistance people. What will happen to her if she is caught?" But excitement and adventure was Sonia's life, and unlike Alex, she never worried.

I found Sonia inside, and heard the whole story. She had gone up to Jean Cazaux's office to discuss hiding places for the prisoners from Hotel Dieu. Jean had just gotten back from Tarbes, with a parachute package from London that included many false ration cards, money and compromising resistance plans. The things lay spread over the table, ready to be packed into small packages for various organizations in the Toulouse region. Jean didn't like the fact that Sonia had turned up just then, but they talked about what to do with the prisoners. She was just about to leave, when there was a knock at the door, and in came two militiamen in civilian clothing!

Sonia had forgotten to lock the door when she went into the office. "Ah, I see we're just in time!" one of the militiamen said as he took in all the compromising material on the table. The other locked the door. When Jean had emptied his pockets, he had put his own identity card on the table. The men discovered it. "My, my, if it isn't Jean Cénac from Tarbes, alias Jean Cazaux? We have been looking for both of you for quite some time, and you turn out to be the same person!" "Get lost, Sonia," Jean said, "This has nothing to do with you." "Aha," said one of them, "Sonia? Haven't we heard that name somewhere as well?" "She has nothing to do with this, she's just a friend." "Hmm, do you know what sort of friends you have; this man is a dangerous terrorist!" "Oh, how awful!" said Sonia, her eyes large. "I had no idea!" and she shot her friend a horrified look.

In the meantime, one of the uninvited guests had gone into the bedroom and was poking around. Suddenly there was a scream. He had pushed a button, and the Murphy bed came down from the wall. The man was hit, and fell to the floor. His colleague ran in, and like a flash Sonia ran out the door, followed by Jean, who managed to grab some of the material from the table and take it with him. They flew down the stairs, and when they got to the bottom, the men shot at them. They ran for their lives, and suddenly Jean tripped and fell. "Run Sonia," he yelled, and Sonia disappeared around the first corner. Jean got to his feet, and ran around a different corner.

Sonia kicked off her awful wartime shoes made of felt with wooden soles, and ran. She threw the papers down one of the few sewer openings. Two terrified old women at an open gate asked: "What's going on? We heard shots." "Oh, I heard them too, and got so scared, I'm completely out of breath. I'm on my way up to my friend who lives in this building to calm down. I have such a weak heart!" Sonia improvised. She went through the gate and up all the stairs. The attic door was unlocked, and she found a dusty little room with a tiny window covered with spider webs. She looked out, finding no escape route there, and it was almost two floors down to the nearest house. She sat down on the floor and waited. An hour later she was back out on the street, her nose powdered, her hair brushed. It was pouring rain and she was wearing only her thin summer dress. She walked calmly, still barefoot, to a nearby food store where she was known, and asked to borrow a coat. She was given a big, brown shop coat that served her purpose, and she got home safely.

Later, we heard that Jean had also gotten away, very lucky to be alive. He was grazed by a bullet on his temple, and fell. He lost everything he had tried to take with him when he ran from his office, but he managed to outrun the soldiers, who were delayed by all the people grabbing the money and papers flying around in the street. Jean ran to rue de la Bourse, and our mutual friend, Madame Prévost.

Both Jean and Sonia had to keep out of circulation. Sonia was so disappointed that she wasn't able to participate in the hospital coup! A couple of days later, when it was all over, Magnus' daughter Nicole and Henriette Léon came to tell about it. A large truck disguised as a Vichy police car, filled with "Vichy" police soldiers, drove up in front of the hospital. They quickly overpowered the militia guards who were fooled by the truck and taken completely by surprise.

Georgette Cassagnavère was one of the few who was permitted to enter the prisoners' room, and she had prepared the patients. She arrived in her Red Cross uniform, carrying a bucket of Quaker soup, and the word spread fast. All the patients, wearing their pajamas and carrying small bundles with their personal possessions, were loaded onto the truck so quickly that they were gone before anyone had time to react. They ended up in a large garage where they received civilian clothing, and each was assigned to a woman who would be responsible for him. They disappeared one by one, on foot, by rail, or – in the case of the weakest – by car. The truck with the police emblems was transformed into a civilian vehicle, and sent back to *le Maquis*.

Both Henriette and Nicole took on several patients. Some members of the FFI General Assembly stayed with Nicole, as well. Nicole shared the title of *La Patronne de la Resistance* with Magali. They were both among Toulouse's most beautiful, spiritual and intelligent women. I must admit that I often wished that I could participate in all these

216

events. But as Helga said, "We have to choose: either the resistance or Quaker work! We must not compromise the Quakers' work."

Ruins in Caen, 1945

IX. The End of the War

The Allies Land at Côte d'Azur

On August 15, 1944 we heard that the Allies landed at Côte d'Azur. First the free French troops by sea, then thousands by air, and then the Americans. The people of Toulouse were filled with excitement and enthusiasm. When would they get here? Would there be fighting? The Americans went directly north through the Rhone valley, and pushed the Germans back along the way.

I had a real scare on August 17. A man came into my office and asked for Dr. Ferry. "He's not here; can I give him a message?" I asked. "No, it's important that I speak with him myself," he answered. This sounded peculiar. We talked a bit. This man could be from the Gestapo or the Militia, but they usually traveled in pairs. He was well dressed and had a trustworthy face, but he wouldn't let me take a message. I decided to take a chance, and sent a messenger to get Alex.

Alex came in, looking a little nervous. I shut the door, but stayed in the room; I *had* to know what was happening. The man took out a letter, and read, "Dr. Alexander Feigenbaum, alias Alex Ferry, is a Polish communist and a dangerous agitator." Alex's face turned green, and he slumped down into a chair. "He is currently working for the Quakers. Every afternoon at 4 p.m. he takes streetcar number 40 from Place Capitol. He must be followed." The letter had been intercepted on its way to the Militia office, so the men there still knew nothing. But more letters could be sent "...so Dr. Ferry has to go underground." Alex managed to stammer out a thank-you. The man said goodbye and left, and so did Alex, as fast as possible!

He suspected that a young soldier who had enjoyed our canteen had reported him. They had met in 1940 when they were demobilized after the cease-fire. He was the only one apart from us who knew of Alex's double identity. Alex was lucky. He only had to endure two days in hiding, because on August 19 we all awoke to the sound of lots of traffic and noise outside. Magnus and I looked out and saw one large truck after another, and countless private cars all loaded with Germans in uniform and their baggage. They were on the run! They had to hurry if they wanted to get home to *das Reich* before the Yankees got them.

We had had an inkling of what was happening, because our young friend Eric Loeb – alias Etienne Lobé – had discovered that the best way to hide was to go right into the lion's den. He got a job as an interpreter in the Gestapo office where he was a double agent for quite some time. He provided lots of interesting information to the resistance. One day he said, with a sly smile, "Now I'll soon be out of a job." And sure enough, he was.

We sat on our balcony enjoying the sight of the Germans leaving the city. The street was full of thrilled spectators. I left for the office around 9 a.m. on foot because the Germans had been confiscating bicycles. What an atmosphere there was in the streets! I met many people I had passed every day for years without ever speaking. But now everyone stopped to talk and laugh, practically hugging each other. At the Place Jeanne d'Arc a fellow came running out of a German employment office. He ran over to a tiny Simca that was filled to overflowing, wearing three hats on his head! When the tiny car raced away, the spectators applauded and yelled "*Gute Reise, Bon Voyage!*" The cars seemed to be coming from all directions, and all the main roads out of Toulouse were filled with *die gefürchteten Terroristen* (the dreaded terrorists) who were doing their best to heckle the fleeing Germans.

We got nothing done at the office. There were no clients and few visitors. Monsieur Zarine, the German Jewish director of the Caffarelli prison told us that the Gestapo had come at 2 a.m, shot fifteen of the prisoners and released all the rest. Zarine was a sort of prisoner himself. I never did understand his job, but he was not a tyrant to the other prisoners. We had set up a sort of infirmary at Caffarelli, so Helga and Toot left right away with a handcart, to save what they could of the Quaker materials. Celine took the whole circus with admirable aplomb. She went down into the courtyard and canned a batch of plums that we had just received from the Branting Farm.

Georges Carél and Andrée Salomon came up to say goodbye and wish us luck. Some errands had kept them in Toulouse for a few days, and now they were on their way back to Chambéry, but the railroad workers had barricaded themselves in the station to protect it from the Germans, so no trains came or went. Georges and Andrée were anxious to get out. They fixed a large package of food, and left on bicycles, headed for Gaillac. We tried to get them to stay in Toulouse, because we felt it was much too dangerous to travel on the country roads.

I just had to get out and see what was happening. I took a camera along to capture Toulouse on this special day, but I was too late. All the signs of occupation had already been torn down by the ecstatic masses. People kept some things as souvenirs, and the rest they burned in the streets. We heard fire trucks and explosions from the early morning on, and saw thick, black smoke climb up toward the sky. When I got home for lunch, Magnus and I went up to the roof where we had a wonderful view of the entire city. The Germans had set fire to everything they could before they left, including the *Magazins Généraux* (the town's food depot), the big central telephone agency, the meat halls, the factories and the Gestapo building at 2 rue Maignan. Then they stood with their machine guns to keep the firemen from putting out the fires. Later in the morning, the French flag was raised over the railway station. We could hear voices singing La Marseillaise. It sent shivers of pride down our spines. We wept for joy.

Then the first trucks arrived with the boys from les Montagnes Noires and the Pyrenees. The cars had no license plates, but they had the French flag and a white FFI flag. The boys were happy and excited, sunburned and armed to the teeth! They were dressed in the strangest clothing: many were wearing only trousers. There was a fistfight. A few Germans remained, but the Militia had nowhere to flee. Most had barricaded themselves on the roofs of the city, and they shot wildly down into the streets to scatter the spectators.

I knew some boys among le Maquis, and they smiled when they saw me. Many of them had become quite familiar during the course of the years, as they relaxed at Lafayette or Frégadé with a glass of some imitation beer or other. They were blasé, dressed in the latest fashion, with long jackets, narrow ties and tight pants with huge cuffs that stopped above the ankle. Now they were thrilled with anticipation of "freeing France." Many of them went on to enlist with General de Lattre de Tassigny and the invasion troops in Provence. They fought valiantly and many fell in Alsace, including our dear Mr. Callebat's son, Pierrot. They were all upstanding young men who died for France.

But first they were ready to fight the Boches, and that afternoon they fought for several hours in the large courtyard in front of the railway station. After lunch, I went down to Pont Jumaux where I saw German soldiers who were supposed to guard their countrymen on their way out of town. When le Maquis showed up, I got out of there as fast as I could! Shots were exchanged, and I heard screams from both sides.

Many people came to our apartment that afternoon. One was an English woman, married to a Frenchman, whose children had been among my foster children. She wept with relief and happiness. She had been in both St. Michel and Cafferelli, and now had been released. "Just like that!" Near dinnertime, my "enfant terrible," Victor Tulman turned up, proud as a peacock, and talking about "those of us in the resistance" although he was every bit as much a scaredy cat as Alex. Victor went up to the rooftop with us. He stayed for dinner, and sang like crazy. He was so thrilled that he didn't have to hide anymore!

Darkness fell, and around 8 p.m. the shooting seemed less. I wanted to go over to the office and Magnus offered to go with me. We asked Victor if he wanted to come along. Victor thought about it for a bit: "Well, it could be dangerous." But he didn't want to stay in the apartment either, so he came along. We heard a single shot here and there as we practically sneaked along the walls of the buildings in the now-empty streets. I had to laugh at us: brave Magnus, then me, and nervous Victor bringing up the rear.

What a sight met us when we got to Bonrepos! A truck had tipped over in front of the office, and the area was covered with barricades. Three dead Germans lay in front of the iron gates to our warehouses. We had to leave them there. Just as I put my key in the lock, Helga opened the door. She was nervous and distraught. She was not happy to see us, and didn't want to talk. She wanted to go home, alone, and she left. I felt guilty and crestfallen. A group of FFI went by, with a few prisoners and wounded Germans between them. Magnus gestured to the dead Germans lying in the street. "Just let them lie there!" they said.

There was no longer any reason to go up into the office, so we locked the gate and returned home. There were barricades everywhere, and shots from the roofs, but no other people. We got to the corner of the boulevard and rue d'Alsace, only to find it closed off. A car filled with

Germans was forced to stop at the barricade. They started shooting wildly out of the car windows. The bullets flew unpleasantly about our ears. Then the car backed down the boulevard. We ran into a man who said, "There are enemies in the tower at St. Sernin, they're shooting like crazy, and someone over on the other side of the street here is returning fire." We got home in one piece, and said goodbye to Victor, who was not at all happy about having to continue on alone, but he had no choice.

Magnus and I each had a solid *Armagnac du Chateau Départ* as we discussed the day's events. Then we went back up to the roof. What a sight! There were flames everywhere, both in the city proper and on the outskirts. We saw sparks from the tower at St. Sernin. The explosions lasted until Sunday morning at 8:30. The Germans managed to clean house thoroughly before they left.

We had a good view of the tower, because our house was on the Boulevard d'Arcole, just in back of the church. On Sunday, August 20 we took another trip up to the roof, to see if it was still standing. In times of great drama, there is often a comical moment: a couple of days later, we read an article in the newspaper. It turned out that that there hadn't been a single living soul in the tower that night. Someone imagined that they had seen a person there, and had fired off a few shots. Then they reported that someone had answered with fire from the tower. The FFI boys streamed into the narrow streets from the Place St. Sernin, and sent up round after round. They believed that they saw smoke and sparks, but it was all created by their own bullets hitting the tower wall. Toulouse laughed.

The atmosphere in the city was euphoric. People were intoxicated with their new freedom, and they filled the streets, setting up chairs, bringing their wine bottles and their knitting. Their jubilation was tempered with nervousness, because the Germans were rumored to be coming closer on their way north from the Pyrenees.

Helga told me all about her adventures the previous day. Everyone had left the office at lunchtime, but she wanted to get a bit of work done. At about 3 p.m. she started for home, but bullets began raining down from a roof so she ran back to the office. A truck full of Germans had stopped in front, followed by an FFI truck. Everyone jumped out, and a fistfight ensued. They built barricades out of handcarts and cars. German cars were tipped over, and people on both sides were hurt. After several hours, Helga opened a shutter just a crack, to look out. Wounded men were lying on the ground. She plucked up her courage, went down to the gate, and asked if she could bring the wounded in. "Keep out of it! This isn't women's work. You'll risk getting a bullet put through your head!"

No sooner had Helga gotten back up to the office than a bullet came flying thorough the shutter, shattered the window and embedded itself into the back wall, followed by another one! She ran down into the courtyard and hid in a tiny shed at the bottom of the property for hours, until she finally dared to try to go home again at around 8 p.m. That's when she ran into us as we were coming in. It would have been all right if it had only been Magnus and me, but Tulman was just too much for her.

In my diary for Monday, August 21, 1944, I wrote:

> *Finally, finally I can write exactly as I wish, without worrying about being "discovered" by the enemy! We are free! I can hardly believe it.*

That Monday was the first work day of the liberation, but it was also a day for celebration. In the office, we just talked and laughed and shared our experiences and impressions and read all the new, free newspapers, called *Patriote, La Republique, Vaincre*. They were issued by the *Dépèche* publishing house (which had sympathized with the Germans), under the headline, *"La Dépèche est Morte!"*

Henriette Léon came and told us that she had been asked to take over leadership of *Secours Nationale*, which had been renamed *Entr'aide Francaise*. Our dear Mademoiselle Georgette Cassagnavère was asked to take over the Vice-Presidency of the Red Cross in Toulouse. She came up to the office and cried on Celine's shoulder. Our dear Cassa with her heart of gold, always ready to help wherever she was needed, said: "No one has any respect for me; they only know me by my bicycle and my soup bucket!" We had worked together since 1941. The former head of the Red Cross was not pleased about her connection to us whom she called "those dangerous spies."

The whole city gathered in front of City Hall at 3 p.m. to celebrate the new Mayor, Mr. Badiou, and Professor Pierre Bertaux, the new *Commisaire du Gouvernement*. We saw our friends from the convent at *La Motte*, standing on the platform Poggioli took the place of Mart y, the dreaded Chief of Police, who fled by airplane when he saw the writing on the wall. The young, smart Colonel Ravanel (who went by the name of Serge Verdun in the resistance) gave a rousing patriotic speech wearing our Nicole's beret on his head. He spoke of the fact that Toulouse had been the first area completely liberated by the FFI. I thought the cheering would never end as *La Marseillaise* rang out over the city!

But beginnings are difficult, and many people used their new freedom to exact revenge for the horrors of the war. They created a Second Bureau that tortured Militia and other "criminals", driving them around the city with their arms tied behind their backs, their faces bruised, and Nazi insignia painted on their naked torsos. Then there were the poor "whores of Germans," women who had had relationships with German soldiers. The crowns of their heads were shaved, and the Nazi insignia was painted onto their bodies. They were also driven around the city for all to see, and people shouted abuse at them. Dear Cassa, who had worked to help the persecuted during all those years, was sad. She said, "Now it will be my job to comfort and smooth the way for all these poor souls." This would cost her dearly – she was later arrested! When the time of adjustment came to an end, those who had taken the law into their own hands were punished and things went back to normal. The trains ran again, at least within the city. The roads outside the city were still barricaded in order to capture Germans and take them prisoner.

There were rumors that an allied delegation would be arriving in Toulouse by airplane. I decided I must have an American, English and a Norwegian flag. Magnus had a French flag. The big Lacroix store, which had bought lots of toys from our workshop in Penne, didn't have any foreign flags, but by some miracle, they had the material! I bought meters of red, white and blue fabric, thinking I could sew the flags. I found the measurements in one of Magnus' encyclopedias, and I – who hated anything having to do with a needle and thread – borrowed the concierge's old sewing machine and managed to sew correct English and Norwegian flags. I am more proud of them than of anything else I've sewn in my life. They went up on the balcony immediately. They looked marvelous and were admired by many. But we saw no Allies in Toulouse. Paris, and the rest of France, was liberated on August 25. Later I wished I had brought my flags home with me. They would have been a wonderful souvenir.

We were showered with gratitude after the liberation in August 1944. Mr. Pierre Bertaux, for example became a Prefect in Haute Garonne after the liberation. His child was one of our foster children during his long arrest and while he was a member of the resistance. He invited Helga and me to a reception for General de Gaulle!

Normandy, Caen

1944 came to an end. We had seen the liberation of France, the invasions in Normandy and on the Mediterranean coast, and the incredible atmosphere in Toulouse. Life slowly returned to normal. It was almost an anticlimax. In fact, the war continued and there were still many difficulties in the south.

We had a shock. Roger Charles, of the French Quakers, sent a letter where he made it clear that Helga was no longer welcome, and she left the Toulouse delegation! I wrote a furious response and collected signatures. Nora and Fred Cornelissan, leaders of the Montauban delegation, sent a wonderful letter of their own. They truly admired Helga. So Monsieur Charles had to give in. Helga went to Paris. The English and American Quakers came back to France eventually and took over the work again. Helga was asked to start a Quaker division in Caen in Normandy, to which she agreed. She asked me to help her, and naturally I said yes.

Helga made a thorough inspection of Normandy, to see what could be done there to relieve the worst pain and suffering. She traveled with José Maria Trias and Madeleine Barot from CIMADE and delivered a report to the American Friends Service Committee, and was then asked to start a delegation in Caen. When she returned to Toulouse, she was once again her energetic self, full of enthusiasm for her new endeavor. She asked me to help dissolve her home and business in Toulouse. She used to call me her "Office Bully," but my goodness how well we worked together.

Since I was to accompany her to Caen, I also had to pack up my work in Toulouse and arrange for my successor. On Christmas Eve we invited all the Toulouse Quakers and some other good friends to the dinner of the century. Magnus brought out the beautiful porcelain and the silver from the basement, and I dug into the treasure chest and produced an elegant damask tablecloth and a long lace border to grace the table, decorated with holly and red candles. The table was much admired. We had a wonderful black-market turkey stuffed with truffles. A magnificent wine and armagnac from our friend Dubos in *Chateau de Départ* topped it all off. The only thing that wasn't perfect was the cold apartment!

The weather was freezing outside and we had no source of heat. But we wrapped our guests in all the blankets we had, over their own coats and wraps, and gave them plenty to drink, so the farewell atmosphere was good. It was a huge success. We celebrated New Year's Eve in front of the open gas heater in the kitchen for warmth, with a large glass of armagnac in our hands.

On January 1, 1945 I went alone to Paris because Helga was quite ill from a bad reaction to vaccinations and influenza. My first visit in Paris was quite naturally to the Quakers, who didn't seem to take much notice of me. I got into a conversation with an English boy in a Quaker uniform, about 28 years old. He didn't seem to have much to do, so I asked if he would like to work in Caen with me. He said he would rather stay in Paris until an English delegation was established. Because the railway lines had been destroyed and all of Normandy was under British and American military control, one needed special permission to travel to Caen, so I asked him how I could get there, and sure enough, a few days later he had found out where I had to apply. I thought I should consult the French Quaker Ellinor Cohu, who was responsible for the transportation division. I didn't want to hurt her feelings by going over her head. She asked me for my papers in a somewhat arrogant and patronizing manner. When I asked her if I needed to apply in person, she replied: "No, that's not necessary, I can manage this myself." But the next time I saw her she was singing another tune. "They want to see you personally," she said with a barely discernable smile.

So early on a Saturday morning, I went down to Major Bramhall at 2 Place de l'Opera. The last time I was at that address was in March 1944, when it was a Boche headquarters! Major Bramhall was extremely helpful and friendly, accompanying me to various offices. One man with the face of a bulldog spoke unpleasantly and tried to dig around in my past, as if I were some sort of criminal. He asked why I wasn't detained in a camp during the war. I told him: "We Norwegians considered ourselves at war with Germany, but they regarded us simply as inhabitants of an occupied country. They didn't imprison *all* Norwegians, just

229

as they didn't imprison *all* Frenchmen, and besides, as Quaker employees we were accorded a certain respect from the Germans. Some of them still remembered being fed by the Quakers after the First World War." *That* gave him something to chew on. After practically two hours of interrogation I got the stamp of approval to accompany a U.S. military truck to Caen.

Major Bramhall accompanied me to the transportation department, asking: "When do you want to leave?" "As soon as possible!" "A transport will be leaving in an hour, can you be ready?" A shock went through me. I was so used to the French bureaucracy, and figured that I wouldn't be leaving before Monday or Tuesday. "There is also a truck leaving at 8 a.m. tomorrow." We agreed that I would leave the next day. To be on the safe side, the transportation office would call me to confirm at the Quaker office before 5 p.m. I sat there and waited and waited. Would the convoy go? No one called. Just before 5:00 I called in desperation. "Oh, it's so good to hear from you! We've been calling the Quaker office, and no one there knew of a Mrs. Synnestvedt!" Major Bramhall personally brought me the final papers. What an example of American service and friendliness!

On Sunday morning at 8 a.m, I was on my way to Caen. Although Helga had laid the groundwork, I had to organize barracks for our work, arrange to have them transported and hire a team to put them together. Everything had to be confirmed and checked. I had many enjoyable lunches and dinners with good friends, so it was actually quite sad to leave in our two enormous 20-ton trucks. My chauffeur was Corporal Woodrow Evans, a friendly fellow from South Carolina, and we talked and laughed over the engine noise. I made the mistake of mentioning the "Yankees" at one point, but he corrected me promptly, saying, "I'm a Rebel!" I had called a southern boy a Yankee! During our break on the road, we swapped sack lunches. He was so incredibly tired of the same military food day in and day out, and thrilled with a little change.

It was pouring rain when we arrived in Caen in the late afternoon, amidst hopeless ruins and bottomless muddy

Caen, January 1945

streets. He dropped me off at the *Convent du Bon Sauveur*, which had been recommended as a place to spend the night. I stood outside the convent and rang the bell a couple of times. Finally, an old nun opened a small window in the door. "Do you have a room for the night?" I asked. "No, absolutely not – we are overfilled as it is," she answered as she shut the window. Someone recommended the Hotel des Ecuyers, but it was practically on the other side of town. I dragged my heavy suitcase in the direction he had told me to go, and got to the hotel after dark. It was full as well, but when the proprietress saw my stricken face, she said, "You can have an easy chair in the salon." So that's where I spent my first, very uncomfortable, night in Caen. The rest of the furniture was taken up with others!

When Helga finally arrived after 10 days, I had managed to get her a miserable room at Hotel des Ecuyers. We waited and waited for our trucks to arrive, using the time to visit the various local social aid organizations. Everywhere, we were told that transport was the most pressing issue. They had practically no trucks left.

Here are some excerpts from a letter I wrote during that time:

Caen, March 4, 1945

I have just come back from Sunday luncheon and am now weeping large tears, struggling to keep the fire alive on wet wood - all the smoke getting into my eyes! We have been plunged in work from morning till night every day now for 3 weeks. Only a few days ago we finally got the electricity installed; so far we lived in moonlight and candlelight in the evenings. We now have one nice barrack — a field operating room from the First World War — with three rooms. We have put stores in one room, clothing in the second, and the third one serves as bedroom offices (for us and our secretary Paulette Baudoux) as well as general sitting room. Two English Quaker boys sleep between the bales in the storeroom.

Any moment now we are expecting four trucks and eight boys from England. We found a ruin whose roof has been patched so they can sleep there until the rest of the barracks are ready. Soon we shall have a whole village of our own here in the courtyard of the lycée.

The country is very desolate and depressing. In village after village one cannot see a trace of what was. The allies have made broad roads for the tanks and all the fields are still full of mines, so it's impossible to pick the snowdrops and other spring flowers that are coming up. In one village, five young men were killed when they tried to plow, so the fields lie uncultivated. Seven months after the battle, one can still see swollen corpses of cattle in the fields, and we cannot go out to bury them. Meat is scarce and the butter ration for March is 150 grams, but despite the Germans, Normandy had enough food all through the war, so one does not see signs of undernourishment.

I had a rather uncanny experience the other day. I took one of the Studebaker trucks and our French driver Charles to fetch several children from different villages: they were off to Switzerland. On our way back, about 10 km outside Caen, a front tire burst, and precious Charles had forgotten his tools! I feared that if I sent hopeless Charles walking to Caen and back, it would be the next morning before he returned! Fortunately there were two social workers with the children, so I set out for Caen myself.

Dusk was falling. The little country road was full of holes and all was quiet except for my hobnail boots on the asphalt. No people and no vehicles passed, so I just had to walk. In the darkness, the rusty tanks and trucks lining the sides of the road took on queer forms. The dreadful ruins gaped at me. I thought I was the only living creature in the whole world. I passed little white crosses, some of them decorated with pierced helmets, soldiers buried where they fell. It was almost a relief when it became pitch dark, protecting me in a way from all the ghosts. And eventually I could see the few lights from the town. Then thank heavens, after 6 or 7 km's walk, my little desolate road joined the highroad, and at last I was picked up by a passing car and returned to our village where Stan found tools, and we went back to rescue our stranded truck and children. We shared a good glass of Calvados when the job was finished!

Helga and I met many interesting people in Caen and the surrounding area. We had something to offer, so people wanted to make friends with us. We gratefully accepted invitations to meals, and the ones with farmers were wonderful! We visited the various official offices – the French Red Cross, *Entr'Aide Francaise* as well as private organizations such as CIMADE, which was led by Mademoiselle Weil and Monique Chauraud. Miss Torr was the impressive leader of the English Red Cross, and "our own sweet Rose Thorndike" from Quaker days in Marseille, represented the American Red Cross.

We visited L'Oasis, a large canteen put together by *Les Soeurs de la Sainte Famille* in the middle of the ruins of their own once-impressive convent. The British had given them two "Nissen" huts: big curved sheets of metal, almost like a half pipe, that can be put together. In these, the nuns had installed their kitchen and canteen. They served more than 1000 meals a day, and gave food to all the people who could take it home. We got to taste the food, and it was first class. We ended up helping a bit there.

Alice, Caen, June, 1945

Strangely enough, salt was scarce in Normandy, so Helga had brought three tons of awful, unrefined salt from Toulouse. It took up a huge amount of space in our storehouse, and smelled horrible because the sacks were wet. But we packed it into small bags for our clients, some of whom were grateful. One day a couple of boys were loading wares to L'Oasis as I stood nearby with the checklist. We were just about to leave when I said, "Oh, take a couple of those awful salt bags so we can get rid of them as fast as possible." They said, "But there's no way we can give something of such inferior quality!" Then we drove off. But when the lovely, aristocratic Mère Supérieure heard about our salt she came out with tears in her eyes. "You have been sent here as an answer to my deep-felt prayers. I have prayed so for help, because we don't have a single grain of salt left, and how can we serve food to 4000 people without salt?" She threw her arms around me. Never in my life have I felt so tiny and worthless as when I referred to God's gift as "awful" salt.

I also had an unusual correspondence with the mother of a British soldier who was killed in France.

Caen, 18/6 - 1945.

Dear Mrs. Wilson,

Anne Crawshay asked me to locate your son's grave at Grasmesnil St. Aignan. We went out yesterday and talked to the Mayor of the village, Monsieur Delrue. He and his wife accompanied us to la ferme Delante, owned by a Mme Massinot. The farm is entirely dead, I could not locate Mme Massinot. But I suppose she is the one who has taken care of the graves. There were about 20 in a group under the apple trees in her garden, and they had been nicely taken care of. The local population had laid stones around them, and there are flowers, and one felt that they cared for the graves with affection. Mme Delrue said she would go regularly to tend them.

It is almost a year since your boy was killed there - and now the spot is so peaceful, with poppies, cornflowers and daisies. But one understands what a fierce battle must have taken place there last summer. The farm is completely ruined – there are big shell holes in the house and in the walls surrounding the property. The village church is very mutilated, but the tower can still be seen from far off.

We took several pictures. It is very difficult to have films developed in France for the moment, so it may last some time before I can send them to you.

You know that when British forces were killed, they were buried on the spot where they fell. But now they are all rapidly being brought to the official cemeteries. I could not find out when or to where the graves in this courtyard will be moved, but the local Gendarmerie or the Mayor will know, when that time comes.

Should there be anything else we can do, please write to my successor, Miss Charlotte Brooks, at the Quakers in Caen.

Yours very sincerely
Alice Resch Synnestvedt.

And here is her response:

> 21 July 1945
>
> *Dear Mrs. Synnestvedt*
>
> *I think you realize what your kind letter from Caen had meant to us and we thank you most sincerely for the work you undertook in tracing the grave of our son Malcolm Wilson. One day we may see it for ourselves at peace in the country - so different from the tortured land he fought over and helped to free.*
>
> *It was thoughtful of you to take photographs and perhaps you may be able to send them but I know only too well the difficulties.*
>
> *I hope that your work in Toulouse is not overwhelming. I am thankful to be able to put in a full day here trying to ease the lot of our allies.*
>
> *Once more I would like you to know how grateful I am for your kindness*
>
> *Yours ever sincerely,*
> Hilda Wilson

Of course we were constantly keeping up with the war news. The English and American columns were often seen in Caen, on their way from Cherbourg to the front. The Allies were advancing slowly, and the Russians were racing ahead. Who would reach Berlin first? Then on May 1, the rumors were flying and everyone was buzzing: "Hitler has disappeared!" "Hitler has committed suicide." On May 4, we heard that Germany had capitulated in Holland and Denmark. Friends and acquaintances came to congratulate Helga. But what about Norway? I was worried about my country. The harbor in Caen was opened for civilian traffic. On the morning of May 7, we met a Norwegian captain who had just arrived with his ship. We were all invited to lunch on board the next day. After work that evening, Helga and I went down to the harbor to see the marvel. A Norwegian boat! I wanted to ask the captain to take me home with him.

We strolled home past all the ruins in the dusk, and then we heard the bells of St. Etienne. It sounded like a celebration! Suddenly the street was filled. People were everywhere, shouting with joy. The great news had finally arrived. The Germans had capitulated in the rest of Western Europe! The war in Europe was over! Oh, my beloved Norway! People were singing and shouting for joy. Suddenly we saw to our horror that two people were climbing up the tower at St. Pierre. The tower was extremely fragile and it was strictly forbidden to go into the church ruins. We stood there with our hearts pounding, following the progress of the two young men on their way up the tower. At the top they unfolded a huge French flag. Then we heard a faint sound. There was still a single bell in the tower, and one of the boys started to hammer on it, then the other joined in. The sound wasn't particularly impressive; it was just one bell, but when we heard it, we broke into a frenzy that seemed it would never end. People sobbed for their beautiful, ruined church, now a symbol of freedom and peace!

On May 8, the capitulation was a fact. The war was over. Peace at last! Helga and I were looking forward to lunch on the Norwegian boat! We were to be picked up at 12:45, and we had informed the kitchen that we wouldn't be having dinner that day. We dressed up in our very best, but no one came to get us. Time passed, the boys came back from lunch. "Are you still sitting here? All dressed up and nowhere to go?" They laughed when they saw how uncomfortable we were. At 2:00 I called to find out what was going on. As soon as they heard of the capitulation, the boat left immediately for Norway! The crew wanted to be the first to arrive home. And I wasn't on it.

Alice with some of the Aspet "children" in Jersualem, 1984
left to right: Uri (Carl) Landau, Martin Eckstein, Ruth Gogol,
Alice's assistant from Aspet, Michael Oppenheimer, Alice, George
Basnizki, Menachem Mayer, Hanna Moses

X. Epilogue – Angel of Aspet

*H*ere ends Alice's account of her experiences during the war years in France. For Europe, the war was over. The American Quakers came back, wanting to resume leadership of the aid work in France. So in July of 1945, Helga Holbek and Alice said goodbye, and left Caen.

Helga quickly obtained permission to travel back home to Denmark. She accepted an invitation to America, where she stayed for six months. After that, she worked in Poland for UNICEF. With her considerable experience in the travel business during the years between the wars, at the age of 60 Helga took a Danish exam to be certified as a guide and group travel leader. She worked for Bennet's Travel Agency, and was quite popular among her clients, traveling all over Europe for many years with Danish and American groups. When she retired in Copenhagen, she started *Hyggehjelpen* (Friendly Help) with another retired woman. Their motto was "Retired People Helping Retired People". It became quite popular, offering "reserve" grandmothers, people to go on walks with, people to read aloud and all sorts of small tasks. The Danish Red Cross continued it under the name of *Besøgsvenner* (Visiting Friends). Helga died on November 23, 1983.

Letter from Alice to her parents in Norway,

August 23, 1945

Dearest Pa and Ma,

I'm writing on Magnus's awful machine just to save space, and to fit more on the page, because there's no more paper here. I bought 12 of these sheets and 12 envelopes with great difficulty for 48 francs. Your letter only took 10 days, and for the first time, it wasn't censored — stirrings of peace. Isn't it wonderful that the war is finally over in the east ... at least we hope that the armistice will be signed on December 31st. ... I think I've gotten all your letters, both those that have come here, and those that came to Toulouse and to Caen, thank you so much. But you understand, I hope, why there is often a lot of time in between my letters to you — it was forbidden to write to Norway, and my English and Swedish sources were on and off — I couldn't continue to use them.

Where did you pick up on that nice title Service International des Amis? Is it known in Norway? Here, of course, the Quakers are officially called Société des Amis, but our work is just called Secours Quaker. ...Just think, it's been 6 years since we've seen each other, and only been able to write more or less undercover. No, it will be a while I suppose until Norwegians can leave the country. All the trouble I run in to in my attempts to get home make me nervous myself. I was at the Norwegian Embassy in Paris right after the war ended in Europe to see what I could find out, and to get a new passport — but they weren't helpful at all. Don't even thiiiiiiiiiiink of tryyyyyyyyying to get home again for at least another year — thank you, but after a bit one hears both this and that about those who have managed to get home inside a year.

I asked for a visa to visit England, thinking I would try from there — I heard that the Norwegians made less trouble with people from England. Haven't even gotten an answer to my application. Then I tried to get a permit to enter Sweden, to come home that way — nope ... I am truly doing everything I can to get home, but I feel like I'm running around in a circle and keep banging my head into a stone wall. ...

Because of my plans to return home, I gave up my Quaker work when I was finished in Caen. I didn't want to go to the trouble of starting up again in Toulouse for such a short time. And everything is quite changed here, so I didn't really want to start again, anyway. We had a wonderful group through all those 5 years; we all had our individual work, and got along well with each other. Now everyone is gone. Helga Holbek, our boss, is in England, and is going to America at the end of September to work with "The American Friends" in Philadelphia. We organized the Quaker work together in Caen, only to have it taken over by the English and American Quaker representatives.

Ima Lieven, who left Toulouse more than a year ago to work in Marseille, is now on her way to the Quakers in Germany. Toot Bleuland van Oordt returned to her father in Holland a month ago, but she is most likely the only one who will come down here in the course of the autumn to continue the work in Toulouse. Celine Rott de Neufville has gone to Switzerland, and will probably not return – she is worn out after all the hard work in these intense years…It's a little odd, all these "foreigners" who are coming down now to direct our work. They don't have any understanding of what we have gone through during these years. But my God that's where the money has come from, so it's reasonable that they would want to decide what and how. You can probably understand how the work isn't the same for us anymore, it's suddenly become complicated and administrative where we were easy and improvised and dealt with the need of the moment without a lot of bureaucracy, knowing full well that waiting would mean that the emergency – and the chance to help – would pass before we finally had all the formalities in order. So I don't regret that I've left my beloved work. And something else is different…now, everything is in the open – no more "secrets" about anything.

Tell Willie that I'm bursting with pride over his clandestine life during the occupation, … We were also in the middle of all that was going on – not officially, though – as Quakers, we had to appear to be neutral. Had it been discovered that the Quakers were doing anything that didn't bear the light of day, all our work would have been put at risk, and our work was truly necessary for all the starving children in the south of France, especially in the concentration camps and prisons. There, we were the only organization that was allowed to enter the stations when the infamous trains left with thousands of people for the deportation camps in Germany. The Germans – and even the Gestapo – gave us permission to give the poor souls a meal before they left. I'll tell you all about that in person sometime.

But we did do other things – under the table. We didn't even tell our good friends – what we didn't know, we couldn't be forced to tell if tortured. ... Magnus and I always had nocturnal guests that first winter we were married, and an architect who lived on the floor above us was arrested by the Gestapo, who then installed two of their men there. So we had the Gestapo living right there in the building with us! Every morning, my first thought upon awakening was, "Well, we managed to make it through another night." The architect has come back from Buchenwald, by the way.

I'll tell you of my trips to the Swiss border and to the foot of the Pyrenees when I get home. I just want to tell you that our life wasn't particularly peaceful here, either, even though we can't compare it to what some others have had to go through. ... But we saw the beginnings of the mass deportation of the Jews from several camps. We were always there to take their last messages and belongings, either to take care of them in hope that they would one day return to claim them, or to send them to their next of kin. It was during the first deportation summer, August of 1942, that we came into contact with the clandestine work – it was only common sense to try to sneak as many as possible out of the camps or the trains.

Oh my little ones, I'd love to be able to send you some packages, but since I've left the Quakers we're on meager rations here in southern France. The situation is a scandal. We used all the money we had during the occupation on black-market purchases, but we don't do that any longer – as a matter of principle, naturally – because someone has to be the first to stop if this country is ever to get back on its feet. But also because we can't afford to anymore,

…Because of this, I'll go to Caen again in the beginning of September to help Helga Holbek, who is coming back from England where she's seen Anne Crawshay, who is the head of at least three relief committees, and who now has got it into her head that it is England's duty to help Normandy get back on its feet, since it was they who ruined it. So she's collected a lot of stuff for Calvados, which she's asked Helga and me to organize…

Love & kisses to you all from LIS

Alice returned to Normandy on one occasion. Her good friend Anne Crawshay, who was forced to leave France in June of 1940, had started an English aid organization for volunteer French soldiers: Friends of the French Volunteers, or *Amis des Volontaries Francais* (A.V.F.). When the war ended, she returned immediately to her beloved France, and started up a huge aid organization, quite like the Quakers, but with headquarters in Falaise. Mrs. Crawshay asked Alice to help her build up the institution, which Alice willingly did. Alice traveled to the enormous American military depots that were closing down, soliciting donations of trucks filled with all sorts of useful material.

In December of 1945, Alice finally received permission to return to Norway, where she stayed with her parents until April of 1946. Then she returned to Paris, where she worked for the American Unitarian Service Committee until it closed down in November of 1948. In January of 1949, she returned to Normandy as secretary for the Swedish *Rädda Barnen* (Save the Children). The Quakers and AVF were long gone, and Caen lay in ruins. For four years, starting in January 1950, Alice was the head of *Rädda Barnen's* home for Jewish children between the ages of 3 and 6, who were regaining their health prior to moving to Israel with their parents. Magnus Synnestvedt died in 1950.

In 1960, Alice closed the door on her French existence of 32 years, and returned home to help her parents in Lofthus. After they died, she moved to Copenhagen. Years passed and then Alice began to hear from some of the Jewish

children she had known during the war, and letters started
to arrive, seeking information about the war years.

Alice's visits to Israel

This letter to her brother and sister-in-law describes Alice's
first visit to Israel, and her reunion with some of the
children from Aspet.

Copenhagen, 1982

My dearest two,

*… my old friend Helga Holbek is still failing. She is now in the
cardiac wing. Luckily, she hasn't lost her good humor – I sat
with her until about 11 p.m. last night, when she suddenly asked
where she was. "You are in intensive care." She smiled and
whispered "the-end-of care… Akk ja." I've known her for 42
years. Now, a little news of "Alice in Wonderland." An
acquaintance asked me recently if my soul had begun to find its
way home again. I had to admit that both my heart and my soul
and thoughts still fly around in that wonderful country (Israel).*

*I was just a regular tourist the first week. Three of "my" children
from the war years were waiting at Ben Gurion airport, with a
huge bouquet of chrysanthemums! They were well intentioned,
but such a bother! I promised of course to water them well, and
had to, because we could risk meeting again somewhere or other.
My Danish companions laughed every time I came dragging out
to the bus with a broom in the mornings. At night, I put them in
the bathtub! Well, the first week I saw Israel from the outside –
we saw all the highlights…*

*…When we arrived at the hotel in Jerusalem, I was again met
with kind letters of welcome and a big bouquet of beautiful roses –
my fellow travelers raised their eyebrows, let me tell you! And
there were phone calls from everywhere…*

*The tourist week was over, and I went over to seeing Israel from
the "inside." One of my war children came to the hotel to discuss
plans. It was strange to see the handsome, middle-aged
gentleman, and think back to when we first met and he was an 8-*

year-old. So far, they've located four people from that particular group of children in Israel. But there is contact with others in America, France, Germany and Switzerland, so they remember that I lived with them those six weeks when they were

Alice and Helga with Joseph Hadass, the Israeli Ambassador to Denmark, 1983

quarantined. We got fifty children out of Camp de Gurs, which was a concentration camp in the Pyrenees. ...

At 11 a.m. Menachem (formerly known as Heinz) Mayer drove me out to "Yad Vashem." It's a large, square, impressive memorial hall for the six million Jews who were killed during the Second World War. Luckily, I had been there the day before with my group, because the sight was so overwhelming that I burst out crying. I could simply not control my emotions. So on Monday, when I was with my Jewish friends, I was able to control myself.

About 20 people had come: my children with wives or husbands, and people we either had worked with, or gotten to know in the concentration camps in the south of France. We went into the large, beautiful hall. The floor is covered with six million tiny black mosaic stones (one for each of the Jews who died) and there is a golden metal box with the names of all the concentration camps around Europe. There are low galleries on three sides, where tourists and visitors can sit. A small distance in front of the third wall, there is a monument, symbolizing high flames – sharp metal sculptures. In front of this burns the eternal flame. The hall is quite dark and solemn, and there is no sound save the crackling of the flame (it's a gas flame, so I don't understand how it crackles). One does not speak in the hall. The day before, there were many tourists – on this occasion, we were alone (so far). Andrée Salomon (the woman I mentioned who worked for Jewish

245

children) took me by the hand, and led me along the galleries all the way to the fourth wall, where there was a staircase down to the floor. We stopped there, and it seemed that a man appeared out of nowhere, down by the monument. He read a speech in French. I couldn't understand a word, because the resonance in the hall created horrible interference in my hearing aid – but suddenly I got a shock: I heard Helga Holbek's name and my own. Later, I asked my good friend Dora Amelan, who had lived in Copenhagen for a year and a half with her husband, about the speech. Dora laughed and said, "A thank-you speech to you and Helga." I almost felt bad, I felt so undeserving. Well, I was led down the staircase and out onto a sort of black carpet in back of the monument. Two of the "boys," who were very religious, went out in front of the monument, and said some prayers in Hebrew. I was then asked to rekindle the holy flame (it's never extinguished completely, but had been turned down quite low).

You can imagine that this was a very emotional moment in my life. A cantor wearing a prayer shawl ... stood in front and sang the most gripping, heart-wrenching psalms. I've never heard anything like it. They went right through my bones. Some tourists stood respectfully near the entrance, and were no doubt just as moved by the ceremony as I. Later, at a reception, I was thanked, along with the American Quakers, as it was they who were being honored through me. Without them, I would never have been able to accomplish anything. When I got home, I told Helga about the whole thing, she was actually part of the ceremony. I don't know which of us was most moved ...

...After the reception, I was driven up to Haifa for three days. My special friend Uri (Carl) Landau*, who visited us in Copenhagen last year, and who organized my whole "private" week, picked me up in Haifa, and we drove to his Kibbutz, where I stayed until Sunday. It was interesting to see a Kibbutz up close. 500 people lived there.

Uri drove me to Tel Aviv, where I saw another child from Aspet, Ruth Gogol, and her exciting husband, Samy. There is a

---

* See page 103

memorial marker for a Polish doctor, Dr. Janusz Kortczak, near
Yad Vashem. He protected small orphans in the Warsaw ghetto,
giving them a home and an education. Samy had been his
student for seven years. Then the Germans came and rounded
them up and took them to the infamous extermination camp at
Auschwitz. All the children were sent to the gas chamber, and Dr.
K. went with them in order to be able to comfort them up to the
last minute. The last one to get out alive was Samy. He was 14,
and a talented harmonica player. When the Germans discovered
this they put him into a children's orchestra. That saved him.
But he had to play with the orchestra time after time at the
crematorium, to drown out the sounds... When the Americans
came, they were all asked where they wanted to go. Samy said
France, without any real thought to the matter. He didn't want to
return to anti-semitic Poland. He was 18, and ended up in the
south of France, where he met my Ruth Beermann, who was also
18. They decided to get married, and of course barely managed
to scrape by for many years, but Samy became famous – he was
much in demand with his harmonica orchestra – so now they are
well-off and live in a wonderful apartment. They have children
and grandchildren, so all is well. Tuesday morning at 5:30 a.m.
Ruth and Samy drove me to Ben Gurion airport, and who do you
think was waiting there – my faithful Uri.

The last I heard as I disappeared up the stairs was "come back
soon!" ...

Letter to her brother telling of Alice's experiences in Israel and posthumous honors that were bestowed on Helga Holbek

Copenhagen, May 5, 1984

Dear Willie!

Finally I've come so far that I can sit down and tell a bit about
my trip to Israel. ... I was met by Eva and Georges and Joav
Basnizki, as well as Ruth and Samy Gogol, the latter bearing an
enormous bouquet of beautiful flowers! "This time you won't have

*to drag it from hotel to hotel and in and out of busses," laughed
Ruth...George and Ruth were among "my" Aspet children....*

*I thought of these "children" often during the ensuing years and
wondered how their lives had turned out. Then, suddenly, after
40 years, I was again in contact with three of them, independent
of each other! And at more or less the same time! By a strange
coincidence they had gotten hold of my address. Letters came
from Israel, from Switzerland and from England — one of them,
Uri Landau, came to Copenhagen with his wife Chasida to say
hello to Helga Holbek and to me. And together we located 14 of
the children. As I said to Uri, "Isn't it strange how everything
from back then turns up now, 40 years later? People are writing
books, memoirs, making movies." Uri said, "Remember that 40 is
a magic number, think of Moses and his 40 years in the desert." I
told this to some friends, whose immediate response was — yes, just
think of Ali Baba and the 40 thieves! ...*

*...Last year, Helga Holbek and I were made members of "The
Righteous Gentiles" (Les Justes des Nations) for the work we had
done for Jews during the war. I have to admit that neither Helga
nor I felt that we had done anything dangerous or heroic — neither
of us felt deserving of the honor. At any rate it seldom occurred to
us that we were risking our lives when we now and then did things
that weren't part of the official Quaker work. "We must under no
circumstances compromise the Quaker work." But it was fairly
unavoidable. Both Helga and I smuggled people into
Switzerland, for example.*

*Along with the title "The Righteous Gentile" we were to be honored
by the planting of a tree on the Avenue of the Righteous, around
Yad Vashem. Last year I simply wasn't up to any more
celebrating, so we were awarded our medal at the Israeli Embassy
here. Then Uri came to Copenhagen in October on business, and
convinced me to go over anyway, so they planted a tree for Helga
and for me on April 25th this year. It's in the beginning of the
avenue, at the bottom of Yad Vashem with a wonderful view of
Jerusalem! ...Helga died before the event, unfortunately. ...In
fact I'm the last of the Toulouse delegation of the American
Friends Service Committee...*

We went to Ben Gurion airport after dinner to pick up Hanna Meyer Moses, one of my Aspet children now living in Switzerland. She wanted to be here to celebrate! She is staying in a marvelous spa hotel nearby, but eats lunch and dinner with us. Eva, George and I drove out to Yad Vashem. We had been told to be there in plenty of time before 11:00, so we were the first to arrive. V.I.P.'s usually come breezing in at the last moment! People started arriving after a bit. It was fun to see so many of "my" children. Uri Landau, who was actually the soul behind the whole celebration, came with his wife, Chasida. Ruth Gogol came without her Samy, who unfortunately had had a heart attack a while ago, and had to take it easy. … Michael Oppenheimer and his wife were there from Paris. They took advantage of the opportunity to visit their son who is a doctor in Beersheva. Jacqueline Salibert from Aspet was there, as was Martin Eckstein from New York. He was one of the children I took to Switzerland. Menachem Mayer came with his Hava and their daughter and of course George Basnizki with his Eva.

From Helga's special group of friends (and mine as well) came Max Ansbacher and Siegfried Rothschild with whom we've had contact since we worked at Camp de Gurs, where they were inmates. Rabbi Kapel was "hidden" in Toulouse. … Andrée Salomon was unfortunately not able to attend; she is quite ill.

To begin with, we entered the memorial hall, where the doors were closed. I laid a lovely bouquet (long-stemmed roses, lilies, irises and chrysanthemums from Eva Have) near the eternal flame, followed by a minute's silence. Then we wandered down to our trees. A tiny coniferous bush had been stuck down into the earth, and I shoveled a bit of dirt around it. Then my seven children came one by one and cast a bit of dirt in the same place. Rabbi Kapel made a nice speech and reminisced about the time in Toulouse.

Then we came to Helga's tree. I shoveled a bit of dirt around it, Max and Siegfried followed. They both approached me to say that they thought my plaque was all wrong: they felt my maiden name ought to be included! They had known me as Miss Resch, after all! I agreed with them of course. Another thing – they had

249

made me Danish! Now it will be changed to: "Alice Synnestvedt - Resch, Norway (France)." It would have made Pa and Ma happy if they'd lived to experience it.

Norwegian I am, and Norwegian I'll remain, despite all my time as a foreigner. France is included because that was where we worked. Some official or other from Yad Vashem took me by the arm, and the procession continued with sightseeing indoors to a new large conference hall, to a gallery of pictures, and to "The Room of Names," where they collect journals on all Holocaust victims. ... We then went into a reception hall and were seated around a table. There were speeches by Monsieur Emmanuel Racine, the honorary president of the Association of French Veterans of War and members of the resistance in Israel (he gave me the Association's Medal of Remembrance). Menachem gave a speech on behalf of the Aspet children. Margot Cohn gave a speech written by Andrée Salomon and then I spoke. My speech was mostly memories of Helga Holbek.

... George took Hanna and me to the large monument for the 80,000 Jews from France who died. It was a huge wall on a cliff in a range of hills, surrounded by forest. The goal is that the forest will eventually have 80,000 trees. One can contribute money and have a tree planted in memory of a relative or an acquaintance. ... All the approximately 75 deportation trains from France are mentioned with their number and place, and with the names of those involved. I saw many names and train information that were familiar to me. ...

And that was the end of my adventure. But I still dream of Israel and the whole experience at night.

NOTE: Alice's brother Wilhelm died September 27, 1997.

Trees planted to honor Helga and Alice

Letters from Al Sperber to Alice

July 8, 1998

Dear Mrs. Synnestvedt,

It is under the most unusual circumstances I received your name from Mr. Jack Sutters of the Archives Department of the Quaker Organization in Philadelphia.

Al Sperber, 1998

During the war in 1942, I was living with my mother near Toulouse, France when we were forced to go into hiding. I was picked up by a lady who brought me to a monastery and my little sister of 4 years to a deaf mute school. I tried to find the name and location of the monastery but so far without success. I had written to several organizations until I contacted the Quakers via Email and finally are you the lady who saved my sister's and my life?

I would love to hear from you. Maybe you can give me your telephone number.

Sincerely

Al Sperber

August 5, 1998

Dear Mrs. Synnestvedt,

I can't tell you how happy I am to have received your letter. I had contacted the Diocese in Paris to get information about a monastery that could have hidden Jewish children during the war. I went to several Jewish organizations that had kept records but to no avail until my wife had the wonderful idea to get on the internet to look for the Quaker organization et voila.

What you did was indeed such a heroic act that words alone are not enough. I am writing to the Holocaust Museum in Jerusalem to recommend that you be given proper recognition. The Talmud says that those who save one life save the world. And you and your organization did just that.

You are asking whatever happened to me and my family after we left Toulouse. We received false travel papers from the underground and came as far as Evian, then with a guide went over the mountains into Switzerland. My little sister saved us as the Swiss guard wanted to send us back into France but saw my sister and he took pity on us and let us in. After a few months in camp, a Swiss family took me in. They were bakers and farmers, so I went to school, and helped on the farm and milked the cows and helped bake the bread. It was a wonderful experience. We are still friends and I just came back from Europe where I visited them. (The children stayed with me for lengthy periods here in New York.) After the war we went back to France where I continued my studies including a couple of years at the Sorbonne. In 1948 we emigrated to the United States. I finished my studies and graduated. I became manager in a very large corporation dealing in electronics and household appliances. In 1950 I married a German girl who herself was hidden for 4 years in Nymegen, Holland in an attic with the family that took her in. Her parents fled to France and were then imprisoned in Rivesaltes. They then fled to Spain. We had 2 children who are married and have each 3 children. My wife died in 1988 after a bout with cancer. I remarried last year and thank God we are very happy. Now I am retired and we do travel a lot. I hope that next year we shall be able to come to Denmark and finally meet you again.

If there is anything I can do for you, please do not hesitate to ask.

With my best wishes,
Al Sperber

Reunion with More of Alice's Jewish Children - by Aase Ingerslev, June 1999

In November 1998, Alice received a phone call from Hugo Schiller, one of her Aspet children now in Myrtle Beach, South Carolina. Alice's 90th birthday was fast approaching, and his good friend the Danish-born Birgit Darby had urged him to visit if he wanted to see her again after 57 years.

Rather than travel to Denmark, Hugo invited Alice to the States and said he would try to bring together the Aspet children who had settled in America. Alice had to decline. Unfortunately, she was simply not up to a trip of that magnitude, but she told me of the invitation. I suggested someone might be willing to accompany her. My husband suggested that I should go, since I knew her story and the story of her "children" as well as anyone else.

Alice agreed at once, but she was uncomfortable calling Hugo Schiller about bringing someone else along, so I called him, and my suggestion was met with great enthusiasm. He even offered to pay my expenses. He set to work at once, and contact was established with eight of the children. Some were not able to participate due to illness or because of other commitments. One came all the way from Iowa.

We landed in New York and the next day Hugo and friends met us with flowers in Myrtle Beach.

It was an unforgettable experience for me. I was deeply touched when I met these people who had lost everything, and now they stood with Alice – their only connection to that period of their lives, and especially to their parents, all of whom perished at Auchwitz. We were met with a generosity and love of life one seldom encounters, and we were all very emotional.

Alice was honored in the synagogue, where Hugo led the formal ceremony. Alice told the childrens' story in her excellent English. Hugo had sung to the other children in the room where they all slept, and now he was singing for her in the synagogue. The next day, Alice and Hugo lit the first candle of the Chanuka festival at a Jewish school. She was named an honorary citizen of Myrtle Beach.

The press covered our visit with articles and photographs in the newspaper every day. The nationally broadcast "Good Morning America," interviewed both Alice and those whose lives she saved. We only wished for more time for private conversations between Alice and her children.

Alice wanted to see the Holocaust Museum in Washington, D.C. and to walk down Fifth Avenue in New York, again after 60 years. So we flew back to New York, where Richard and Sheila Weilheimer were our guides, taking us around Manhattan in all its Christmas glory. Before going up to our rooms, we were presented with a large box of chocolates! Tired but happy, we took the elevator up to the roof to see the Empire State Building and then we sat on our beds eating chocolate like a couple of schoolgirls.

The next day we took the train to Washington, D.C. The train station in Washington had a Norway exhibit: a Christmas tree decorated with Norwegian flags, and information about Norway as a tourist destination, even Norwegians in Viking garb "working" at their various tasks. Alice greatly enjoyed this coincidence!

Together with Richard and Sheila we went to the Holocaust Museum where we were met by the Director, who took us to the wall where Alice's name is inscribed as one of the Righteous Gentiles. She was photographed and we explored the museum at our own pace, an unforgettable, gripping experience. What a contrast when we went out into the sunshine and freedom!

During our last dinner, the young people gave each of us wonderful books from the museum. The next morning we took the train

Hugo Schiller, Alice, Ruth Oppenheimer David, Eva Hertz Boden, Myrtle Beach 1998

back to New York and then we flew back to Denmark. We were both sad to say goodbye.

Another reunion of Alice and her Aspet children took place in Denmark, from August 15 though 19, 2002. The "children" came from Israel, Germany, France, Switzerland and the USA to honor Alice at our home in Fredenborg. The days were full of joy and happiness. Throughout the afternoon and Sunday evening – accompanied by Jewish and Norwegian music, and lovely warm weather – everyone who wanted to say something to Alice, or just tell about the past, was able to do so.

Richard Weilheimer, Alice, Ernest Weilheimer, Myrtle Beach 1998

The Woman Who Saved My Life

By RICHARD WEILHEIMER

Fifty-six years is a long time. But it is not too late to thank someone for saving your life. Two years ago, I rediscovered the identity of my rescuer during the time of the Holocaust.

I had remembered Alice Resch Synnestvedt only as "the Quaker lady." Alice is American, born of Norwegian parents, and herself a citizen of Norway. She studied in Germany between the world wars, lived in France for many years and is now a resident of Denmark. During World War II she was a volunteer with the Toulouse delegation of the American Friends Service Committee, a Quaker organization.

When the Gestapo rounded up the first group of Jews to be deported from Germany on Oct. 22, 1940, my whole family spent three days without provisions on a train taking us to the concentration camp in Gurs at the base of the Pyrenees in Vichy France. This camp, notorious for death by starvation and diseases, turned out to be a holding area until the construction of the infamous death camps was completed. The Quakers were on the scene trying to ease the hardship of our daily existence. My 39-year-old

---

We left Marseille...just five days before the infamous Adolf Eichmann came to Paris to order the implementation of the "Final Solution" in France.

---

mother died there in 1941, and my father was 55 years old when he was gassed at Auschwitz two years later.

After four months at the camp, the Quakers successfully negotiated the release of 48 children which included my brother Ernest and me, and placed us in Maison des Pupilles, an orphanage in Aspet. We spoke no French and no one at the orphanage spoke German. Thirty-two-year-old Alice Resch, as she was then known, moved into our dormitory, becoming "mother" to us all. While other rescue work soon took her from us, she would always return to "her children." Sixteen months later, she handpicked six boys, including my brother Ernest and myself, for a clandestine operation by which we were smuggled out of Europe. We left Marseille on June 25, 1942, just five days before the infamous Adolf Eichmann came to

Paris to order the implementation of the "Final Solution" in France. I believe we were on the last ship out of Europe before the mid-July round-up of Jews for transport to Auschwitz started in the orphanages and in Gurs, Récébédou, Rivesaltes and other camps.

Staying one step ahead of the Nazi and Vichy murderers, Alice placed children with Trappist Monks in a French monastery and in various convents. She worked with her Quaker team in providing false documentation and created escape routes for countless others. Some were taken to the Protestant Huguenot village of Le Chambon Sur-Ligon and hidden there. Four children were taken on a "skating" outing near the Swiss border. A dry run for the crossing was rehearsed several times. However, at the actual escape attempt, the guards unexpectedly stepped onto the children's path. To Alice's dismay, three of them ran back to her while the fourth raced to freedom, never looking back.

The world will always produce perpetrators and therefore their unfortunate victims, but then there are the majority of people, the bystanders, who for lack of concern or fear of involvement do nothing. By far, the smallest group consists of resisters and rescuers, those heroic, righteous individuals whose humanity and selflessness motivates them to act, to do "the right thing."

Recently, some of Alice's now aging child-survivors, who located each other through a series of coincidences, used the occasion of her 90th birthday to bring her to the United States from Copenhagen. Alice's eyes no longer see well, but the glimmer is as strong as the smile on her face. After all those years, she was reunited with some of "her children," each of whom she remembers very well. Her retentive memory for details is incredible. Alice's joy at meeting survivors, their spouses, children and grandchildren, was an indescribable emotional experience.

We convened in Myrtle Beach, S.C., where Alice stayed for several days. There were luncheons, dinners and parties in her honor. The local Chabad invited her to light the Chanukah menorah as the rabbi declared "when you light a candle, it chases a lot of darkness away." She was given the keys to a couple of cities and appeared with the survivors on several television programs. "Good Morning America" sent its crew for a taping to be aired, and the press followed and reported on her activities daily.

She had not been to the United States in 6 years and was elated to stop over in New Yor to see the city in all its holiday glitter. We wer on to Washington, D.C., where a director o The Holocaust Memorial Museum greeted u and pointed out Alice's name on the wall of th "Righteous Among the Nations."

Dozens of high school students surrounded he asking questions and thus bringing the reality o the heinous crimes into a personalized focus Alice insists she did nothing to deserve the atten tion and honors. "I only did my job," she kep repeating. But this was a time when giving ai

> *I have often wondered if I would have the courage and strength to do what she did.*

to a Jew could lead to summary execution or a best, deportation to a concentration camp. In he modesty, Alice states: "But there were others.

Yes, there were, but Alice was not the com manding officer operating from behind the lines she was in the trenches, in harm's way, fightin for "her children."

I have often wondered if I would have the courage and strength to do what she did. would want and hope to, but the crucial tes comes only when one is faced with life's try ing situations. For weeks prior to her comin here, I tried to devise ways to thank her. How does one thank someone who was so instru mental in saving your life at the risk of sucl personal danger? Perhaps the only way is to lead a commendable life and instill humanity into one's own children. Then hope that th lineage to follow will always remember tha their existence was possible because of Alice Resch Synnestvedt.

Ancient rabbinic writings state "Anyone whe saves one life saves the world."

Alice Resch Synnestvedt saved the world.

Richard Weilheimer lives in Torrington.

"Angel of Aspet"

Hal Myers' tribute to Alice at the July 1, 2002 gathering of One Thousand Children, in Chicago.

I am grateful for this opportunity to acquaint you with a remarkable lady.

Hal Myers, in Aspet, 1940 and Cleveland, 1999

I was nine years old in 1940 when I first met Alice Resch at Camp de Gurs in southern France. Alice is the person to whom I owe my life. She first came with a group of Quakers to feed the children a daily ration. This was the first time we were aware that outsiders knew of our plight since that awful morning in September, when the Gestapo gave us one hour to pack four days rations and one suitcase, each. I will always remember the silence on the

Kaiserallee in Karlsruhe as the Gestapo escorted us to the railway station.

Three days later, we arrived at Camp de Gurs, in a pouring rain. Children and women were separated from the men. The sanitation facilities were platforms over some tubs where many elderly women slipped and drowned. Others drowned in the mud that was two and three feet deep. The death wagon came through daily to remove the bodies that had drowned or died of dysentery.

Food was very scarce and the soup, which was the standard ration, was mostly water and fat with a few vegetables. When my mother got a job in the kitchen, I was permitted to visit her. I put sugar on bread and heated it next to the soup pots on the open fire. That was my only treat.

In February of 1941, Alice Resch escorted 48 boys and girls from Gurs to the *Maison des Pupilles de la Nation*, an orphanage in Aspet, about 50 miles south of Toulouse. Alice had convinced the Vichy authorities that the Quakers would care for these children and relieve the French from any further responsibility. Because one boy refused to be parted from his parents, I became number 48 on the list.

The *Maison des Pupilles* was located on a beautiful hilltop overlooking the Garonne River Valley and the Pyrenees Mountains. Some of the older children took care of the younger ones, who risked a beating from the Director for bedwetting and other such infractions, but the major problem was the shortage of food. The French ate a vegetable that was a cross between a turnip and a rutabaga and it tasted like sawdust. It was served in soup, mashed, hashed and fried and we ate almost none of it. I still taste that awful stuff in my sleep. I had always been pudgy and this was the only time in my life that I became quite skinny. I had one friend who was three years older. I wrote his name and that of Alice Resch in a tiny address book that my parents had given me when I left them at Gurs.

Alice lived with the boys during our thirty-day quarantine period. She became our teacher and our friend with a listening ear and a cheery word. She would take us for walks along the river and in the meadows. We would beg for apples from the farmers and occasionally receive a slice of real bread. A taste of Heaven! Alice returned to Toulouse, but she continued to spend time at the orphanage, teaching us English, French and mathematics.

In August, the Director told me that I would be going to America. Great Excitement! No one knew anything more. I was put on a train and told that a Quaker lady would meet me in Toulouse. I stayed on the train until the conductor told me to get off. Then I waited on a bench. Since I was to be met by the Quakers in Toulouse, I determined that somehow I should be able to find them. I walked out of the vast train shed. I saw a taxi stand outside and asked the driver *"Qvakers?"* in a German accent that I was not sure he understood. He was grumpy and pointed to the canal that ran in front of the train station, and said "Alla." So I headed across the square, carrying my treasured little suitcase. After walking for a few blocks, I saw a most beautiful brass sign that said, "Society of Friends, *Société Quaker.*"* With no hesitation and little wonder at my incredible good fortune, I went inside.

No one had been advised of my arrival. Alice was on holiday. One of the ladies gave me a bowl of thick soup and they found a bed for me at another orphanage. The next morning a man appeared. He had business in Marseilles, my destination, and instructions to not let me out of his sight.

So, I and about a hundred others came to America on the SS *Serpa Pinta* via Madrid, Lisbon, Casablanca, Bermuda, Ellis Island, and a lot of seasickness. I was lucky. Through the Joint Distribution Committee of the Jewish Welfare Fund I came to Cleveland and was taken in by the Myers

---

* This must have been 16 Boulevard Bonropos. see page 74.

family. I became a chemical engineer, and spent four years in the Air Force as a meteorologist. I now own an electroplating company. I am married to Nora and we have six children and 14 grandchildren.

But in 1942 the Germans and French began rounding up all "foreign aliens" in France. That meant Jews. My parents went on transport 27 to Auschwitz. Of 15,000 German Jewish children in southern France, 234 came to America. A few others went to Israel. Most went in cattle cars to Auschwitz.

Alice made sure that her remaining children were spared the deportations. She placed them in remote orphanages, in monasteries, with private families, in nunneries, and she managed to take some across the border into Switzerland. In all, Alice managed to save 47 of the 48 children who were at Aspet. She takes credit for 206 others. She has been justly honored as a Righteous Gentile at the Holocaust Museum and at Yad Vashem.

I managed to bury the holocaust deep inside, but suddenly in 1996, with one phone call everything changed. Paul Niedermann, an old friend from my Karlsruhe days, found me through the Red Cross. He had escaped from Camp de Gurs and lived in the country with other children. He now lives outside Paris, and is a frequent speaker on the Holocaust. He testified in the Klaus Barbie trial. Then in 1998, I received a phone call from a lady in Cincinnati, Ohio who had just interviewed Paul for a book about the children in Vichy France. I described some of my experiences and she told me that she had interviewed one of the ladies from Toulouse, now living in Copenhagen. She gave me her address and phone number. When I came home and looked at that little address book from long ago, I realized that the lady in Copenhagen was indeed the Alice Resch of my childhood. That has changed everything.

Throughout these years I had nurtured the dream of someday locating the Quakers in order to repay them for saving my life. I had made several attempts without success. I immediately called Alice. She still remembered her brave little Hansl who went alone to Toulouse and was lost. My wife and I had plans to visit Germany, so we took a detour to Copenhagen for an emotional reunion. We arrived at Alice's apartment in a large housing complex for the elderly. Even at 94 she did her own cooking and she served us pastries and tea. She introduced us to the list of Aspet children with whom she remained in contact. I am now in touch with thirty-one of them. Eight couples of the Aspet alumni celebrated Alice's 95th birthday with her in Copenhagen.

She will always be my Angel of Aspet.

From an AFSC *news release April* 24, 1945

"Rodolfo Olgiati, A Swiss Friend who visited in the United States last year and now is director of *Don Suisse*, a Swiss relief organization, recently sent from Bern a postcard conveying his greetings to his many friends here. The postcard was a poem in German, 'Ruf Aus Gurs,' written by a group of refugee children. The following translation was made by Mary Campion

Plea from Gurs

We, far from our native forest,
  Lost in a foreign land
Are tender young trees that a woodman
  Uprooted with violent hand.
Surely there must be another;
  Somewhere on this earth
To plant in a friendlier climate
  Our roots as they seek a new birth.
Alive are the delicate fibers
  In every tender shoot;
Which need but the help of a gardener
  To help them take new root.
Richly would we reward him
  His toil and ardent care.
Resplendent foliage render –
  In return for his being there.
In the spreading shade of our branches
  Would all mankind rejoice;
And from our limbs heavy-laden
  Pluck fruits of the finest choice.
Where are you, gentle gardener?
  From the north blows a wind of hate
Take us into your keeping – before it is too late.

Additional Resources

Each of these books sheds additional light on the work of Quakers in France during the Nazi occupation.

David, Ruth. *Child of Our Time; A Young Girl's Flight from the Holocaust.* London, I.B. Tauris, 2003. Ruth went to England on the *kindertransport*; her brother, Michael Oppenheimer was among the children whom Alice cared for at Aspet.

Hallie, Philip. *Lest Innocent Blood Be Shed; The Story of the Village of Le Chambon and How Goodness Happened There.* New York, Harper & Row, 1979.

Kershner, Howard. *Quaker Service in Modern War; Spain and France 1939-1940.* New York, Prentice Hall, 1950.

Marrus, Michael R. and Paxton, Robert O. *Vichy France and the Jews.* New York, Basic Books, 1981.

Pickett, Clarence. *For More than Bread.* Boston, Little, Brown, 1953.

Schmitt, Hans A. *Quakers and Nazis; Inner Light in Outer Darkness.* Columbia, Missouri, The University of Missouri Press, 1997. This is the definitive work on Quaker service throughout Europe, during WWII.

Wriggins, Howard. *Picking Up the Pieces from Portugal to Palestine; Quaker Refugee Relief in World War II, A Memoir.* Lanham, Maryland, University Press of America, 2004.

Index